HISTORY OF INITIATION

IN TWELVE LECTURES;

COMPRISING A DETAILED

𝔄ccount of the ℜites and ℭeremonies,

DOCTRINES AND DISCIPLINE,

OF ALL THE

SECRET AND MYSTERIOUS INSTITUTIONS

OF THE

ANCIENT WORLD.

BY THE REV. GEORGE OLIVER, D.D.,

INCUMBENT OF THE COLLEGIATE CHURCH, WOLVERHAMPTON; D. P. G. M. FOR
LINCOLNSHIRE; DOMESTIC CHAPLAIN TO THE RIGHT HONOURABLE
LORD KENSINGTON.

PUBLISHED BY
THE LOST LIBRARY
GLASTONBURY, ENGLAND

First Published by
Leon Hyneman, in 1829
This edition 2016

This facsimile edition has been carefully scanned
and reprinted in the traditional manner by
THE LOST LIBRARY
5 High Street,
Glastonbury UK BA6 9DP

The LOST LIBRARY is a publishing house based in
Glastonbury, UK, dedicated to the reproduction
of important rare esoteric and scholarly texts for
the discerning reader.

Cataloguing Information
The History of Initiation
George Oliver

ISBN 978 1 906 62141 4

Printed and bound in Great Britain by
Clays Ltd, St Ives plc

THE LOST
LIBRARY

TO THE RIGHT HONOURABLE

CHARLES TENNYSON D'EYNCOURT, M. P.

M. A., F. R. S., F. A. S., ETC.

ONE OF THE EQUERRIES OF HIS R. H. THE DUKE OF SUSSEX, PROVINCIAL
GRAND MASTER OF FREE AND ACCEPTED MASONS FOR
THE COUNTY OF LINCOLN.

My Dear Sir,

Whilst I was engaged in arranging these papers for the press, I received the gratifying intelligence that the friend and supporter of all my literary labours had been elevated, by His Royal Highness the Duke of Sussex, to the superintendence of Freemasonry in Lincolnshire, in the capacity of its Provincial Grand Master. It required no deliberation to determine at whose feet these Lectures should be placed; for duty and inclination alike concur in the propriety of inscribing them to you, as the ostensible guardian of Masonry within the Province, and the legitimate patron of all its collateral pursuits.

To your energies I confidently look for the spread of Masonry in this extensive county. From your enlightened understanding and vigorous superintendence I anticipate measures that will secure to the man of letters a profitable employment for his time in the tyled recesses of the Lodge; for it may be fairly presumed that if his mind be not deeply interested in the investigations, he will soon bid adieu to Freemasonry.

Experience is a species of wisdom that is seldom erroneous; and it amply confirms the opinion that a masonic

Lodge is founded upon an insecure basis if it rejects from its illustrations the philosophy, and contents itself with the technicalities of the science; like one possessing the keys of a rich casket of splendid jewels, which he has not the curiosity to open, that their rarity or value may be correctly estimated.

It is well known that in our Lectures, much scope is afforded for amplification both in science and morals; it cannot then be a futile expectation, while knowledge is making such a rapid progress in the present age of free inquiry, that by the judicious rule and masterly elucidations of our legitimate governors, our Lodges will maintain their proper character of schools of virtue and dispensers of the liberal arts.

Imbued with these sentiments, it affords me no inconsiderable degree of pleasure to associate your name with these Lectures, assured as I am that it will recommend them to the notice of the fraternity.

I have the honour to be, my dear Sir,

Your faithful servant and Brother,

GEORGE OLIVER, D. D.

Wolverhampton,
Dec. 7th, 1840.

ANALYTICAL TABLE OF CONTENTS.

LECTURE XI.

LECTURE XII.

COROLLARY.

PREFACE.

THE excellent Preston says, with much justice, "Many are deluded by the vague supposition, that our mysteries are merely nominal; that the practices established amongst us are frivolous; and that our ceremonies may be adopted or waived at pleasure. On this false basis we find too many of the Brethren hurrying through all the degrees of the Order, without adverting to the propriety of one step they pursue, or possessing a single qualification to entitle them to advancement. Passing through the usual formalities, they consider themselves authorised to rank as Masters of the Art, solicit and accept offices, and even assume the government of the Lodge, equally unacquainted with the rules of the Institution that they pretend to support, and the nature of the trust which they are bound to perform. The consequence is obvious; anarchy and confusion ensue, and the substance is lost in the shadow.—Hence men, who are eminent for ability, rank, and fortune, frequently view the honours of Masonry with indifference; and, when their patronage is solicited, either accept office with reluctance, or reject them with disdain.

"Masonry has long laboured under these disadvantages, and every zealous friend of the Order must earnestly wish for a correction of the abuse. Of late years, it must be acknowledged, our assemblies have been in general better regulated; of which the good effects are sufficiently displayed, in the judicious selection of our members, and the proper observance of our general regulations.

"Were the Brethren who preside at our meetings to be properly instructed previous to their appointment, and duly apprised of the offices they are chosen to support, a general reformation would speedily take place. This conduct would establish the propriety of our government, and lead men to acknowledge that our honour were not undeservedly conferred; the ancient conse quence of the Order would be restored, and the reputation of the Society preserved. Till genuine merit shall distinguish our claim to the honours of Masonry, and regularity of deportment display the influence and utility of our rules, the world in general will not be led to reconcile our proceedings with our professions."*

In coincidence with these sentiments, I am decidedly of opinion that much general knowledge is necessary to expand the mind, and familiarise it with masonic discussions and illustrations, before a Brother can be pronounced competent to undertake the arduous duty of governing a Lodge. A Master of the work ought to have nothing to learn. He should be fully qualified, not only to instruct the younger Brethren, but to resolve the doubts of those who are more advanced in masonic knowledge; to reconcile apparent contradictions; to settle chronologies, and to elucidate obscure facts or mystic legends, as well as to answer the objections and to render pointless the ridicule of our uninitiated adversaries.

Impressed with these ideas at a very early period of my masonic career, it occurred to me that some aid was wanting to convey a species of information on the subject of our antiquities which was not generally attainable in the common routine of our Lodge pursuits; and that desideratum I entertained the ambition of attempting to supply. How far I have succeeded must be submitted

* Illustr., p. 12, Edit. xiv. and xv.

to the fiat of the literary and intelligent portion of our community. The series is before them, and to their decision I implicitly bow.

The comprehensive nature of the inquiries embraced in the present volume has not been without its difficulties. The arrangement is in a great measure new, and proportionably abstruse, and, therefore, I have advanced with much caution, and have not ventured to introduce any single fact without its accompanying authority. Hence, any person who may be desirous of following in the same track, will be comparatively free from the intricacies with which I have been surrounded; and may refer without difficulty to the original sources from whence I have drawn my information.

It is to be hoped that this work will display the beauty of Christianity with some degree of effect, by portraying the abhorrent superstitions and revolting customs which were introduced amongst all nations during the prevalence of idolatry, and the absence of LIGHT from the mind; for, during the entire period from the Dispersion to the Advent of Christ, the whole world, with a very inconsiderable exception, sat in DARKNESS AND THE SHADOW OF DEATH, and were enveloped in a veil of delusion so impervious that all the exertions of their wisest philosophers were ineffectual to obtain the least glimmering of light, until it burst upon the world with effulgent glory in the person of our blessed Redeemer.

It will be seen by those who have perused the former edition, that I have altered my original plan, and have comprised the whole work in twelve Lectures, that the arrangement may correspond with my former publications on Freemasonry.

The whole of the original work has been retained except a few paragraphs which have been struck out of the fifth Lecture, because they were considered irrelevant. Much additional matter has been substituted·

and it is hoped that the general value of the work is greatly increased.

The notes with which each Lecture is accompanied are of great extent and variety. By this means I have been enabled to embody a considerable portion of interesting matter without swelling out the volume to an unwieldy and inconvenient size; and I flatter myself that the general reader will meet with a fund of entertaining information which will materially assist him in any researches he may be inclined to make, either into the antiquity of Masonry, or the parallel institutions of the heathen world.

ADVERTISEMENT.

The Publisher of this Edition being desirous that I should subjoin a list of the authorities which I originally consulted to elucidate the various subjects of which it treats, under an impression that such a means of reference might be useful to the Fraternity, I have endeavoured to comply with his request, although the task has been attended with some difficulty. It is several years since the History of Initiation was written, and at that period I had access to many valuable works which were not in my own collection. I am now resident in a distant part of the country, and, to supply such a catalogue, I must depend principally upon the strength of my memory, which is not particularly retentive; for even the greater part of my own library is in Lincolnshire. Should there be any inaccuracies, therefore, in any of the titles, size, or number of volumes, I must claim the indulgence of my readers. The list does not contain all the works which I found it necessary to consult: and I regret to add, that I do not possess the means of making it more extensive and correct.   G. O.

ABULFARAGII Historia Pocockii, 2 vols 4to.
Acosta's History of the Indies.
Æschylus, by Potter, 8vo.
Ammiani Marcellini, Historia, fo.
Anderson's Constitutions, 4to.
Aneurin's Gododin, in Davies's Druids.
Annales Usheri, fo.
Apuleii Opera, 2 vols. 8vo.
Arabian Nights Entertainment, 4 vols. 12mo.
Aristophanes, Greek and Latin, square 12mo.
Asiatic Researches, 12 vols. 8vo.
Ayeen Akbery, 3 vols. 4to.

Babylon, Ruins of, 8vo.

Banier's Mythology, 4 vols. 8vo.
Bardwell's Temples, 8vo.
Barruel's History of the French Revolution, 8vo.
———— Memoirs of Jacobinism, 4 vols. 8vo.
Bacchic Mysteries, on the,—Pamphleteer, vol. viii. 8vo.
Bacon, R. Opus Majus, fo.
Bernier's Travels in the Mogul Empire, 2 vols. 8vo.
Berosus apud Eusebium, fo.
Bhagvat Geeta, 4to.
Bilson's Survey of Christ's Sufferings.
Bin Washish's Ancient Alphabets, by Hammer, 4to.
Blair's Chronology, fo.

Bocharti Sacra Geographia.
Bower's History of the Popes, 4to.
Brady's Clavis Calendaria, 8vo.
Brand's Popular Antiquities, 2 vols. 4to.
Brown's Vulgar Errors, 4to.
Bryant's Analysis, 6 vols. 8vo.
Buchanan's Researches in Asia, 4to.
———— Journey from Madras, 3 vols. 4to.
Buckingham's Travels in Palestine, 2 vols. 8vo.
Buxtorfii Synagoga Judaica, 12mo.
———— Lexicon Rabbinicum.

Calcott's Candid Disquisitions on Freemasonry, 8vo.
Calmet's Dictionary, 5 vols. 4to.
————Antiquities, 4to.
Camden's Britannia, by Gough, 4 vols. 4to.
Carne's Letters from the East, 8vo.
Cave's Lives of the Fathers, fo.
Celsus apud Origen contra Celsum, 4to.
Chardin's Travels in Persia, 2 vols. 8vo.
Chronicon Paschale, fo.
Ciceronis Opera, 8vo.
Clarke's Travels, 6 vols. 4to.
Clemens Alexandrinus Stromata, fo.
Couplet's History of China.
Cudworth's Intellectual System, 2 vols. 4to.
Cumberland's Sanchoniatho, 8vo.
———— Origines Gent. Antiquissima, 8vo.

D'Anville on Ancient Geography, 2 vols. 8vo.
Davies's History and Mythology of the Druids, 8vo.
———— Celtic Researches, 8vo.
———— on British Coins, 8vo.
Dean's Worship of the Serpent, 8vo.
Denon's Travels in Egypt, 2 vols. 8vo.
Dermott's Ahiman Rezon, 8vo.
Desaguliers' Constitutions, 4to.
D'Hancarville's Recherches sur les Monumens Antiques de l'India, 3 tom. 4to.
Diodori Siculi Bibliotheca Historica, fo.
Diogenes Laertius, Greek and Latin, square 12mo.
Dionysius, de Divinis Nominibus.
Dow's History of Hindostan, 3 vols. 4to.
Dubois on the Institutions of India.
Du Halde's History of China, 4 vols. 8vo.

Eddas of Snorro and Saemund, in Mallet's Northern Antiquities.
Eleusinian Mysteries, on the,—Pamphleteer, vol. viii. 8vo.

Encyclopedia Britannica, Londinensis, Metropolitana, Rees's, Perthensis, &c.
Euripides, by Potter, 8vo.
Eusebius de Preparatio Evangelica, fo.

Faber's Mysteries of the Cabiri, 2 vols 8vo.
————Pagan Idolatry, 3 vols. 4to.
Fenton's Hist. of Pembrokeshire, 4to.
Fleury's Manners of the Ancient Israelites, 12mo.
Forbins' (Count de) Travels in the Holy Land, 8vo.
Freemasons' Magazine.

Gael and Cimbri, 8vo.
Gage's Survey of the West Indies.
Gale's Court of the Gentiles, 3 vols 4to.
Godwyn's Moses and Aaron, 4to.
Goranson's Histories in Mallet's Northern Antiquities.
Grabe's Septuagint, 4 vols. fo.
Greaves's Pyramidographia, 8vo.
Greek Minor Poets, Greek and Latin, 12mo.
Grose's Voyage to the East Indies, 2 vols. 8vo.
———— Provincial Glossary, 8vo.
Grotius de Veritate, 12mo.

Hales's Analysis of Chronology, 4 vols. 8vo.
Halhed's Code of Gentoo Laws, 4to.
Hamilton's Egyptiaca, 4to.
Hectopades, 8vo.
Helvetian Ritual, a MS.
Herodoti Historia, fo.
Hesiod, Greek and Latin, 12mo.
Holwell's Historical Events, 2 vols. 8vo.
————, on the Feasts, &c., of the Hindoos, 2 vols. 8vo.
Hope's Architecture, 8vo.
Horapollinis Hieroglyphica.
Humboldt's Personal Narrative, 7 vols. 8vo.
———— Monuments of the Ancient Inhabitants of America, 2 vols. 8vo.
Hutchinson's History of Cumberland, 2 vols. 4to.
———— Spirit of Masonry, 12mo.
Hyde, Veterum Persarum Religionis Historia, 4to.

Jamblichus de Mysteriis, fo.
Jamieson's Scottish Dictionary, 4to.
Jones's (Sir W.) Works, 6 vols. 4to.
Jones's (Stephen) Masonic Miscellanies, 12mo.
Josephus on the Antiquities of the Jews, 4 vols. 8vo.
Isocrates, by Dinsdall, 8vo.
Julius Firmicus de Errore.

Kæmpfer's History of Japan, 2 tom. fo.
Keightly's Mythology, 8vo.
Kellet's Tricænium Christi, fo.

Laurie's History of Freemasonry in Scotland, 8vo.
Le Compte's Memoirs of China, 8vo
Lamb's Hieroglyphics, 8vo.
Ledwich's Antiquities of Ireland.
Le Noir, L'Antiquité de la Franc-Maçonnerie, 4to.
Lord's Banian Religion
Lucian de Deâ Syria.

Macrobii Opera, 8vo.
Maimonides de Idolatria.
Malcolm's History of Persia, 2 vols. 4to
—————— Memoirs of Central India, 2 vols. 8vo.
Mallet's Northern Antiquities, by Bishop Percy, 2 vols. 8vo.
Manetho apud Eusebium, fo.
Marsh's Horæ Pelasgicæ, 8vo.
Maundrell's Journey, 8vo.
Maurice's Indian Antiquities, 7 vols. 8vo.
—————— Ancient History of Hindostan, 4to.
—————— Modern History of Hindostan, 3 vols. 4to.
Meyrick's History of Cardigan, 4to.
Mills's History of the Crusades, 2 vols. 8vo.
—————— Chivalry, 2 vols. 8vo.
Milman's History of the Jews, 3 vols. 12mo.
Montfaucon, L'Antiquité expliquée, 5 tom. fo.
Moor's Hindoo Pantheon, 8vo.
More's Apocalypsis Apocalypseon, 4to.
Mounier's Influence of Freemasonry on the French Revolution, 8vo.

Newton's Chronology, 4to.
Niebuhr's Voyage in Arabia, 3 tom. fo.
Nieuhoff's Travels to India, fo.
Norden's Travels in Egypt and Nubia.

Oliver's Signs and Symbols, 8vo.
—————— Antiquities of Masonry, 8vo.
—————— Star in the East, 12mo.
—————— History of Beverley, 4to.
Orme's Transactions in India, 3 vols. 4to.
—————— Historical Fragments, 8vo.
Owen's Welsh Dictionary, 8vo.
—————— Introduction to Llywarch Hên, 8vo.
—————— Serpent Worship, 12mo.

Palmyra, Antiquities of, 8vo.
Pamphleteer, vol. viii. 8vo.
Parsons's Remains of Japheth, 4to.

Patricii Oracula Zoroastr, fo.
Pausanias, by Taylor, 3 vols. 8vo.
Pennant's Tour in Scotland, 4to.
—————— Journey to Alston Moor, 4to.
Perron's Zendavesta, 3 tom. 4to.
Philonis Judæi Opera, fo.
Philostrati Opera, fo.
Philpot's Heraldry, 12mo.
Pierii Hieroglyphica, fo.
Pignorii Mensa Isiaca, 4to.
Pinkerton's Collection of Travels, 4to.
Platonis Opera, 2 vols. fo.
Plinii Naturalis Historia, fo.
Plutarchi Opera, 8vo.
—————— Iside et Osiride, 4to.
Pocockii Specimen Historiæ Arabicæ, 4to.
Poli Synopsis, 5 vols. fo.
Pontoppidon's History of Norway, fc.
Porphyrius de Antro Nympharum, 12mo.
Potter's Archæology, 2 vols. 8vo.
Preston's Illustrations of Masonry, 12mo.
Prideaux's Connection, 2 vols. 8vo.
Purchas's Pilgrim, fo.
—————— Voyages and Travels, 6 vols. fo.
Pyramids, Description of the, fo.

Raleigh's History of the World, fo.
Ramsay on the Theology of the Pagans 12mo.
Religious Ceremonies of all Nations, fo.
Richardson's Dissertation, 8vo.
Robertson's History of America, 8vo
Robison's Proofs of a Conspiracy, 8vo.
Rollin's Ancient History, 10 vols. 12mo.
Rowland's Mona, 4to.
Runic Poems, in Mallet's Northern Antiquities.

Sacontala, Sir W. Jones's Works.
Sale's Koran, 2 vols. 8vo.
Samme's Britannia, fo.
Satires of Perseus, 8vo.
Savary's Letters on Egypt, 2 vols. 8vo.
—————— Letters on Greece, 8vo.
Deely's Wonders of Elora, 8vo.
Delden de Diis Syriis, 8vo.
Shuckford's Connection, 3 vols. 8vo.
Smith's Use and Abuse of Freemasonry, 8vo.
Southey, Notes to his Poems.
Spencer de Legibus Hebræorum, fo.
Spineto's (Marquis of) Lectures, 8vo.
Stanley's Chaldaic Philosophy, fo.
—————— History of the Philosophers, 3 vols. fo.
Stillingfleet's Origines Sacræ, 4to.
Strabonis Geographia, fo.
Stukeley's Itinerary, 2 vols. 4to.

Stukeley's Stonehenge and Abury, 2 vols. 4to.
Syncelli Chronographia, fo.

Tavernier, les Six Voyages, 6 tom. 4to.
Taylor's Proclus, 2 vols. 4to.
Tenison's Idolatry, 4to.
Thevenot's Travels into the Levant, fo.
Toland's History of the Druids, 8vo.
Turnbull's Voyage round the World, 4to.
Turner's History of the Anglo-Saxons, 3 vols. 8vo.

Universal History (Ancient,) 18 vols. 8vo.
Universe Displayed, 4 vols. 8vo.

Valpy's Classics.

Vancouvre's Voyage round the World, 3 vols. 4to.
Verstegan's Restitution of Decayed Intelligences, 4to.
Volney's Travels in Syria, 2 vols. 8vo.

Wait's Oriental Antiquities, 8vo.
——— Jewish Antiquities, 8vo.
Warburton's Divine Legation of Moses, 5 vols. 8vo.
Ward's View of the Hindoos, 8vo.
Webb's Freemason's Monitor, 12mo.
Welsh Archæology, 3 vols. 8vo.
Willett's Hexapla in Exodum, fo.
Wormius's Danish Monuments, fo.

Young's Egyptian Antiquities, 8vo.

Zimmerman's Tract on the Illuminati.

HISTORY OF INITIATION.

LECTURE I.

GENERAL INTRODUCTION.

INITIATION may be traced to a period of the most remote antiquity. In the infancy of the world the ceremonies would be few and unostentatious, and consist,
perhaps, like that of admission into Christianity, of a
simple lustration, conferred alike on all, in the hope that
they would practise the social duties of benevolence and
good will to man, and unsophisticated devotion to God.[1]
It was after the stream of iniquity had inundated the
world, and bad men had turned a sacred institution into
ridicule from its simplicity[2] and easiness of access, that
some discriminations became necessary, and the rites assumed a higher and more imposing form. The distinguished few who retained their fidelity, uncontaminated
by the contagion of evil example, would soon be able to
estimate the superior benefits of an isolated institution
which afforded the advantage of a select society, and kept
at an unapproachable distance, the profane scoffer, whose
presence might pollute their pure devotion and social
converse by contumelious language or unholy mirth. To
prevent such intrusion, therefore, the rites of initiation
would become progressively more complicated, and some

---

[1] This was, doubtless, primitive Masonry;—in reality nothing more
than the practice of those simple moral precepts which were enjoined
by a religion, pure as it came from the hand of God, and unadulterated
by the innovations of man.

[2] Warburton says, that it was an universal opinion that *the heathen
Mysteries were instituted pure;* (Div. Leg., vol. i., p. 172,) referring,
doubtless, to the primitive Science here described, which was the great
original from whence they were derived.

distinctive *tokens* would be adopted as infallible tests to exclude the uninitiated; and enable the pious worshipper to detect with unerring certainty the truth or falsehood of any pretensions to a fraternity with the faithful followers of the true God.[3] Their ordinary employment was in the cultivation of the mind, by pursuits of literature,[4] the study and contemplation of God's wisdom, in making, ordering, and governing the world; together with observations on the motions of the heavenly bodies, and the sciences of astronomy and geometry .therein employed; which are sublime studies, and suppose or involve some skill in Letters, first used in writing and in numbering.[5] The study of Astronomy was indeed a favourite pursuit with the Freemasons, so to call them,[6] who flourished before the Deluge, and would doubtless be one of the Sciences inculcated on the initiated. Whether it led to the practice of the Sabean superstition is matter of conjecture;[7]

[3] The divine Enoch gave to these rites a decisive character, and added to the practice of divine worship the study and application of human science. "Enoch was the first who invented books, and different sorts of writing. The ancient Greeks declare that Enoch is the same as Mercury Trismegistus, and that he taught the sons of men the art of building cities, and enacted some admirable laws. In his days 180 cities were built; of these, that which was the least, was Edessa. He discovered the knowledge of the Zodiac and the course of the Planets; and he pointed out to the sons of men, that they should worship God. that they should fast, that they should pray, that they should give alms, votive offerings and tenths. He reprobated abominable foods and drunkenness, and appointed festivals for sacrifices to the Sun at each of the Zodiacal Signs, &c., &c." (Bar Hebraeus, cited by Wait. Orient. Ant., p. 182.) It will be observed that in the latter part of the above quotation, Enoch is converted into an idolater; but the author evidently blends into one, the characters of Enoch and Enos. According to our traditions, Enoch was a very eminent Freemason, and the conservator of the true name of God, which was subsequently lost even amongst his favourite people, the Jews.

[4] According to the Bechinath Happerushim, the doctrine of the Patriarchs before the flood consisted of traditions of the Creation, Paradise, the Seventh day, the Fall of Man, Cain's fratricide, &c., to which, after the Flood, were added the Seven precepts of Noah. Vid. Wait. ut supra. Pref., p. viii.; and the Antiquities of Freemasonry, by the Author of this Work, p. 93.

[5] Cumb. Sanch., p. 226.

[6] This was the race which the Freemasons of the present day regard as their most early predecessors in the practice of rites, to which accident gave the name of Masonry. Vid. Ant. of Masonry, p. 17.

[7] Bishop Cumberland says, "the chief suggestion which Moses has given us concerning the beginning of idolatry before the Flood, is in

but we have no certain evidence that it produced any
surreptitious rites, bearing a character similar to the
polluted Mysteries of the postdiluvians.[8] Such was Ini
tiation in these primeval ages, and thus it passed through
the hands of the antediluvian patriarchs, unalloyed by
any innovations which might tend to vitiate its benefits
or circumscribe its blessings.[9]

Gen. iv., 26: the words being translated, as in the margin of our Bibles,
then, while Enos lived, men began to call THEMSELVES *by the name of
the Lord ;* i. e. to be deified." (Cumb. Sanch., p. 304.) Maimonides,
however, was decidedly of opinion that the antediluvians were addicted
to the solar and sideral worship. These are his words: "In the days
of Enos, the son of Seth, men fell into grievous error, and even Enos
himself partook of their infatuation. Their language was, that since
God had placed on high the heavenly bodies, and used them as his
ministers, it was evidently his will, that they should receive from man
the same veneration as the servants of a great prince justly claim from
the subject multitude. Impressed with this notion, they began to
build temples to the stars, to sacrifice to them, and to worship them,
in the vain expectation that they should thus please the Creator of all
things. At first, indeed, they did not suppose the stars to be the only
deities, but adored in conjunction with them, the Lord God Omnipotent. In process of time, however, that great and venerable Name
was totally forgotten, and the whole human race retained no other
religion than the idolatrous worship of the host of heaven." (Maim.
de Idol. apud Fab. Mys. Cab., vol. i., p. 10.) The patriarch Noah,
however, should have been excepted from this general charge of
idolatry, for we know from an authority higher than that of
Maimonides, that Noah was a just man and walked with God.
(Gen. vi. 9.)

[8] The early attachment to this science thus displayed, produced
some very curious fables in subsequent ages. Thus Atlas is represented
as supporting the heavens on his shoulders ; a fiction arising entirely
out of his reputed hnowledge of astronomy, for Atlas was but a personification of Enoch, who is said to have invented or greatly improved
this sublime science. Heraclitus (de incred., c. 4,) tells us that Atlas
was the first eminent astronomer of the antediluvian world, and
Eupolemus in Eusebius (Præp. Evan., c. ix., 17,) ascribes the invention of astronomy to Enoch, which is no inconsiderable proof of their
identity.

[9] A Masonic tradition is in existence, that our antediluvian Brethren
engraved their ineffable secrets on pillars, and deposited them in a
cavern of the earth. In corroboration of this legend, the authors of
the Universal History say, that "Manetho extracted his history from
certain pillars which he discovered in Egypt, whereon inscriptions had
been made by Thoth, or the first Mercury, in the sacred letters and
dialect ; but were, after the Flood, translated from the sacred dialect
into the Greek tongue, and laid up in the private recesses of the
Egyptian temples. These pillars were found in subterraneous caverns,
near Thebes, and beyond the Nile, not far from the sounding statue of
Memnon, in a place called Syringes, which are described to be *certain*

But after the Flood the altar of Darkness[10] was arrayed
against the altar of Light; the patriarchal ordinances were
perverted; the rites of Buddha were engrafted on the
pure ceremonies of the masonic ritual,[11] and the plains of
Shinar resounded with the frantic yellings of the rebellious Cuthites.[12] By subsequent corruptions, the arkite
rites thus boldly introduced,[13] at length assumed the more
complex form of Brahmenism,[14] and were solemnized with

winding apartments under ground, and which, as it is said, *those who
were skilled in ancient rites*, foreseeing the coming of the Deluge, and
fearing lest the memory of their ceremonies should be obliterated,
built and contrived vaults, dug with vast labour, in several places;
cutting on the walls many sorts of birds and beasts, and innumerable
kinds of animals, which they called hieroglyphical letters." (Vol. i.,
p. 39.)

[10] It may be observed here, that in all the idolatrous systems, *Darkness* was honoured with peculiar marks of veneration, by reason of its
supposed priority of existence; for those who were unable to extend
their ideas beyond the creation of this world, always considered darkness to have been of greater antiquity than light; and hence their
cosmogonies all commence with dark chaos. This principle was identified with the Great Mother, (for Venus and Night were the same
individual deity, Orph. Hymn. 2.) who, representing equally the earth
and the ark of Noah, remained enveloped in the blackest shades of
darkness, both before the creation and during the prevalence of the
diluvian waters. (Vid. Signs and Symbols, by the Author of this
Work, Lect. 6.) And this awful goddess was no other than the Isis,
or Ceres, or Rhea, or Ceridwen of the Mysteries. (Signs and Symb.,
pref.)

[11] "It has been often supposed," says Malcolm, "that Buddhism
resembles Brahmenism, which is a great mistake. No two systems
can be more opposite, or bear less evidence of being derived from each
other. Brahmenism has incarnations, but Buddhism admits of none,
for it has no permanent god. That has a host of idols; this only one.
That enjoins bloody sacrifices; this forbids all killing. That requires
atrocious self tortures; this inculcates few austerities. That makes
lying, theft, and other vices sometimes commendable, and describes
the gods as excelling in those enormities; this never confounds right
and wrong, and never excuses any sin. That makes absorption into
deity the supreme good; this annihilation.

[12] Faber contends that idolatry commenced at Babel, from that passage in which " the prophet of the Apocalypse styles Babylon or
Babel, the mother of harlots and abominations of the earth; (Rev.
viii., 5,) by which is meant, in the figurative language of scripture, that
all the abominations of apostate idolatry originated from that city as
from a common parent." (Pag. Idol., vol. i., p. 77.

[13] Signs and Symbols, Lect. 5.

[14] The mysterious systems of polytheism branched off into two great
sects, which have been distinguished by mythologists, under the names
of Buddhism and Brahmenism, each possessing its own peculiarities,

such splendour of ceremonial pomp and imposing magnificence of decoration, that they excited universal notice,
and their peculiar symbols were introduced into the
celestial sphere.[15] The apostacy was attractive, and the
spurious initiations aimed at extinguishing the unpre-
suming blaze of truth, which is now denominated Masonry,
supported only by the unpopular recommendations of
silent devotion to God and unoffending simplicity to man ;
accompanied by a life which coveted no distinctions in this
world, but such as emanate from piety and virtue. At the
dispersion, the architects of Babel travelled into distant
countries, each tribe under its ostensible leader, bearing
the sacred ark of the favourite deity, under whose protection they penetrated into unknown climes, and settled
in such situations as promised to yield them shelter and
support.[16] The surreptitious initiations accompanied each
tribe, increasing in pomp and celebrity, until they literally
covered the earth as the waters cover the sea.[17] They
sprang up in the East like some insignificant plant, but

which marked a distinctive character; separating their professors
from each other by conflicting ordinances, and often producing inex-
tinguishable hatred and sanguinary hostility. The mixed tribes, who
emigrated from Shinar under the direction of a Cuthite priesthood
and nobility, adopted the latter system, while the unmixed tribes
adhered to the former. (Fab. Pag. Idol., vol. ii, p. 36.) The Indians,
the Greeks, (except Pythagoras, who practised a modification of
Buddhism,) and the Britons were Brahmenists, while the Chinese, the
Japanese, the Persians, and the Saxons were Buddhists. The distinctions between these two sects were arbitrary. The Buddhists
were Magians, the Brahmenists were Sabians; and how abhorrent
soever it may appear from the mild and bloodless character of the
primitive Buddha, the former maintained their superiority by the
sword, the latter were peaceable, and addicted to the arts of civil and
social life. In some nations the two systems became, in subsequent
ages, so intimately blended, that the minute distinctions of each were
swallowed up in the broad outline of the general scheme. Of these,
the Indians and the Britons may be marked out as the chief.

[15] Fab. Mys. Cab., vol. i., p. 203.

[16] It is evident from Josephus, (Ant. Jud., l. i., c. 1.) that a regular
idolatrous priesthood was established prior to that dispersion ; for he
says, citing from Hestiæus, " *the priests of Jupiter the conqueror,* sur-
viving the general destruction, having preserved the holy vessels and
ornaments, repaired with them to Babylon."

[17] Zosim., l. iv., apud Warb. Div. Leg. It is a melancholy fact, that
before the advent of the Messiah, the whole earth was polluted with
these abominations ; and every country had its system of religious
mysteries ;—all partaking of the source from which they undoubtedly
sprang.

grew and enlarged with such prodigious rapidity and
strength, that soon their vigorous branches spread from
east to west, from north to south. The continent of Asia
was pervaded in every part of its vast and spacious surface ; the shores of Africa basked under their shade, and
disseminated their abominations; they imparted activity
to the adventurous designs of the Phenician merchants,
and gave distinction to the Greek and Roman name;
the distant isles of Britain and Hibernia; the cold and
inhospitable regions of Scandinavia and Iceland, alike
yielded to their sway; and even the distant and unknown
colonies which peopled the woods and forests of the new
world, felt and acknowledged their utility in enslaving
and reducing to abject submission the savage nature of
their fierce inhabitants.[18]

The universal Deluge would produce a tremendous
effect on the minds of the survivors, and as a knowledge
of this terrible event was propagated amongst their posterity, it would naturally be accompanied by a veneration
for the piety, and afterwards for the persons of the favoured few who were preserved from destruction by the visible interference of the Divinity. This veneration, increasing with the march of time, and with the increasing
oblivion of the peculiar manner in which their salvation

[18] The Mysteries, after they were once instituted, which probably
took place on the plains of Shinar, before the dispersion of mankind,
spread over the world with a rapidity which is truly astonishing. They
were introduced into India by Brahma, into China and Japan by
Buddha, into Egypt by Thoth the son of Mizraim, (Ant. Mas., p. 148,)
into Persia by Zeradusht, (Pococke. Spec. Hist. Arab., p. 147,) into
Greece by Melampus, (Herod., l. ii., c. 4.,) or Cadmus, (Epiphan. adv.
Hær., l. i.) into Bœotia by Prometheus and his son, (Etnæus. Pausan.
Bæot., p. 300,)into Crete by Minos, into Samothrace by Eumolpus or
Dardanus, (Bp. Marsh. Horæ Pelasg., p. 9,) into Messenè by Caucon,
(Pausan. Messen., p. 281,) into Thebes by Methapus, into Athens by
Erectheus, into Etruria by Philostratus, (Apoll. Bibl., l. iii., c. 5,) into
the city of Arene by Lycus, into Thrace by Orpheus, into Italy by the
Pelasgi, (Bp. Marsh. Hor. Pelasg., p. 9,) into Cyprus by Cinyras, into
Gaul and Britain by Gomer or his immediate descendants, into Scandinavia by Sigge or Odin, (Mal. North. Ant., v. i., p. 62,) into Mexico
by Vitzliputzli, (Purch. Pilg., b. viii., c. 10,) and into Peru by Manco
Capac and his wife. (Garcilasso. b. i., c. 15.)   Hence it will follow,
by a clear induction, that all the Mysteries throughout the world
were the same in substance, being derived from one source, and celebrated in honour of the same deities, though acknowledged under
different appellations.

was accomplished, at length assumed the form of an idolatrous worship, and Nimrod, the first open apostate, instituted a series of divine honours to Noah and his triple offspring, who were identified with the Sabian worship, and gave the original impulse to the helioarkite superstition. Hence the Sun and Noah were worshipped in conjunction with the Moon and the Ark,[19] which latter subsequently represented the female principle, and was acknowledged in different nations, under the various appellations of Isis, Venus, Astarte, Ceres, Proserpine, Rhea, Sita, Ceridwen, Frea, &c., while the former, or male principle, assumed the names of Osiris, Saturn, Jupiter, Neptune, Bacchus, Adonis, Hu, Brahma, Odin, &c.,[20] which by degrees introduced the abominations of the phallic worship; while Vesta represented the Ark itself, Minerva the divine wisdom and justice, which produced the Deluge and preserved the ark upon its waters, Iris was the rainbow, and Juno the arkite dove. On these rude beginnings the whole complicated *machinery* of the Mysteries was formed, which completely banished from the political horizon of idolatry the true knowledge of God, and of a superintending providence. Each of these deities had legitimate and appropriate symbols, which ultimately became substituted for the antitype, and introduced amongst mankind the worship of animals, and the inanimate objects of the creation.

Added to this, the doctrine of the influences of the heavenly bodies over the affairs of men was assiduously inculcated, and as the supernal deities were consecrated into the principal stars, their priests were supposed to be invested with a power of directing those influences at pleasure; and the high rewards of a residence with them in the same happy mansions was held out to all the virtuous *who embraced their opinions;* which may afford an additional reason why the system extended itself so generally over

[19] Mr. Faber conceives that "the ancient mythologists considered the whole frame of the heavens in the light of an *enormous ship.* In it they placed the Sun, as the fountain of light and heat; and assigned to him, as the acknowledged representative of the great father, the office of pilot." (Pag. Idol., vol. i., p. 36.)

[20] These were the various appellations which different people bestowed on the same divinity, the founder of their nation, male or female. They constitute the same false principle to which the Mysteries were universally consecrated.

the face of the earth; for the priests, thus potent and
despotic, would not fail to consign to universal execration
and contempt in the present world, and eternal torment
in the next, the impious contemner of their rites, while
rewards and honours would be accumulated on those who
distinguished themselves in the defence of their apostacy
from the simplicity of primitive worship.[21]

And the triumph of this diabolical system was complete by the invention of the Metempsychosis,[22] in which
they were taught to believe that the unhappy soul of the
wicked despiser of the Mysteries was doomed to a transmigration of three thousand years' duration. This doctrine
was a fearful engine in the hand of a politic priesthood to
enslave the mind through the influence of imaginary
fears. What could be more terrible than the contemplation of a punishment which degraded the human soul
beneath its natural superiority of character, and consigned
it to a long succession of transmigrations through the
polluted bodies of ravenous beasts, or loathsome reptiles?[23] And who would be bold enough to reject or

[21] Maurice asserts, from Porphyry in Eusebius, that in the most
early times, "the whole Thebais united in acknowledging a supreme,
presiding Spirit, whom they called Cneph, *upon which account they
were excused from paying the public taxes,* levied to defray the ex-
pences of maintaining the sacred animals adored in the cities of
Egypt." (Ind. Ant., vol. iv., p. 672.) Cneph was a serpent-deity, and
was affirmed to be the creator of the world. (Euseb. præp. Evan., l.
iii., c. 11.)

[22] The greatest philosophers of all ages and nations considered this
doctrine to be perfectly orthodox. Malcolm gives a curious account of
the transmigration of Godama, the Buddhist king. "Godama was
the son of a king, who had previously lived in four hundred millions
of worlds, and passed through innumerable conditions in each. In
this world he had been almost every sort of worm, fly, fowl, fish, or
animal, and in almost every grade and condition of human life.
Having in the course of these transitions, attained immense merit, he
at length was born son of the above-mentioned king. The moment he
was born, he jumped upon his feet, and spreading out his arms, exclaimed—'Now I am the noblest of men! This is the last time I shall
ever be born!' When in this state his mind was enlarged, so that he
remembered his former conditions and existences, of which he rehearsed many to his followers. Five hundred and fifty of these narra-
tions have been preserved, one relating his life and adventures as a
deer; another as a monkey, elephant, fowl, &c."

[23] Thus, in the ordinances of Menu, it is decreed, that, "a man who
designedly takes away the property of another, or eats any holy cake
not first presented to the deity *at a solemn rite,*" in defiance, I suppose,

contemn a system which bore the ensigns of such a dreadful retribution?

Meanwhile the true light of Masonry declined in public estimation as the rapid progress of its earth-born[24] adversary made all nations and people and languages bend before it, until it gave portentous intimation of approaching decay; and nought could have saved it from extinction, had it not been reinvigorated by the Essenes, a well-intentioned sect of people amongst the Jews, who took charge of the forsaken Institution,[25] cherished it in

or contempt of the holy ordinance, "shall inevitably sink to the condition of a brute." (Sir W. Jones, Works, vol. iii., p. 453.) "The slayer of a Brahmin must enter, according to the circumstances of his crime, the body of a dog, a boar, an ass, a camel, a bull, a goat, a sheep, a stag, a bird, chandala, or a pucassa". (Ibid., p. 451.) *"He who steals the gold of a priest, shall pass a thousand times into the bodies of spiders, of snakes and chameleons, of crocodiles and other aquatic monsters, or of mischievous blood-sucking demons."* (Ibid., p. 451.) In the Bhagvat Geeta this degrading species of punishment is still more pointedly denounced on the despisers of the sacred Mysteries. "Because of their folly," says the good Crishna, *"they adopt false doctrine and continue to live the life of impurity ;* therefore I cast down upon the earth those furious, abject wretches, those evil beings who thus despise me, *into the wombs of evil spirits and unclean beasts.* Being doomed to the wombs of Assoors, (dæmons) from birth to birth, at length, not finding me, they go into the most infernal regions." (p. 116, 117.)

[24] I have denominated the surreptitious initiations *earth-born,* in contradistinction to the purity of Freemasonry, which was certainly derived from above. And to those who contend that Masonry is nothing more than a miserable relic of the idolatrous mysteries, (vid. Fab. Pag. Idol., vol. iii., p. 190,) I would reply in the emphatic words of an inspired apostle: "Doth a fountain send forth at the same place sweet water and bitter? Can the fig tree bear olive berries? either a vine figs? so can no fountain both yield salt water and fresh. The wisdom that is from above is first pure, then peaceable, full of mercy and *good fruits.*" (James iii., 11, 12, 17.) I wish to be distinct and intelligible on this point, as some misapprehensions are afloat respecting the immediate object of my former volume of Signs and Symbols; and I have been told, that the arguments there used afford an indirect sanction to the opinion that Masonry is derived from the Mysteries. In answer to this charge, if it require one, I only need refer to the general tenor of that volume; and to declare explicitly my firm opinion, founded on intense study and abstruse research, that the Science which we now denominate Speculative Masonry was coeval, at least, with the creation of our globe, and that the far-famed Mysteries of idolatry were a subsequent institution, founded on similar principles, with the design of conveying unity and permanence to the false worship, which it otherwise could never have acquired.

[25] Vid "The Progress of Light," a Sermon, by the author of this

their bosom, until its rays of light once more began **to** illuminate the surrounding darkness; and it thence continued to enlighten a narrow and restricted path, terminating, however, in the broad and glorious blaze of splendour that dissipated the unholy shades of idolatry in the person of Jesus Christ.

Long antecedent to the time when this benevolent dispensation was promulgated, which brought life and immortality to light, and clearly revealed those important truths which the metaphysical reasonings of heathen philosophy could never fathom, were the practices exhibited which form the subject of the following pages. In those distant times, and amongst the people who had renounced the homage which the creature owes to the Creator, the rites of initiation were so indispensable, that no one could rise to any degree of celebrity in the religious or political institutions of polytheism, but by passing through this preliminary form; it was the only avenue to honour, wealth, or fame; and the peculiar blessings of immortality were restricted to those alone, who had borne without shrinking or complaint, the privation and actual terrors of this rigorous ordeal.   To despise the Mysteries, or omit the process of initiation, were to relinquish all the title to preferment;[26] and even the comforts and charms of domestic life were scarcely attainable without this indispensable qualification, which was supposed to restore the fallen soul to its original state of perfection;[27] for the uninitiated person was virtually an outcast from society, an eternal object of suspicious jealousy, and almost without the pale of legal protection.   Hence the extreme utility, in these times of superior light, of investigating a subject of such extensive application and high importance towards elucidating many abstruse points in the history and mythology of

Work. Laurie, in his History of Freemasonry in Scotland, has also taken a clear view of this subject; and has instituted a comparison between the usages of the Essenes and those of Freemasonry. Laurie was an intelligent Mason, and has written an useful book; although I differ from him on some important points.

[26] The first initiation was a sort of baptism, and simple introduction to religious privileges, conferred on persons in their infancy.

[27] Plato. Phædone. The Orphic mysteries were dignified with the high appellation of *Orphotelestæ*, because the initiated were assured of certain happiness in a future state.

the ancient world, which are at present wrapt up in the
mantle of obscurity, and need this Master-Key to bring
them into light. The Casket, which contains a splendid
collection of antique jewels of inestimable value, has
long been closed, and its riches inaccessible to the eager
eye of curiosity; but by the prudent use of this talismanic key, the bolts may be withdrawn, and the contents
exposed to the penetrating gaze of antiquarian research.

Initiation involved all the confused and complicated
mechanism of heathen mythology; and many of the political and domestic customs of antiquity may be traced
to the same inexhaustible and prolific source. It was
considered to be a mystical death, or oblivion of all the
stains and imperfections of a corrupted and an evil life, as
well as a descent into hell, where every pollution was
purged by lustrations of *fire and water;* and the perfect
Epopt was then said to be regenerated[28] or new born, restored to a renovated existence of life, light and purity,
and placed under the Divine protection. This was a
figurative representation of the descent of Noah into the
Ark, which was a place of refuge from the punishment
inflicted on the sins with which the old world was stained.[29] Here he remained in darkness and solitude, impressed with feelings of horror and apprehension, not
unaptly termed *death,* until the earth had been purified
by a general lustration;[30] and then with the seven just

[28] This Regeneration originated the very curious ceremony of the
Taurobolium and Criobolium, or the bloody baptism of the Bull and
Ram. (Vid. Ant. of Masonry, p. 115.) The ram as well as the bull
was a legitimate symbol of the Ark of Noah, and hence the motives
which produced the superstition will not be difficult to account for.

[29] The eastern Christians had a curious tradition, derived, probably, from some ceremony in the mysteries, which were decidedly
ark'te, that when God ordered Noah to build the Ark, he also directed
him to make an instrument of wood, such as is used in the East at
this day instead of bells, to call the people to worship, and named in
Arabic, *nakus,* which he was to strike three times every day, not only
to call together the workmen that were building the Ark, but to give
him an opportunity of daily admonishing them of the impending
danger of the Deluge. (Univ. Hist., vol. i., p. 43.)

[30] If the theory be correct which supposes the *natural* cause of the
Deluge to be the near approach of a powerful comet to the earth, as
is advanced by Mr. Whiston, whose power of attraction not only
elevated the tides to a prodigious height above their customary level,
but burst the central abyss and caused the waters to rush out with a
dreadful concussion—then the lustration may be said, as it **actually**

persons who were incarcerated with him, he emerged
into the light and hope of a new and perfect world on
which the favour of heaven once more smiled, as it did
on the first created man in the garden of Eden. The
candidate, at his initiation, was a representative of the
patriarch during his erratic voyage and subsequent de-
livery from destruction.[31] Like Noah, he beheld, in a
figurative manner, the uncontrolled licence of the iron
age,[32] the anarchy and contentions of the impious race
before the Flood, under the sway of their prince Ophion,[33]
—like Noah, he descended into Hades or the Ark, a place

was in the Mysteries, to have been accomplished by *fire and water;*
and it is remarkable that all the heathen accounts of the Deluge
ascribe that event to the agency of fire. (Ovid. Metam., l. i.) And
the account in Hesiod's Theogony of the destruction of the Titans,
who were no other than the impious antediluvians. is replete with
the same terrific machinery; thunder, lightning, fire, and water. In
the highly figurative account of the Deluge exhibited in the Courma
Avater of the Hindoos, the mountain Mandar, which represents the
earth, is said to be involved in *raging flames* which spread destruction on every side. (Bhagvat Geeta. p. 148.) It was, indeed, a common belief amongst all nations that the Deluge was accompanied by
a torrent of fire. " Pionus, who suffered martyrdom in the year 250,
under the Emperor Decius, among other things, spake thus to his
unbelieving persecutors:—' Ye yourselves, from your old traditions,
acknowledge that the Deluge of Noah, whom you call Deucalion,
was *mingled with fire,* yet do you but half understand the real truth
of this matter.' " (Pontoppidon. Hist. Norway, p. 52.) Sale, from
Al Beidâwi says, that the waters of the Deluge were reputed to have
burst from a *hot-oven* at Cufâ; (Koran, Edit. 1825, vol. ii., p. 44, in
notâ. b.) and the Parsees similarly fabled that the waters proceeded
from the *hot-oven* of an old woman named Zala. On this curious
subject the authorities are numerous and convincing. The intelligent
reader may profitably consult Hyde de Rel. vet. Pers., c. 10. Vid.
etiam Plat. Tim., p. 22. Plin. Nat. Hist., l. ii., c. 25. Cedren. Hist.
Comp., p. 10. Strabo. Geogr., p. 197. Cudw. Int. Syst., p. 328.
Wilkins. Bhagvat. Geeta, p. 147. Fab. Pag. Idol., vol. ii., b. iii., c.
4. Myst. Cab., vol. i., p. 82. Dav. Celt. Res., p. 157. Maur. Ind.
Ant., vol. ii., p. 344. Edda Snor., Fab. 32. Mal. North. Ant., vol. ii.

[31] The Mysteries, in all their forms, were *funereal.* They celebrated the mystical death and revivification of some individual, by the
use of emblems at once impious and disgusting. David accuses the
Israelites of this abominable practice in Psalm cvi. (v. 28, 29.) "They
joined themselves to Baal Peor, (*Dionusus,* Orph., Hymn 5.) and *ate
the sacrifices of the dead.* Thus they provoked Him to anger with
their inventions."

[32] Vid. Ovid. Metam., l. i.

[33] Apollon. Argon., l. i. Ophion was no other than the infernal
Serpent, the equal foe of God and man.

of solitude and darkness, and here in safety he heard the
dissolution of the world, the rush of waters, the dismemberment of rocks and mountains, the bitter cries and
shrieks of despairing sinners in the agonies of remorse
and death;—like Noah, he passed unhurt through the
purifying element;[34] and being thus regenerated, like the
diluvian patriarch, he emerged into a new life of purity
and perfection,[35] and rejoiced in the distinction which, he
was taught to believe, his piety had conferred.[36]

The legend of initiation was this. Osiris,[37] king of
Egypt, to confer benefits on the nations around him, left
the government of his kingdom to the care of his wife
Isis, and travelled for three years to communicate to
them the arts of civilization. On his return, he fell a
sacrifice to the intrigues of his brother Typhon, who had
formed a conspiracy in his absence to destroy him and
usurp his throne. He was invited to a grand entertainment in the month of November, when the Sun was in
Scorpio, at which all the conspirators were present.

---

[34] Ablutions were profusely used during the initiations. Nationes
extraneæ—sacris quibusdam initiantur *Isidis* alicujus, aut Mithræ
per lavacrum. (Tertull.) Apuleius thus describes those of Isis: Sa-
cerdos, stipatum me religiosâ cohorte, deducit ad proximas balneas;
et prius *sueto lavacro* traditum, præfatus Deum veniam, purissimè
circumrorans abluit. (Metam., lib. ix.)

[35] The aspirant *figuratively*, like Noah in *reality*, was thus said to
be an inhabitant of two worlds; and to be equally acquainted with
things past, present, and to come; in præteritorum memoria et pro-
videntia futurorum. Cic. de Senect.

[36] Thus introduced to all the blessings of a new mythological existence, the aspirant was represented under the figure of a new born
infant seated on the lotos or water lily, which was a symbol of the
Ark of Noah. But the infant and lotos was an emblem of the Sun,
(Plut. de Isid. et Osir., p. 355,) as well as of the *aphanism* and
euresis; and, therefore, the regenerated aspirant was an emblem of
the Sun; which agrees with the patriarch Noah in the helio-arkite
superstition.

[37] The fable respecting the birth of Osiris is thus related by the
authors of the Universal History, (vol. i., p. 268): "On the day
Osiris was born, a voice was heard crying out—'the Lord of all
things is come into the world;'—or, according to others, a damsel
called Pamyles, going to fetch water from the temple of Jupiter, at
Thebes, heard a loud voice commanding to proclaim—'The great
and beneficent king Osiris is born.' He was delivered to this damsel,
who was directed to nurse him, which she did with all the veneration
due to such a charge; performing the mysteries called **Pamylia, like**
those styled Palephoria, in honour of the infant."

Typhon produced a valuable chest, richly inlaid with gold, and promised to give it to any person present whose body it would most conveniently contain. Osiris was tempted to try the experiment; but was no sooner laid in the chest, than it was nailed down and thrown into the river. This was the *aphanism* of the Mysteries; and it must be observed that the candidate was put through a corresponding series of ceremonies to produce a strong and lasting impression upon his mind. The first persons who discovered the above transaction were Pan[33] and the Satyrs, who communicated the intelligence to the inhabitants, and they were filled with horror and amazement.

The body of Osiris, thus committed to the mercy of winds and waves, was cast up at Byblus, in Phenicia,[39] and left at the foot of a tamarind tree. Isis, in the extremity of sorrow and despair at the loss of her husband, set out in company with Thoth, and traversed the earth in search of the body, making the air re-echo with her lamentations. After many extraordinary adventures, they at length gained possession of her husband's corse, with which she returned to Egypt in triumph, intending to give it a splendid interment. By the treachery of Typhon she was again deprived of the body, which was severed into *fourteen* parts, and secreted in as many different places. Isis, with unparalleled zeal and perseverance, undertook a second journey to search for the scattered fragments; and after considerable fatigue, and repeated disappoint-

[38] This is said to be the origin of the word *panic* to express exceeding great amazement and fear." (Plut. Is. et Osir., p. 19.)

[39] The present appearance of the caverns at Byblus, where these ceremonies were solemnized, is thus described: "About half a mile to the southward of the court are two towers, supposed to be sepulchral monuments, for they stand on an ancient burying place. [The initiations were always funereal.] They are about ten yards distant from each other, one in form of a cylinder, crowned by a multilateral pyramid, thirty-three feet high including the pedestal, which is ten feet high and fifteen square. The other is a long cone, discontinued at about the third part of its height; and, instead of ending in a point, wrought into an hemispherical form: it stands upon a pedestal six feet high, and sixteen feet six inches square, adorned at each angle with the figure of a lion in a sitting posture. Under ground there are square chambers of convenient height for a man, and *long cells branching out from them, variously disposed and of different lengths.* These subterraneous chambers and cells are cut out of the hard rock." (Univ Hist., vol. ii., p. 9.)

ments, she succeeded in finding every part, and buried them in the several places where they were discovered, erecting an altar over every grave, to mark the situation where her beloved husband's remains were deposited. It was then proclaimed that Osiris was risen from the dead ; and the most extravagant demonstrations of joy were used to express the sincere delight of the mystæ on this interesting occasion. This was the *euresis*.

It will be observed that the main facts in this fable were in all countries the same, although the names of the individuals in whose honour the rites were celebrated, varied with the varying language of the people.

> Ogygia me Bacchum vocat ;
> Osirin Egyptus putat ;
> Mysi Phanacem nominant ;
> Dionuson Indi existimant ;
> Romana sacra Liberum ;
> Arabica gens Adoneum.[40]

As in Egypt Osiris and Isis were the prominent deities, so in Greece the rites were celebrated in honour of Bacchus and Rhea ;[41] at Byblus, to Adonis and Venus ; in India, to Mahadeva and Sita ; in Britain, to Hu and Ceridwen ; in Scandinavia, to Woden and Frea, &c. ; and amongst the Pelasgi they were called the mysteries of the Dii Magni. In every instance these divinities represented the two most obvious lights of heaven, the sun and the moon.[42] On the above legend the dramatic scenes of initiation were constructed. They were pompous and imposing, and conducted with great splendour, as vehicles intended to uphold false systems of religion ; and

---

[40] Auson. Epig. 30.

[41] The emblems by which this goddess was designated are so striking, that I cannot resist the opportunity of quoting them from the learned Bryant. (Anal., vol. iii., p. 247.) She is figured as a beautiful female personage and has a chaplet in which are seen *ears of corn* like rays. Her right hand reclines on a pillar of stone, in her left are spikes of corn, and on each side *a pomegranate*. Close by her side stands the *beehive*, out of the top of which there arise corn and flowers, to denote the renewal of seasons, and promise of plenty. In the centre of these fruits, the favourite emblem, the pomegranate, appears again and crowns the whole.

[42] Dion. Hal., l. 2, c. 12. Macrob. Saturn., l. c. 21. Diod. Bibl., l. p. 10. Varro de Ling. Lat., l. 4, p. 17. Orph. Fragm., iv., p. 364. Virg. Georg., l. 1. Montif. Ant., tom. 2, p. 189. W. Arch., vol. i., p. 365.

while they embodied important truths of revelation, studiously concealed them from the knowledge of all but those who were interested in perpetuating the imposture.

A new language, mysterious and symbolical, was adapted to these celebrations ; and a system of hierogly phics, legible only to the initiated, placed the learning, the morality, and the politics of every nation as decidedly out of the reach of popular acquirement, as if they had been incased in a rock of adamant.[43] And the jealousy of the hierophants, or dispensers of these Mysteries, became at length so strongly excited, that trembling for their secret, they subsequently invented a new hieroglyphic or sacred symbolical character[44] and language, which was exclusively appropriated to the highest Degree of their Order ;[45] in which it is probable that nearly the same symbolical *characters* were made use of, but the hidden meaning attached to each was entirely changed ;[46] so that even those who had been initiated into the preliminary Degrees, and made acquainted with the common *curiologic* and *tropical* hieroglyphics, were as completely ignorant of the nature and secrets of the ineffable Degrees, to which but few were admitted, as the uninitiated themselves.[47] So artfully were these mysteries constructed, that they were perfectly understood by none but the hierophants and mystagogues, whose interest and personal welfare were bound up in their concealment; and they succeeded so effectually in establishing an absolute control, by the influence of visionary and preternatural

[43] Vid. Pococke. Descr. of Egypt, vol. i., p. 227.

[44] Herod., l. ii., 36.

[45] So effectually was the meaning of these hieroglyphics hidden from all but the distinguished few, that in process of time the interpretation was entirely lost. At the invasion of Cambyses it was but imperfectly understood ; and in the time of Alexander the Macedonian, none could be found to show the meaning of, or design anew, a hieroglyphical inscription.

[46] Thus, if in the common hieroglyphic, a hawk signified the *human soul*, in the sacred hieroglyphic it would stand for *Expedition ;* and thus essentially would the signification of every particular emblem be altered.

[47] An opinion was industriously promulgated, that the sacred hieroglyphic and language was the same as was used by the celestial deities. (Jambl. de Myst., § 7, c. 4.) A phonetic alphabet has recently been discovered amongst these hieroglyphics, which is described and explained in my Theocratic Philosophy of Freemasonry, p. 122.

terrors, that the very name of INITIATION, though possessing a wild charm, whose effects on the mind were indescribable,[48] yet would conjure up unheard of fears, and blanch the cheek with imaginary apprehensions. Its process, by artful changes, introduced at different periods, in shades so delicate as to be unobserved, had become revolting;[49] its probations were severe. Innumerable ceremonies, wild and romantic, dreadful and appalling, had been engrafted on the few expressive symbols of primitive observance; and instances have occurred where the terrified aspirant, during the protracted rites, has absolutely expired through excess of fear.[50]

It has been observed that the priests were peculiarly interested in the general dissemination of the Mysteries,[51] and therefore it is no wonder that they should endeavour to induce as many as possible to participate in the advantages which were ostensibly attached to the process of initiation. For this purpose the Mysteries were proclaimed the beginning of a new life of reason and virtue;[52] and the initiated, or esoteric companions were said to entertain the most agreeable anticipations respecting

[48] Whence the Greek proverb, when any one was transported with extraordinary sensations of pleasure, Ἐποπτεύειν μοι δοκῶ, I feel as though I had been initiated. (Vid. Warb. Liv. Leg., vol. i., p. 166.)

[49] Clemens of Alexandria exclaims with indignation : " Such are your voluptuous symbols—your insulting theologies—the institutions of your libidinous gods—your satyrs, naked nymphs, and contests of buffoons exposed in shameless nudity." It is a melancholy fact, that in the mysteries practised at Alexandria, children of both sexes were slain ; divination being effected by their entrails, and their flesh eaten. (Socr.. l. 3., c. 13.)

[50] Vid. infra, Lect. vii.

[51] The whole of Egypt, says Diodorus, being divided into a number of parts called nomes by the Greeks, each of these is governed by a Nonarcha, to whom the care of its public concerns is entrusted. The land being everywhere divided into three portions, *the first is occupied by the priesthood*, who are held in the greatest respect by the inhabitants, as being devoted to the worship of the gods ; and as possessing the greatest power of understanding, from the superiority of their education ; and from the revenues of these lands they perform all sacrifices throughout Egypt, and support the servants of the temples as well as their own families; for they hold that the administration of the honours of the gods ought not to be fluctuating, but to be conducted always by the same persons, and in the same manner; and that those who are above all their fellow citizens in wisdom and knowledge, ought not to be below any of them in the comforts and conveniences of life. [52] Cic. de Leg., l. ii., c. 14.

death and eternity ;[53] to comprehend all the hidden mysteries of nature ;[54] to have their soul restored to the
state of perfection from which it had fallen, and at their
death to be elevated to the supernal mansions of the
gods.[55]   They were believed also to convey much temporal felicity, and to afford absolute security amidst the
most imminent dangers by land or water.[56]   On the other
hand a public odium was studiously cast on those who
refused the rites.[57]   They were considered as profane
wretches, unworthy of public employment or private
confidence ;[58] sometimes proscribed as obdurate atheists,[59]
and finally condemned to everlasting punishment.   And[60]
to heighten the impression, the despisers of the Mysteries
were considered marked men.   They were exhibited in
the dramatic machinery of initiation as enduring the
pains of Tartarus—a doom which was pronounced to be
everlasting.   These motives were strengthened by that
undefined principle of curiosity, which is always excited
by a system in which secrecy forms a prominent feature ;
for the human mind, reaching forward to extended information, seeks for it in those institutions where it is supposed to be preserved;   and the knowledge which is
enveloped in mystery is frequently courted with greater
eagerness than that which is open to public inspection.
We do not esteem the sciences or languages which we
know equally with others of which we are ignorant; and
those are always deemed the most abstruse, of which we
possess the least degree of information.   From the prevalence of this general feeling it was that such a high
degree of public curiosity attached to the Mysteries.
They professed to be a short and certain step to universal
knowledge, and to elevate the soul to absolute perfection ;
but the *means* were shrouded under the impenetrable veil

[53] Isoc. Paneg.   [54] Clem. Alex. Strom. 5.
[55] Plat. Phæd. The evidences of this fact are numerous and weighty ;
and serve to prove that a future state of rewards and punishments
formed a prominent doctrine in the Mysteries.
[56] Schol. in Aristoph. Iren., v. 275.   Thus the Argonauts are fabled
to have been initiated at Samothrace, to procure an auspicious voyage
(Apollon. Rhod. Argon.)   The faith in such protection, however
was suspended on the possession of amulets which were delivered to
the candidates at their initiation.
[57] Warb. Div. Leg., vol. i., p. 140.   [58] Plat. Phæd.
[59] Lucian. Demon.   [60] Orig. cont. Cels., l. viii.

of secrecy, sealed by oaths and penalties the most tremendous and appalling."[61] This feeling was not a little encouraged by the hieroglyphical characters with which the walls, columns, and ceilings of the most sacred temples were curiously decorated. A laudable thirst after knowledge prompted the youth of all ranks to aspire to the ambition of decyphering the meaning and illustration of these obscure symbols, which were said to have been communicated to the priests by revelation from the celestial deities. Initiation was the only means of acquiring this knowledge, and it is therefore no wonder that initiation was so much in request.[62]

There was also another quality of the mind which served to recommend the mysteries :—that strange attachment to the marvellous by which every grade of human nature is swayed. To excite this sentiment in all its sublimity of horror, the initiations were performed at the dead of night (εν σκοτω και νυκτι.)[63] No severity of probation could deter the bold and determined aspirant from encountering terrors and actual dangers which led to the gratification of his curiosity; and the shades of darkness imparted vigour to the passion which looked forward to a recompense of such an exalted nature.[64]

---

[61] See Meurs. Elusin., c. 20, and many other authorities which will satisfy the most sceptical, that the system was a kind of Inquisition, based on terror, and supported by superstition of the very worst kind.

[62] All persons were initiated into the Lesser, but few into the Greater mysteries.

[63] Eurip. Bacchant., Act. 2. *Black*, the emblem of night, was considered the proper colour to shadow the mysteries : (Strabo. Georg., l. 17,) and hence the early idolatry of most nations was directed to a *black stone* ; (Porph. apud. Euseb. præp. even., l. iii., c. 3. Appollon Rhod. Argon., l. i., 1176,) and when this stone was in the form of a *Cube*, it was emblematical of the altar of Noah. Even the detached tribes of wandering Arabs venerated the *black stone* Kaábah, which is described as being originally "whiter than snow and more brilliant than the sun." At the time of the Flood, say the Arabian writers, "it was taken up to heaven, or elsewhere, where God chose, and restored to Abraham, by the angel Gabriel, when he built the temple." (Al Azáli, cited by Wait, Orient. Ant., p. 41.)

[64] Darkness was an emblem of death ; and death was a prelude to resurrection. It will at once be seen, therefore, in what manner the doctrine of the resurrection was inculcated and exemplified in these remarkable institutions.

But the potent spell which sealed the authority of the hierophant was the horrid custom, resorted to in times of pressing danger or calamity, of immolating human victims,[65] the selection of which was commonly the prerogative of the chief hierophant.[66] It is difficult to pronounce, with any degree of precision, what was the origin of this revolting practice, although it might probably have arisen from an imperfect knowledge of the prediction of the Messiah.[67] Thus were the initiated placed, by the sanction of supernatural apprehensions, at the absolute disposal of the hierophant; and the most exalted rank was not exempt from an abject subserviency, which was cemented by fearful oaths and heavy and destructive penalties.[68] Few, however, of the myriads who sought admission into the lesser Mysteries, attained to the higher and more perfect Degrees, for here were imbedded the real secrets of the Institution.[69] The most careful selection and preparation were necessary to determine who were fitted for these important disclosures; and for this purpose they were subjected to a lengthened probation of four years[70] before it was considered safe to admit them into the Sanctum Sanctorum, to become depositaries of those truths, the disclosure of which might endanger, not only the Institution, but also the authority of the civil magistrate. Hence to reveal the Mysteries was the highest crime a person could commit, and was usually punished by an ignominious

[65] Diod. Sic., l. v.   Strabo, l. iv.   Euseb. Orat. ad Const.

[66] Sammes. Brit., vol. i., p. 104.

[67] Vid. Ces. bel. Gal., l. vi., c. 16.

[68] The inviolable *oath* of Jupiter, by Styx, was referred to in the initiations, and is thought by Mr. Faber to bear a reference to the oath of God, at the Deluge, that he would no more drown the world; "for which reason, Iris, the rainbow, the daughter of Thaumas, is represented by Hesiod as hovering over the broad surface of the ocean, when this oath of Jupiter was taken. Now that such a phenomenon appeared immediately after the Deluge, we are expressly informed by Moses; and it is observable, moreover, that it was made a special sign of God's oath to Noah. Vid. Gen. ix., 13." Faber. Mys. Cab., vol. i., p. 261; and see Fab. Pag. Idol., vol. i., p. 372, with authorities.

[69] Clem. Alex. Strom. 5. And these were the Creation, Fall, and promise of a Mediator; the unity and trinity of the Godhead; the Deluge; redemption by a bloody sacrifice; and the soul's existence in a future state.

[70] Tertul. adv. Valentin.

death,[71] embittered by denunciations of the hottest pains
of Tartarus in another world.[72]

The places of initiation were contrived with much art
and ingenuity, and the machinery with which they were
fitted up was calculated to excite every passion and
affection of the mind. Thus the hierophant could rouse
the feelings of horror and alarm; light up the fire of
devotion, or excite terror and dismay; and when the soul
had attained its highest climax of apprehension, he was
furnished with the means of soothing it to ·peace, by
phantasmagoric visions of flowery meads, purling streams,
and all the tranquil scenery of Nature in its most en-
gaging form, accompanied with strains of heavenly music,
the figurative harmony of the spheres. These places
were indifferently a pyramid,[73] a pagoda, or a labyrinth,[74]
furnished with vaulted rooms, extensive wings connected

[71] Clem. Alex. Strom. 2. Sam. Petit. in lege Attic. p. 33. Si quis
arcanæ mysteria Cereris sacra vulgâsset, lege morti addicebatur.

[72] Virg. Æn. l. vi.

[73] The pyramids were doubtless erected very soon after the dispersion, as copies of the great phallic tower on the plain of Shinar; and
as the latter was designed for initiation, so were the former. We are
told, by an acute observer, that the second pyramid has two elaborate
pieces of cavern architecture attached to the north and west sides,
thirty feet in depth, and fourteen hundred feet in length, hewn out of
the solid rock on which the pyramid rests; and hollowed into an
extensive range of apartments. The entrance is narrow, and the construction of the cells intricate, all involved in darkness, and many of
them closed up with an accumulation of dust and rubbish. They had
a communication with the interior of the pyramid, which cannot now
be discovered, as many of the cells are entirely choked up (Greaves.
Pyram., vol. ii., p. 34); and it may be added, that perhaps the only
entrance was from the caverns beneath, into which the egress from
the pyramid was by a shaft or well; for we know that pits or wells
were occasionally used in the mysteries (Fab. Pag. Idol., vol. iii.,
p. 187, Maur. Ind. Ant., vol. v., p. 1061), and a well did actually exist
in the pyramid, the use of which is otherwise unknown. "At the
extremity of one of the passages" says Sir R. Wilson, "is a well, the
depth of which was never ascertained." (Vid. also Pococke's Descrip.
of the East, vol. i., p. 243.) Mr. Greaves thinks that these apartments were for the priest to lodge in; but independently of the consideration that such extensive excavations would never have been
made out of the hard rock with the chisel for mere dwellings, when
buildings on the surface would have been erected at one hundredth
part of the labour and expense, it is clear from the internal construction of these spacious caverns, that they were intended to contain the
apparatus of initiation into the mysteries and were exclusively devoted to this important purpose.

[74] The labyrinths of Egypt, Crete, Lemnos, and Italy, were **equally**

by open and spacious galleries, multitudes of secret dungeons, subterranean passages, and vistas, terminating in adyta,[75] which were adorned with mysterious symbols carved on the walls and pillars, in every one of which was enfolded some philosophical or moral truth.[76] Sometimes the place of initiation was constructed in a small island in the centre of a lake;[77] a hollow cavern natural or artificial, with sounding domes, tortuous passages, narrow orifices, and spacious sacelli;[78] and of such magnitude as to contain a numerous assembly of persons.[79] In all practicable instances they were constructed within the recesses of a consecrated grove, which in the torrid regions of the east conveyed the united advantages of secrecy and shade; and to inspire a still greater venera-

designed for initiation into the mysteries. (Fab. Pag. Idol., vol. iii., p. 269.)

[75] Plut. de Isid. et Osir., p. 639.

[76] In the Divine Legation of Moses, the learned Warburton has given some plates from the Bembine Table, which is an invaluable specimen of the secret symbols concentrating the leading principles of Egyptian politics, learning and religion.

[77] One of the most sacred places which ancient Egypt could boast, was the small island of Phile in the Nile, near the cataracts. The whole island was dedicated to Osiris and Isis, and appropriated to their worship: and a superb temple was erected, which almost covered its entire surface, where the relics of Osiris were said to be preserved. "Throughout the whole of this famous island," says Mr. Maurice (Ind. Ant., vol. iii., p. 536), "where anciently the solemn and mysterious rites of Isis were celebrated with such distinguished pomp and splendour, there appeared to Mr. Norden to run subterranean passages. He attempted to descend several of the steps that led down into them, but was prevented, by the filth and rubbish with which they were filled, from penetrating to any depth. It was in these gloomy caverns that the grand and mystic arcana of this goddess were unfolded to the adoring aspirant, while the solemn hymns of initiation resounded through the long extent of these stony recesses. It was there that superstition at midnight waved high her flaming torch before the image of Isis borne in procession; and there that her chosen priests, in holy ecstacy, chaunted their sweetest symphonies."

[78] Plut. de Isid. et Osir., p. 639.

[79] Strabo. Georg., l. ix In the *particular* mysteries of every nation, these places will be described with some degree of minuteness; suffice it to say here, that such complicated excavations are common in every part of the world, and were indubitably used as places of initiation. (Vid. Pag. Idol., vol. iii., p. 254.) Even the stable, or rather the cave at Bethlehem, in which Jesus Christ was born, if we may credit the testimony of the learned Calmet, was afterwards devoted by the Emperor Adrian, to the celebration of the mysteries of Thammuz or Adonis. (Cal. Dict. in v. Bethlehem.)

tion, they were properly denominated *Tombs*, or places of sepulture.[80]

Thus invested by superstition with tremendous powers, which assigned to them the province of executing the will and pleasure of the *infernal*, as well as the *celestial* deities, these potent priests became possessed of absolute authority, as the accredited agents of invisible beings, and frequently beheld even monarchs crouching at their feet, and submitting, without murmur or complaint, to their arbitrary or wanton inflictions, against which, indeed, there was no appeal. Thus despotic, it is scarcely to be supposed that this proud hierarchy would exercise its influence with moderation. They had the privilege of nominating human victims; but as the devoted offering might be redeemed by a heavy fine proportionate with his wealth or rank, it is reasonable to believe that the ransom would be paid, even though the unbounded avarice of the priest might assess the penalty at a large proportion of his temporal possessions. Thus they controlled senators and kept monarchs in awe: and as they increased in riches, the inevitable result of the system, they imbibed a corresponding love of magnificence and luxury. The crimes and indecencies of their order were soon transferred to the initiations; and, at length, this haughty priesthood fell with greater rapidity than it had risen; for the open debaucheries of the one, and the unbounded licentiousness which pervaded the other, excited public horror and aversion, against the effects of which, their wealth and power were equally unavailable. At this period of the degeneracy and degradation of the Mysteries, the blaze of Christianity, like a glorious PILLAR OF FIRE, penetrated into their darkest recesses; the demons fled,[81] at the approach of Truth, and the

[80] Jul. Firm. de. error., p. 4. Diod. Bibl., p. 194. Hence the pyramids of Egypt were accounted to be Tombs. And justly; for the rites of initiation there celebrated were funereal.

[81] Strabo, l. vi., tells us, that in the times of Augustus Cesar, the Oracle ceased to give responses; and to the same effect Suidas (in voc. Delphi.) says, that after the birth of Christ, Augustus enquiring of the Oracle whom he should appoint as his successor to the imperial diadem, was answered, that the God of gods was incarnate amongst the Hebrews, and had commanded him to return to his place; that he could not disobey, and therefore no responses would be given. (Vid. Antiq. of Masonry, p. 82.) And the Christian has no reason to doubt

institutions which they upheld, finally sank to rise no more.

These united causes were the precursors of their destruction; for the reality having appeared, the types, whether Jewish, or heathen, were no longer necessary. In the year 364, says Zosimus,[82] Valentinian published a law forbidding nocturnal sacrifices, for the purpose of preventing the indecencies which were perpetrated in the Mysteries. But the pro-consul of Greece, Pretextatus, thinking that the law would impel the people to despe-ration, if they were prevented from performing the sacred Mysteries, upon which, as they believed, the welfare of mankind solely depended,[83] permitted them to be cele-brated, provided everything was done decently and in order. Subsequently, however, Theodosius sent Cyne-gius into Egypt, with orders to close the temples and places of initiation, who executed his commission to the letter. He shut up the temples, and prohibited the cele-bration of the Mysteries all over the East, and even in Alexandria itself; and finally abolished these institutions, and every branch of the ancient and religious rites; although it has been said,[84] and probably with some truth, that these rites were secretly performed in Greece and Rome, for several centuries after the Advent of Christ,[85] under the pretext of convivial meetings. Psellus

the accuracy of this account, from the numerous instances, in his own Scriptures, of infernal spirits being ejected at the command of Christ and his Apostles.

[82] Zos., l. 4, p. 735.

[83] The pagans entertained such a very high opinion of the Mysteries, that one of their best writers attributes the dissolution of the Roman polity to their suppression. He says (Zos., l. 2. p. 671), "whilst, therefore, the Mysteries were performed, according to the appointment of the oracle, and as they really ought to be done, the Roman Empire was safe, and they had, in a manner, the whole world in subjection to them. But the festivals having been neglected from the time that Dioclesian abdicated, they have decayed and sunk into oblivion."

[84] Gibbon, vol. v., p. 110.

[85] The legend of initiation was subsequently interwoven into Chris-tianity by a sect of heretics who flourished soon after the time of the Apostles, called the Basilideans. The founders of this sect, in imita-tion of Pythagoras, enjoined on the candidates for admission into his school a five years' silence; and adopting some of the astronomical absurdities which he had learned in Egypt, engrafted them into his system, which caused his followers to be anathematized by the Church. Assuming Osiris to be the sun, Isis the moon, and Typhon

says, that in Athens they were practised till the eighth century; and we are assured, on undoubted authority, namely, from the Bardic writings of that period, that they were celebrated in Wales and Scotland, down to the twelfth century of Christianity.

Scorpio, he taught his disciples to frame crystals bearing these emblems, which were used as amulets or talismans to protect them from danger. Mr. Hutchinson, in an early edition of his "Spirit of Masonry," has given an engraving of one of these gems, in which the above symbols bear a conspicuous figure; and they are accompanied by a brilliant star and the serpent. The moon is depicted in its increase as a crescent, because Isis is represented with horns, like a new moon. These were a transcript of the talismans of Persia and Arabia, which were delivered to every candidate at his initiation into the Mysteries. By the former they were termed *azimet;* by the latter, *alakakir;* and subsequently *abrac, abraxas,* or *abracadabra.*

LECTURE II.

HISTORY OF INITIATION IN HINDOOSTAN.

INDIA is a very ancient nation; derived, if its own annals are deserving of credit, from the seven Rishis or penitents, whose exemplary virtues elevated them to a residence in the stars. These seven holy persons, according to the Abbe Dubois,[1] were the seven sons of Japhet,[2] who formed colonies in the neighbourhood of Mount Caucasus, and from thence their posterity spread over the vast continent of ancient India.[3] And Mr. Maurice is of opinion that they proceeded thence to the remotest regions of the west. These primitive inhabitants practised the patriarchal religion, and, consequently, worshipped the true God, until they were conquered and subjected to the yoke by the idolatrous Cuthites, under Rama, the victorious son of Cush;[4] and then the diluvian Mysteries were introduced, with all the horrible rites

[1] Description of India, pt. i., c. 6.

[2] The Indian Records present us with this information, in language very similar to our own Sacred Writings. "It is related in the Padma-Pooraun, that Satyavrata, whose miraculous preservation from a general deluge is told at large in the Matsya, had three sons, the eldest of whom was named Jyapeti, or Lord of the Earth; the others were Charma and Sharma; which last words are in the vulgar dialects usually pronounced Cham and Sham, as we frequently hear Kishn for Chrishna. The royal patriarch, for such is his character in the Pooraun, was particularly fond of Jyapeti, to whom he gave all the regions to the north of Himalaya, or the Snowy Mountains, which extend from sea to sea, *and of which Caucasus is a part*; to Sharma he allotted the countries to the south of those mountains; but he cursed Charma, because when the old monarch was accidentally inebriated with strong liquor made of fermented rice, Charma laughed; and it was in consequence of his father's execration that he became a slave to the slaves of his brothers." (Maur. Hist. Hind., vol.ii., p. 45.)

[3] It is highly probable, however, notwithstanding the authority in the text, that the seven Rishis were the seven persons who were preserved with Noah in the Ark.

[4] Gen. x., 7.

and disgusting superstitions' which had polluted the religion of the descendants of Ham. The system of divine worship, after this innovation, soon became divided into two discordant Sects; the one mild and benevolent, addressed to Vishnu,[5] the other, which proclaimed the superiority of Siva, was a system of terror and penance, barbarity and blood.[6] The professors of these sectarial divisions bore an irreconcilable hatred to each other, and were equally distinguished by feelings of such interminable hostility, that if an individual of each adverse party accidentally met, they considered themselves polluted, till by some purifying rite of devotion, they had obliterated the stain.[7]

The chief deity of this vast empire was the tri-une Brahma—Vishnu—Siva,[8] who was said to dwell on the holy mountain Meru, whose three peaks were composed of gold, silver and iron; the central peak was appropriated to Siva, and the two others to Brahma and Vishnu.[9] But the Indians " saw God in every object

[5] " The religion of the Vishnu sect," according to Maurice, " is of a cheerful and social nature. Theirs is the festive song, the sprightly dance, and the resounding cymbal; libations of milk and honey flow upon his altars; the gayest garlands decorate his statues; aromatic woods eternally burn before him; and the richest gems of the east disperse fragrance through the temples of the Preserver." (Ind. Ant., vol. v, p. 856.)

[6] Speaking of a temple near Bereng, the Persian historian says, " in the centre of the reservoir is an idol temple of stone—a beautiful fabric. At this place, the devotees surround themselves with fire till they are reduced to ashes, imagining they are, by this act, pleasing the deity." (Ayeen Akbery, vol. ii., p. 158.)

[7] Maur. Ind. Ant., vol. v., p. 863.

[8] This triad was variously represented by emblems in this quarter of the globe. The mystical zennar was a cord of three threads; the emblem borne in the hands of some of these deities, was a trident, similar to that of the Grecian Neptune; the mode of worship was ternary, and consisted of bowing the body three times; the principal deity in the cavern of Elephanta was depicted with three heads; the summit of the massive pyramidal pagoda of Tanjorn is surmounted by three peaks, &c., &c.

[9] Fab. Pag. Idol., vol. iii., p. 205. This custom of accounting the three peaked mountain holy, was not confined to the idolatrous nations, so called, but was venerated by the Jews. Thus Olivet, near the city of Jerusalem, had three peaks, which were accounted the residence of the deity, Chemosh—Milcom—Ashtoreth. (2 Kings xxiii., 13.) See, also, Zachariah, (xiv., 4.) where, by a sublime figure, the feet of the Almighty are placed on the two outer peaks of this mountain, during the threatened destruction of Jerusalem; while the

under the sun," and had consecrated and paid divine
honours to such a multitude of different substances, that
their Pantheon is said to have contained three hundred
and thirty millions of deities.[10]

The mysteries of India formed one of the earliest corruptions of the pure science which is now denominated
Freemasonry, and bore a direct reference to the happiness of man in paradise, the subsequent deviations from
righteousness, and the destruction accomplished by the
general Deluge.   They were celebrated in subterranean
caverns and grottoes,[11] formed in the solid rock by human
art and industry; or in the secret recesses of gloomy
pyramids and dark pagodas;[12] and the adoration of the
Solar Fire,[13] and the reputed perfection which its worship,
conveys, appear to have been the object and the end of
the initiated.   These caverns were frequently excavated in
the bosom of a grove of trees, which was thus converted
into a permanent residence of the deity;[14] and became a
source of high and superstitious terror to all the world
besides.   A brief description of the caverns of Elephanta
and Salsette, both situated near Bombay, will afford a
competent specimen of the inner apartments exhibited
in the places of secret celebration, which abound in the
vast continent of ancient India.   These stupendous edifices, carved out of the solid rock, and charged with
statues of every description and degree of magnitude,

mountain itself is made to split asunder, by a tremendous concussion,
at the centre peak, from east to west, leaving a great valley between
the divided parts.   Tatian (Orat. contra. Grœcos.) says that it was
Hiram's daughter, whom Solomon married, who seduced him to the
worship of this unholy triad on the above mountain.

[10] Statues of the principal Indian Gods may be seen in the Museum
of the Asiatic Society, London.

[11] Fab. Pag. Idol., vol. iii., p. 184, 254.

[12] Fab. Cab., vol. ii., p. 386.

[13] The earliest religious dance with which we are acquainted, was
in honour of the Solar Fire.   It was a wild and frantic movement,
accompanied with the clashing of swords and shields, and called
Betarmus; symbolical, according to Bryant, of the confusion which
occurred when the Noetic family quitted the ark.   But in process of
time, when the Sabian worship was engrafted upon the rites of the
ark, its influence extended also to the sacred commemorative dance.

[14] The solemnity of an extensive wood, or grove of ancient trees,
appears to have suggested to all nations the probability that it was
the sacred abode of the divinity.   And in the Heetopades, p. 243, it is
represented as a place of penance and mortification.

are of doubtful origin.[15]   Their antiquity is infolded in
the veil of obscurity; and the name of the monarch,
whose bold and aspiring mind, could project, and whose
power could execute such imperishable monuments of
human ingenuity and labour, is lost and forgotten in the
lethean stream of time.[16]

The cavern of Elephanta, the most ancient temple in
the world, framed by the hand of man,[17] is one hundred
and thirty-five feet square,[18] and eighteen feet high.   It
is supported by four massive pillars, and its walls are
covered on all sides with statues and carved emblematical
decorations.[19]   Maurice[20] says "that some of the figures
have on their heads a kind of helmet of a pyramidal
form; others wear crowns, rich with devices, and splendidly decorated with jewels; while others display only
large bushy ringlets of curled or flowing hair.   Many
of them have four hands, many have six, and in those
hands they grasp sceptres and shields, the symbols of justice and ensigns of religion, the weapons of war and
the trophies of peace."   The adytum, placed at the
western extremity of this extensive grotto, was accessible
by four entrances, each guarded by two gigantic statues,

[15] Fab. Pag. Idol., vol. iii., p. 361.
[16] They may probably be ascribed to the first Cuthite conquerors
of India, whose enterprising genius would be applied, in times of
peace, to such stupendous works as might practically exhibit a striking
indication of their superiority over the vanquished people.
[17] Maur. Ind. Ant., vol. iv., p. 736.
[18] Goldingham, in Asiat. Res., vol. iv., p. 407.
[19] All the temples and pagodas of Hindoostan were ornamented
in the same style.   The temple of Jagan-nath "is a stupendous fabric,
and truly commensurate with the extensive sway of Moloch, horrid
king.   As other temples are usually adorned with figures emblematical
of their religion, so, Jagan-nath has representations, *numerous and
various*, of that vice which constitutes the essence of his worship.
The walls and gates are covered with indecent emblems, in massive
and durable sculpture." (Buchan. Res. in Asia, p. 133.)
[20] Ind. Ant., vol. ii., p. 245.   "Some of these figures have aspects
that inspire the beholder with terror; and, in the words of Lins-
choten, are distorted into such horrible and fearful forms, that they
make a man's hair stand upright; others are distinguished by a placid
serenity and benignity of countenance, and others betray evident
marks of deep dejection and inward anguish.   The more conspicuous
figures are all gorgeously arrayed, after the Indian fashion, with
heavy jewels in their ears, with superb collars of precious stones, with
belts sumptuously wrought, and with rich bracelets on their arms and
wrists." (Ibid.)

naked, and decorated with jewels and other ornaments.
In this sacellum, accessible only to the initiated, the
deity was represented by that obscene emblem, which
was used in a greater or less degree by all idolatrous
nations, to represent his generative power.[21]   On each
side were ranges of cells and passages, constructed for
the express purpose of initiation;[22] and a sacred orifice,
as the medium of regeneration.[23]

The caverns of Salsette, excavated in a rock whose
external form is pyramidal, and situated in the bosom of
an extensive and fearful wood, infested by enormous serpents and ravenous beasts,[24] very greatly exceed, in
magnitude, those of Elephanta; being in number three
hundred, all adorned with an abundance of carved and
emblematical characters.[25]   The largest cavern is eighty-
four feet long, forty-six broad, and forty high; full of
cavities on all sides, placed at convenient distances, for
the arrangement of the dreadful apparatus of initiation,
which was so constructed as to overwhelm the unconscious aspirant with horror and superstitious dread.   The
different ranges of apartments were connected by open
galleries; and the most secret caverns, which contained
the ineffable symbols, were accessible only by private
entrances, curiously contrived, to give greater effect to
certain points in the ceremonial of initiation; and a
cubical cista, for the periodical sepulture of the aspirant,
was placed in the inmost recesses of the structure.   In
every cavern was a carved basin, to contain the consecrated water of ablution. on the surface of which floated
the flowers of the lotus, this element being considered
the external medium by which purity was conveyed
And amongst an innumerable multitude of images and
symbolical figures with which the walls were covered,
the Linga,[26] or Phallus,[27] was everywhere conspicuous;
often alone, and sometimes in situations too disgusting to

---

[21] Maur. Ind. Ant., vol. ii., p. 332.   [22] Archæol., vol. vii., p. 287.
[23] Fab. Pag. Idol., vol. iii., p. 185. This orifice is used at the present
day, for the same mysterious purpose.
[24] Maur. Ind. Ant., vol. ii., p. 273.   Archæol. Ant., vol. vii., p. 333.
[25] Vid. Signs and Symbols, Lect. 9.
[26] Maur. Ind. Ant., vol. ii., p. 156.
[27] A specimen of this obscene emblem is preserved in the Museum
of the Asiatic Society, London.

be mentioned;[28] and typified equally by the petal and calyx of the lotos, the point within a circle,[29] and the intersection of two equilateral triangles.

The periods of initiation were regulated by the increase and decrease of the moon;[30] and the mysteries were divided into Four Steps, or Degrees, called *Char Asherum*, which were equally the dispensers of perfection in a greater or less degree.[31] The candidate might perform his first probation at the early age of eight years.[32] It consisted of an investiture with the Zennar, or sacred cord of three threads, which was explained to refer to the three elements, earth, fire, and air; for water, according to the Brahmins, is only air in a condensed form.[33] This investiture was attended with numerous ceremonies; with sacrifices to the Solar fire, to the planets, and to the household gods; with aqueous ablutions, and purifications with the dung and urine of the cow,[34] and ended with an extended lecture from his preceptor, usually too abstruse for his juvenile comprehension; the principal subject of which related to the unity

[28] "The tower of Jaggernaut," says Dr. Buchanan, (Res. in Asia, p. 145,) "is covered with indecent emblems, which are newly painted when it is exhibited in public, and are objects of sensual gaze *by both sexes*.

[29] Vide Signs and Symbols, Lect 9.

[30] I do not find what particular stage was the most auspicious for this purpose, except it was the ninth day of the decrease; at which time began the great festival in honour of the goddess Durga, who was the same as Juno, or, perhaps, the Minerva of the Greeks. The rites of this goddess bore a great similarity to those of Egypt and other nations. After various ceremonies, the image of the goddess was committed to the Ganges, and her mystical death was celebrated with lamentations; while the utmost joy prevailed when the idol emerged from the purifying stream. A great annual festival was held in January, on the seventh day of the New Moon, which was celebrated in honour of the Sun. (Holwell. Gent. Fast., p. 134.)

[31] "Let even the wretched man," says the Hitopadesa, "practise virtue, *whenever he enjoys one of the three or four religious Degrees*; let him be even-minded with all created things, and that disposition will be the source of virtue." (Hitop., b. iv.)

[32] Ordin. of Menu. Sir W. Jones' Works, vol. iii., p. 88. In Greece, children were, in like manner, initiated into the Lesser Mysteries.

[33] Maur. Ind. Ant., vol. v., p. 966.

[34] "They use *cowdung* in purification, because it is the medium by which the barren soil is rendered prolific; and, therefore, reminds them of the famous Indian doctrine of corruption and reproduction." (Maur. Ind. Ant., vol. v., p. 935.) The cow was a sacred animal.

and trinity of the godhead; the management of the
consecrated fire, and the holy rites of morning, noon,
and evening.[35] He was then clothed in a linen garment
without seam;[36] a cord was put over his right ear as a
medium of purification, and he was placed under the
exclusive care of a Brahmin, who was thence termed his
spiritual guide, to be instructed in the necessary qualifications for the Second Degree. He was inured to hard-
ships, suffered the infliction of rigid penances[37] until he
attained the age of twenty years; was restricted from
all indulgences, whether carnal or intellectual, and
passed the whole of his time in prayer and ablution.[38]
He was taught to preserve the purity of his body, which
was figuratively termed the city with nine gates, in
which the soul is imprisoned,[39] by avoiding external
defilements; to eat becomingly;[40] and was instructed in
all those minuter ceremonies which were adapted to
every act of his future life, and by the use of which he
was to be distinguished from the uninitiated. Much of
his time was devoted to the study of the sacred books;
for a competent knowledge of the institutions, ceremonies, and traditions of religion, were an essential
qualification for another Degree.

When he had attained the specified age, if he were
found, on examination, to have made due progress in the
mythological lore of the First Degree, he was admitted
to enter on the probationary ceremonies for the Second,
which was called Gerishth.[41] Here his austerities were
doubled; he was obliged to support life by soliciting
charity; his days were passed in prayer, ablutions and
sacrifice, and his nights in the study of Astronomy; and
when exhausted nature demanded repose, he stretched
his body under the first tree,[42] snatched a short sleep, and

---

[35] Ordin. of Menu. Sir. W. Jones. Works, vol. iii., p. 92.

[36] Maur. Ind. Ant., vol. v., p. 969.

[37] These penances were indeed rigid, if Mr. Maurice be correct in
his information, for he says, (Ind. Ant.; vol. iv., p, 574, in nota,) that
the candidates were plunged in alternate baths of fire and water!

[38] Ayeen Akbery. Maur. Ind. Ant., vol. ii., p. 346.

[39] Bhagvat Geeta, p. 48. The *nine* gates are the avenues of
evacuation, as the nose, mouth, ears, &c.

[40] A phrase meaning, literally, a total abstinence from animal food.

[41] Maur. Ind. Ant., vol. v., p. 972.

[42] Ayeen Akbery, vol. iii., p. 219.

rose speedily to contemplate the monsters of the skies,[43] personified in his imagination by the appearance and situation, of the fixed stars.[44] "In the hot season he sat exposed to five fires, four blazing around him, with the Sun above; in the rains he stood uncovered, without even a mantle, when the clouds poured the heaviest showers; n the cold season he wore wet clothing, and went on ncreasing by degrees the austerity of his devotion."[45] His probation being at length completed, he was admitted by initiation to participate in the privileges which the mysteries were believed to confer.

Sanctified by the sign of a Cross,[46] which was marked on every part of his body, he was subjected to the probation of Pastos,[47] which was denominated the door of Patala, or hell.[48] His purification being completed, he was led at the dead of night to the gloomy cave of mystery, which had been duly prepared for his reception.

The interior of this holy cavern blazed with a light equal to that of the meridian sun, proceeding from myriads of brilliant lamps.[49] There sat in rich and costly robes[50] the three chief hierophants,[51] in the East, West and South, to represent the great Indian triad, Brahma—Vishnu—Siva.[52] The attendant Mystagogues,

[43] The singular arrangement of the Fixed Stars into Constellations by the ancient Indians, was of a nature calculated to encourage the indulgence of this feeling.

[44] Maur. Ind. Ant., vol. vi., p. 974.

[45] Ordin. of Menu. Sir W. Jones. Works, p. 228.

[46] The Christian reader may start when he beholds the sacred emblem of his faith used as a symbol of heathen devotion; but it is even so. The holy Cross pointed to the four quarters of the compass; and was honoured as a striking emblem of the universe, by many ancient nations. It is found engraven on their monuments; and even the erection of many of their temples was conducted on the same cruciform principles. The two great pagodas of Benares and Mathura are erected in the form of vast crosses, of which each wing is equal in extent, (Maur. Ind. Ant., vol iii., p. 360, 377,) as is also the pyramidal temple of New Grange, in Ireland (Ledwich. Ant. Irel., p 316.) and many others. A specimen of the Crux Ansata may be seen in Pococke's elaborate description of the East. Plate 69, fig. 19.

[47] Signs and Symbols, Lect. 6.

[48] The Tartarus of the Grecian mysteries.

[49] Maur. Ind. Ant., vol. v., p. 898.

[50] Ibid. vol. ii., p. 357.

[51] Signs and Symbols, Lect., 7.

[52] When the Sun rises in the east, he is Brahma; when he gains his meridian in the south, he is Siva, and when he sets in the west, he is

clad in sacred vestments, having their heads covered each with a pyramidical cap, emblematical of the spiral flame, or the solar ray, were seated respectfully around. Thus disposed in solemn guise, the well-known signal from the sacred bell[53] summoned the aspirant into the centre of this august assembly; and the initiation commenced with an anthem to the great God of nature, whether as the Creator, Preserver, or Destroyer. The sacred business was then solemnly opened, with the following apostrophe to the Sun :—" O mighty being, greater than Brahma, we bow down before thee as the prime Creator! Eternal god of gods ! The world's mansion ! Thou art the incorruptible being, distinct from all things transient ! Thou art before all gods, the ancient Pooroosh,[54] and the supreme supporter of the universe! Thou art the supreme mansion! And by thee, O infinite form, the universe was spread abroad."[55]

The aspirant, already weakened by abstinence and mortification, was overawed by the display now exhibited before him; but, resuming his courage during this apostrophe, he prepared himself for the active business of initiation, in some doubt as to what results this unexpected scene would lead. His reflections were interrupted by a voice, which called upon him to make a formal declaration, that he will be tractable and obedient to his superiors; that he will keep his body pure, have a tongue of good report, observe a passive obedience in receiving the doctrines and traditions of the Order, and the firmest secrecy in maintaining inviolable its hidden and abstruse mysteries. This declaration having been

Vishnu. (Asiat. Res., vol. v., p. 254. Moor. Hind. Panth., p. 277.) Sir W. Jones thinks that Siva, like the Sabazius or Bacchus of the Greeks, was a corruption of Jehovah Sabaoth. (See also Cic. de nat. deor., l. iii., c. 23.)

[53] Ramayuna of Valmic. Saib Ibn Batric pretends that Noah had a bell in the Ark, made of the wood of the Indian plane. (Wait. Orient. Ant., p. 82.) The bells used in the Jewish ministrations, were imitated in the spurious Freemasonry, where they were profusely introduced ; and as they were attached to the priestly vestments, so were they worn by the Bacchantes in the Dionysiacal celebrations.

[54] Pooroosh literally means no more than *man* ; but in the Geeta it is a term in theology used to express the vital soul, or portion of the universal spirit of Brahm, inhabiting a body. (Vide Wilkins, Notes on the Geeta, p. 142.)

[55] Bhagvat Geeta, p. 94.

assented to, he was sprinkled with water; a mantra or incantation was pronounced over him, or more frequently whispered in his right ear;[56] he was divested of his shoes,[57] that the consecrated ground on which he stood might not be polluted, and was made to circumambulate the spacious cavern three times, in reference to the Tri-murti, whose representatives were stationed triangularly in the east, west, and south points of the circumference of the mystical circle. While performing this ceremony, he was taught to exclaim, on his arrival each time in the south, "I copy the example of the Sun, and follow his benevolent course." This being completed, he was again placed in the centre, and solemnly enjoined to the prac-tice of religious austerities, as the efficient means of preparing his soul for ultimate absorption; and was told

[56] The *mantra* is merely an invocation of the deity. According to Mr. Ward, in his "View of the Hindoos," the initiary incantation was this: Haree, Haree, Haree, Rama, Haree, Rama, Rama, Rama, Haree, &c.;" which is merely a repetition of the two names of the deity,; (Vid. Bhagvat Geeta, p. 156,) and they believe that this repetition has abundance of merit; and that, like fire, these names will consume and destroy their most inveterate sins. How contrary to the simple com-mand of the true God, "Thou shalt not take the name of the Lord thy God in vain!" The Hindoos are further persuaded, that by medi-tating on the perfections of the deity, and pronouncing those meritori-ous names, they are enabled to penetrate into futurity, and to obtain every wish of their hearts.

[57] This was the common practice of antiquity. "Moses at the Bush, and at the Mount, was enjoined to take the shoes from off his feet, because the place on which he stood was holy ground. Herodotus and Diodorus Siculus assure us. that when the Egyptian priests adored any of their deities, their feet were uncovered. According to Strabo, such was the practice with the sacerdotal Order among the Germans; and such was the case in the worship of Diana and Vesta, which the fathers assert to have been borrowed from Moses. Silius Italicus (Bel. Pun., l. iii.,) says of the priests of Hercules,

——— Nec discolor ulli
Ante aras cultus; velantur corpora lino,
Et Pelusiaco præfulget stamine vertex,
Distinctis mos thura dare, atque, à *logo parentum*,
Sacrificam, lato vestem distinguere clavo.
Pes nudus, tonsæque comæ, costumque cubile,
Inrestricta focis servant altaria flammæ.

In 2 Chron. xxviii., 15, the captives taken by the children of Israel from the cities of Judah and Jerusalem are depicted as barefooted, previously to the harangue of Oded; and Isaiah walked barefooted, to typify the captivity in Babylon. Several gentile philosophers affected to do the same to enforce reverence from their disciples." (Wait, on Jewish, &c., Antiquities, p. 69.)

that the merit of such works will emit a splendour which renders man not only superior to the gods, but makes those immortal beings subservient to his wishes.[58]

After this admonition, the aspirant was placed under the care of his gooroo or spiritual guide, and directed to observe a profound silence during the whole of the succeeding ceremonies, under the denunciation of summary punishment from the presiding Brahmin, who, he was told, possessed unlimited power, even to strike him dead on the spot with a malediction, should he presume to violate the injunction now imposed upon him. Thus instructed, the subdued candidate endeavoured to preserve the utmost equanimity of temper during the process of initiation; fearing, lest by any involuntary expression which might imply cowardice or disapprobation, he should elicit the dreaded resentment of this potent avenger; for the gooroo was usually possessed of much discrimination, and was always prepared to punish the indiscreet disciple who should fail in any point, either of deference or respect; or betrayed any symptoms of dread or irresolution.

The bewailings for the loss of Sita then began.[59] The aspirant was passed through seven[60] ranges of dark[61] and

[58] It is no uncommon thing to read in the Puranas, and other writings, of a religious ascetic, who has attained the high distinction of Brahma's blessing, by the performance of the prescribed observances, tyranizing over the whole host of deities, and commanding them to perform the most menial services to gratify his curiosity, or to amuse his imagination. These austerities do not necessarily include the practice of morality; for the Hindoos hold that though they live in the habitual commission of every known sin throughout the whole period of their lives, yet if they are able to repeat the name of a god with their dying lips, it is a certain passport to heaven. Mr. Ward, (View of the Hindoos, b. i., c. 2, § 11,) says, "A Hindoo shopkeeper one day declared to the author, that he should live in the practice of adultery, lying, &c., till death; and that then repeating the name Krishnu, he should without difficulty ascend to heaven!" How nearly allied is this to the creed of some Christian sects.

[59] In some of these celebrations, the death of Cama was lamented with solemn dirges and bewailings. This god, who was the Cupid of Hindoostan, is said to have been slain by Iswara, and committed to the waves inclosed in a chest, like the Grecian Bacchus, and the Egyptian Osiris. The chest was swallowed by a fish, which being caught, the infant was taken from its entrails, and nurtured by Reti, &c. (Asiat. Res., vol. iii., p. 187.)

[60] Niebuhr. Voy. in Arab., tom. ii., p. 28.

[61] Maur. Ind. Ant., vol. v., p. 274.

gloomy caverns, amidst the din of howling, shrieks, and dismal lamentations, to represent the bewailings of Mahadeva, who is fabled to have circumambulated the world *seven* times, with the remains of his murdered consort on his shoulders.[62] Amidst all this confusion a sudden explosion was heard, which seemed to rend the mountains whose gloomy recesses they were now exploring, and this was instantaneously followed by a dead silence. Flashes of brilliant light streamed before their eyes, which were succeeded by the blackest darkness. To his utter astonishment, the candidate now beheld shadows and phantoms of various and compound shapes, surrounded with rays of light flitting across the gloom.[63] Some with many hands, arms, and legs; others without any of those appendages; here a shapeless trunk, there a human body with the head of a bird, beast or fish; now a human trunk with bestial extremities, succeeded by the body of an animal with the- head of a man.[64] Some with "fiery eyes, yellow bodies, red faces, long ears, armed with tridents and axes in their right hands, and holding human skulls and vases in their left. Others having three eyes and strings of human skulls suspended round their necks, with long, straggling, frightful teeth."[65] Amongst these he saw one terrible figure, who had "a gorgeous appearance, with a thousand heads, and on each of them a crown set with resplendent gems, one of which was larger and brighter than the rest; his eyes gleamed like flaming torches, but his neck, his tongues, and his body were black; the skirts of his habiliments were yellow, and a sparkling jewel hung in every one of his ears; his arms were extended, and adorned with

[62] Another account states, that when Mahadeva received the curse of some devotees, whom he had disturbed at their devotions, he was deprived of his Lingam, which in the end proved fatal to his life. His consort wandered over the earth, and filled the world with her bewailings. Mahadeva was at length restored, under the form of Iswara, and united once more to his beloved Sita.

[63] Vid. the Wisdom of Solomon, (c. xvii.,) in the Apocrypha of our Bible, where this part of the ceremony of initiation is minutely described.

[64] These were the initiated, disguised for the purpose, and passing in processional review before him. In these processions the Stolistes were distinguished by a *Square;* and their duty was to take care that the sacred symbols were not improperly exposed.

[65] Calica. Purana. Asiat. Res., vol. v., p. 390.

rich bracelets, and his hands bore the holy shell, the
radiated weapon, the mace of war, and the lotos."[66]
This was no other than Mahadeva himself, in his character of the Destroyer. These appearances were intended to typify the first generation of the gods; for it was
figured that while the body of Sita was carried by the
sorrowing Mahadeva, it burst and the gods contained in
her capacious womb[67] were scattered over the face of
the earth; and the places where each of them fell were
accounted sacred.[68]

The candidate was then made to personify the god
Vishnu, and to perform his numerous Avaters; which,
if my conjecture be correct, would produce the following ceremonies. He was plunged into the waters to
represent the fish-god, who descended to the bottom of
the ocean to recover the stolen Vedas.[69] A heavy burden was placed on his back, and he was said to resemble
a Tortoise supporting the earth.[70] He was instructed to

[66] Sir W. Jones, on the gods of Greece. Asiat. Res., vol. i., p. 249.
[67] Bhagvat Geeta, p. 90.   [68] Vid. Asiat. Res., vol. vi., p. 477.
[69] This was called the Matse Avater, and contains an account of the
general Deluge. Brahma having fallen asleep, the demon Hayagriva
stole the Vedas, and, swallowing them, retired to a secret place at the
bottom of the sea. The sacred Books being lost, mankind soon fell
into vice and wickedness, and becoming universally corrupt, the world
was destroyed by a flood of waters, except a pious monarch, with his
family of seven persons, who were preserved in a vessel constructed
under the direction of Vishnu. When the waters had attained their
greatest elevation this god plunged into the ocean, attacked and slew
the giant Hayagriva who was the cause of this great calamity, and
recovered three of the books from the monster's belly, the fourth
having been digested. Then emerging from the waves, half man,
half fish, he presented the Vedas to Brahma; and the earth resuming
its former state was repeopled by the eight persons who had been
miraculously preserved. (Maur. Ind. Ant., vol. ii., p. 353.)
[70] This Avater was also a figurative account of the Deluge. Satyavrata, a king of India, was instructed by a fish that in seven days the
world would be inundated, but that a ship should be sent in which
himself and his seven holy companions might be preserved. These
persons accordingly entered the vessel, and the waters prevailed so
extensively as to produce the entire destruction of all created matter.
The Soors then held a consultation on the summit of mount Meru to
discover the Amreeta, or water of immortality, allusive to the reani-
mation of nature; and learned that it could be produced only by the
violent revolution of the mountain Mandar, which the Dewtahs found
themselves unable to move. In despair they solicited the aid of
Brahma and Vishnu: who instructing them how to proceed, the serpent Vasookee wound the folds of his enormous body round the

descend into a lower cavern on all fours, through a passage scarcely large enough to admit his body. Here he was received by an antagonist who offered him battle. A mimic conflict ensued, in which the aspirant was victorious.[71] While elated with this conquest, he was again attacked by a gigantic monster, whom, as the representative of Vishnu, he subdued.[72] He was then taught to take three steps at right angles, which referred to the fifth manifestation;[73] and the remaining Avaters[74] in-

mountain like a cable, and Vishnu becoming incarnate in the form of a Tortoise, took the mountain on his back. Thus loosened from its foundation, Indra began to whirl the mountain about with incessant motion, with the assistance of the Assoors, who were employed at the serpent's head, and the Soors, who were engaged at his tail. Soon the violence of the motion produced a stream of smoke, fire, and wind, which ascending in thick clouds replete with lightning, it began to rain furiously, while the roaring of the ocean was tremendous. The various productions of the waters were torn to pieces; the fruits of the earth were annihilated, and a raging fire spread destruction all around. At length a stream of the concocted juice of the dissolved matter ran down the mountain, mixed with molten gold, from whence the Soors obtained the water of immortality, or, in other words, the restoration of Nature from the power of the triumphant waters. (Maur. Ind. Ant., vol. ii., p. 343.) Then the Soors and Assoors commenced a dreadful battle for the possession of this glorious water, which at length decided in favour of the Soors, and their opponents fled; some rushing headlong into the ocean, and others hiding themselves in the bowels of the earth. The mountain Mandar was then carefully replaced in its former station, and the waters retired to their primitive caverns and recesses. (Bhagvat Geeta, p. 150.)

[71] This was done to commemorate the third manifestation of Vishnu; who, in the shape of a Boar, penetrated through the earth, by means of his snout, in search of the monster Hiranyakshana, who had taken refuge in the lowest of the seven inferior worlds. The god found him out and slew him.

[72] Vishnu, in the form of an animal compounded of a man and a lion, attacked the brother of the former giant, who had received an assurance from Brahma, that no being of any known form should have power to hurt him. To evince his contempt of the divinity, therefore, the giant dared him to come forth from a marble pillar. The column immediately burst with a violent concussion, and Vishnu issuing forth in flaming fire, tore the giant in pieces, drank his blood, and decorated himself with his entrails as a trophy of victory.

[73] As a diminutive Brahmin, Vishnu demanded of the impious tyrant Bali, who was a huge giant, as much ground for sacrifice as would suffice to place three feet upon. The tyrant granted his demand; and Vishnu resuming his own form, with one foot covered the earth, with the other he filled all the space between earth and heaven, and with a third, which unexpectedly started from his belly he crushed the monster's head, and hurled him down to the infernal regions.

[74] In the sixth manifestation, Vishnu, in the human form, encounter-

volved him in a series of furious conflicts from which he seldom escaped without wounds and bruises; for to make him equal with the gods, it was necessary that he underwent the same trials, and exposed himself to similar dangers.

Having reached the extremity of the seven[75] mystic caverns,[76] a cheerful peal of bells was heard to ring;[77] which he was instructed to believe would expel from these dark caves the evil demons who might be inclined to disturb the sacred ceremonies in which they were engaged.[78]   Before the candidate was enlightened and

ed and destroyed whole hosts of giants and tyrants.   The seventh Avater forms of itself a complete and voluminous Romance, of which Vishnu is the hero, under the name of Rama, who is represented as a valiant and successful warrior.   With the assistance of a vast army, composed of an incredible number of monkeys or satyrs, led on in battle array, he accomplished so many wonderful adventures, that their recital actually fills several volumes.   In the eighth Avater, he slew a host of giants, armed only with an enormous serpent; and in the ninth he transformed himself into a tree, for the purpose of gratifying a criminal passion with a king's daughter.   The Hindoos still expect a tenth Avater, with the same impatience which the Jews manifest for their Messiah.   Sir W. Jones informs us, that this Avater "is expected to appear mounted (like the crowned conqueror in the Apocalypse,) on a white horse, with a cimeter blazing like a comet, to mow down all incorrigible and impenitent offenders who shall then be on the earth." (Asiat. Res., vol. i., p. 236.)

[75] Vid. Signs and Symbols, Lect. 8.

[76] These seven caverns bore an allusion to the metempsychosis, as well as to the seven places of reward and punishment which different nations have received into their creed.   And it may perhaps be asserted without profanation, that the Christian system gives a sanction to the same hypothesis.   If an inspired Apostle speaks of a third heaven : (2 Cor. xii., 2,) of the righteous differing from each other in glory, as one star differs from another ; (1 Cor. xv., 41,) if the plural number be commonly used by Christ and his apostles, when speaking of the place of supreme bliss; (Mark i., 10.   Acts vii., 56.   Eph. iv., 10. Heb. i., 10.   2 Pet. iii., 5, &c.,) and if the Saviour himself should acknowledge that heaven contains many mansions; (John xiv., 2,) then we may also conclude that as there are many heavens, so there are also degrees of reward proportioned to the measure of man's faith and obedience.

[77] From time immemorial, bells were employed in religious rites all over the eastern world. (Wait. Orient. Ant., p. 83.   See also the Ramayuna of Valmic.)   In India no religious ceremony was esteemed efficacious if unaccompanied by this indispensable appendage. (Maur. Ind. Ant., vol. v., p. 900.)

[78] These wicked and mischievous beings were said to be struck with horror at the sound of a bell; and even the undulations of the air produced by it were so detestable to them, that they would flee with

introduced into the presence of the holy Altar, he was told that "whatever is performed without *faith*, whether it be sacrifices, deeds of charity, or mortifications of the flesh, is not for this world or that which is above;"[79] and was strictly admonished against the commission of five crimes, which were prohibited under heavy penalties in this life, and punished with eternal vengeance in the next. And these particulars form a part of the Oath under which he was now solemnly bound; and he seals it by a sacred ablution.[80]

The awful moment was now arrived when the ceremony of initiation had attained its highest degree of interest; the pealing Conch was blown,[81] the folding doors were suddenly thrown open, and the candidate was introduced into Cailasa or Paradise,[82] which was a spacious apartment blazing with a thousand brilliant lights;[83] ornamented with statues and emblematical figures, scented with the rich fragrance of odorous flowers, aromatic gums, and costly drugs;[84] decorated profusely with gems and jewels;[85] the unsubstantial figures of the airy inhabitants of unknown worlds carved on the roof, in the act of volitation; and the splendid sacellum

precipitation from the hated spot, and take refuge in deep caves and inaccessible recesses, to avoid a sensation at which their nature revolted. (Sacontala. Translated by Sir W. Jones. Works, vol. vi.) The Christians of this country, before the Reformation, were addicted to the same superstition.

[79] Bhagvat Geeta, p. 123.

[80] The terms of this oath are curious. He swears, in addition to the usual points relating to secrecy, that he will never have any carnal knowledge of his mother, sister, or daughter, but will always extend his protection towards them; that he will not assassinate a Brahmin, or rob him of gold or other property, but rather relieve him; that he will not be addicted to intemperance in eating or drinking; and that he will not associate with any person who has polluted himself by the commission of these crimes

[81] Vid. Bhagvat Geeta, p. 29. Facts in natural history were made subservient to the purposes of superstition. This sacred Shell, which had nine valves, or foldings, was referred to the nine incarnations of Vishnu. (Maur. Ind. Ant., vol. v., p. 906.)

[82] This was the actual name of one the grottoes in the subterranean temple of Elora, and is supposed by Faber (Pag. Idol., vol. iii., p. 255,) to have been the illuminated sacellum into which the aspirant was introduced at the close of his initiation.

[83] Maur. Ind. Ant., vol. ii , p. 281.

[84] Ibid. vol. v., p. 897.

[85] Philost. in vit. Apollon , l. ii., p. 2.

thronged with priests and hierophants, arrayed in gorgeous vestments, and crowned with mitres and tiaras of burnished gold.[86] With eyes rivetted on the altar, he was taught to expect the descent of the deity in the bright pyramidal fire that blazed upon it.[87] The sudden sound of the shell or trumpet,[88] to which the hollow caverns reverberated in long and continued echoes; the expansion of the folding doors; the brilliant display so unexpectedly exhibited before him; the instantaneous prostration of the priests, and the profound silence which followed this ceremony, filled the mind of the aspirant with admiration, and lighted up the holy fervour of devotion in his heart; so that, in the moment of enthusiasm, he could almost persuade himself that he actually beheld the expected descent of the great Brahma seated on the lotos, with his four heads[89] and bearing in his hands

---

[86] The riches of many of these temples is incredible. The pillars were covered with plates of gold, intermixed with precious stones. (Maur. Ind. Ant., vol. iii., p. 368.) The images were of gold and silver, and many thousands were often found in the same temple. (Ib. p. 369. And when Mahmed broke in pieces the idol of Sunmaut, to his astonishment he found the hollow body full of " diamonds, rubies, and pearls, of a water so pure, and of a magnitude so uncommon, that the beholders were filled with surprise and admiration." (Ib. p. 373.) The idol of Krishna in the temple at Mattra had two great rubies in the place of eyes; and the floor of the hallowed temple at Naugracut was covered with plates of gold. (Mandeslo. Travels, p. 21.) The principal idol in the Pagoda at Benares was decorated with chains of precious stones, some being rubies, others pearls, and others emeralds. (Voyage de Tavernier, tom. iv., p. 151.) In some of the Pagodas, the ears of the monstrous idols were gilded and full of jewels, their teeth and eyes of gold. (Purch. Pilgr., vol. i., p. 579.) And the priests were as proud of these trophies, as if they were their own personal property.

[87] " God is in the fire of the altar." (Bhagvat Geeta, p. 54.)

[88] Vid. 1 Thess. iv., 16, where the Judge of all the world is represented as descending to the sound of the eternal trumpet.

[89] The four heads of Brahma represent equally the four elements, and the four quarters of the globe. The history of the production of these four heads is somewhat curious, and I therefore introduce it here from the Matsya Purana, in Fab. Pag. Idol., vol. i., p. 319. " When Brahma assumed a mortal shape, he was pleased to manifest himself in Cashmir. Here one half of his body sprang from the other, which yet experienced no diminution; and out of the severed moiety he framed a woman, denominated Iva and Satarupa. Her beauty was such as to excite the love of the god; but deeming her his daughter, he was ashamed to own his passion. During this conflict between shame and love he remained motionless, with his eyes fixed upon her.

the usual emblems of eternity and uncontrollable power,[90] the circle,[91] and fire.[92]

Satarupa perceived his situation, and stepped aside to avoid his ardent looks. Brahma, being unable to move, but still desirous to see her, a new face sprang out upon him towards the object of his desires. Again she shifted her situation, and another face emanated from the enamoured god. Still she avoided his gaze, until the incarnate deity, become conspicuous with four faces directed to the four quarters of the world, beheld her incessantly, to whatever side she withdrew herself. At length she recovered her self-possession, when the other half of his body sprang from him, and became Swayambhuva or Adima. Thus were produced the first man and woman, and from their embrace were born three sons, in whom the Trimurti became incarnate."

[90] Maur. Ind. Ant., vol. v., p. 852.

[91] The Circle or Ring was received as an expressive symbol of the Ark all over the world; and as the great Father was hidden within its enclosure during the prevalence of the diluvian waters, many fables sprang out of this connection. I shall mention only one, the mysterious Ring of Gyges, which was reputed to render the wearer invisible. 'Gyges, according to Plato, found a brazen horse in a cavern. Within the horse was hid the body of a man of gigantic stature, having a brazen ring on his finger. This ring Gyges took, and found that it rendered him invisible. The cavern, the ring, and the giant, show pretty evidently whence this fable originated. The mare was a form of Ceres or Hippa, the mystic nurse of the ark-exposed Bacchus or Noah; the man, therefore, was the Ark. The dead giant was the gigantic Buddha, or the great father, during the period of his death-like slumber while enclosed within the ark. And the cavern was one of those sacred grottoes, within which the mysteries were perpetually celebrated; and from which both he and his initiated votaries were feigned to be born again." (Fab. Pag. Idol., vol. ii., p. 440, in notâ. 1.

[92] "Suddenly a golden temple appeared, containing a chain of wrought gold. On the summit of the temple Brahma alighted, and held a canopy over the head of Sacya; while Indra, with a fan in his hand; Naga, prince of serpents, and the four tutelary deities of the four corners of the universe, attended to do him reverence and service." (Asiat. Res., vol. ii., p. 385.)

LECTURE III.

THE fatigue attending the protracted ceremonies described in the preceding lecture exhausted the aspirant; and therefore to renovate his spirits, he was made to drink a fermented liquor out of a human skull. And now being fully regenerate, a new name was given him, expressive of his recently attained purity, and he was introduced to the chief Brahmin, in the midst of the august assembly, who received him as a brother and associate, invested him with a white robe and tiara, seated him in an elevated situation, and solemnly delivered the signs, tokens, and lectures of the Order. His forehead was marked with a cross,[1] which was explained as symbolical of the four cardinal points of the compass. An inverted level was inscribed on his breast,[2] to express his recently acquired dignity, by which he was advanced to an equality with the superior order of the priests. He was invested with the sacred sash or belt,[3] the consecrated chaplet, the Kowsteke-Men, or Kowstoobh,[4] and the

---

[1] The sectarial mark on the forehead is called *Tiluka*. (Valmic. Ramayuna, p. 2.) Mr. Maurice (Ind. Ant., vol. v., p. 849) says he has no doubt but this mark was the hermetic cross.

[2] Or, in other words, the tau cross; which was considered equally as a badge of innocence, and a symbol of eternal life.

[3] Mr. Maurice is very particular in his description of this sacred cord. It can be woven by no profane hand; the Brahmin alone can twine the hallowed threads that compose it, and it is done by him with the utmost solemnity, and with the addition of many mystic rites. *Three* threads, each measuring ninety-six hands, are first twisted together; then they are folded into *three* and twisted again, making it consist of *nine*, i. e., *three times three* threads; this is folded again into three, but without any more twisting, and each end is then fastened with a knot. Such is the *zennar*, which being put on the left shoulder, passes to the right side, and hangs down as low as the fingers can reach. (Ind. Ant., vol. iv., p. 740.)

[4] Vid. Signs and Symbols, Lect. 10.

talismanic label for the left arm. The salagram,[5] or magical black stone, was delivered to him,[6] as an amulet which would insure to him the protection of Vishnu, whose multiform shapes he was emblematically said to have assumed; and the serpent stone, an amulet similar to the anguinum of the Druids, was presented as an antidote against the bite of serpents, or other venomous reptiles.[7]

He was then instructed in the secret art of composing amulets, for his own personal protection,[8] and incantations, to procure the torture or destruction of his enemies,[9] and being now fully invested, the candidate was entrusted with the sublime NAME,[10] which was known only to the

[5] Specimens of the Salagram may be seen in the Museum of the Asiatic Society.

[6] Maur. Ind. Ant., vol. v., p. 908.   [7] Ibid. vol. iv., p. 660.

[8] " A branch of Snuhi (Euphorbia) in a whitened vessel, placed with ʼn red flag on the house-top, on the fourteenth day of the dark half *Chartra*, drives away sin and disease." (Rájamártanda, in Asiat. Res., vol. iii., p. 279.) A charmed paste, to procure good fortune, is said, in the Drama of Sacontala, to be prepared as follows:—" I have filled," says Anusúyá, " the shell of a cocoa nut, which you see fixed on an Amra tree, with the fragrant dust of Nágacésaras; take it down and keep it in a fresh lotos leaf, whilst I collect some Góráchana from the forehead of a sacred cow, some earth from the consecrated ground, and some fresh Cusa grass, *of which I will make a paste, to insure good fortune.*" (Sir W. Jones. Works, vol. vi.)

[9] This was a most horrible ceremony in a country where the people were superstitiously addicted to the belief of preternatural acquirements. We are not informed what was the absolute nature of this charm; but the following was considered sufficiently efficacious to destroy an enemy. He who wished to use it, waited patiently for the ceremony of burning a widow on the funeral pile of her husband; from the flames of which he snatched the half-consumed bamboo lever by which the bodies had been secured, and retreated rapidly to his hut. Here, in the dead of night, he formed this purified bamboo into a bow, and having set up a clay image to represent his unconscious adversary, he aims an arrow at its breast. which is believed to inflict a similar wound on his enemy. that would, undoubtedly, prove fatal unless averted by a counter incantation. The Hindoos used charms on every occurrence in life, and generally had the Lingam suspended from their neck (Maur. Ind. Ant., vol. v., p. 935); for protection against serpents and ravenous beasts; to cure diseases; to ensure success in litigated suits; to appease or destroy an enemy, &c., &c. The remnant of this ancient superstition is observable amongst the uneducated rustics in almost every part of Europe; but in India it still exists in all its primitive force.

[10] The Mahometans, in common with the Jews and idolaters, attach to the knowledge of this sacred Name the most wonderful powers.

initiated; and which signified the solar fire, or more properly the sun itself, the sacred emblem of the supreme
deity; and united in its comprehensive meaning the great
Trimurti, or combined principle, on which the existence
of all things is founded. This word was OM;[11] or as it
was expressed in a triliteral form in the mysteries, AUM,[12]
to represent the creative, preserving, and destroying
power of the deity,[13] personified in Brahma, Vishnu,
Siva, the symbol of which was an equilateral triangle.[14]
This ineffable word formed the subject of incessant and
pleasing contemplation, which could be indulged only in
silence,[15] and seclusion; for the pronunciation of this awful Name A. U. M. ॐ,[16] was said to make earth tremble,

"They pretend that God is the Lock of the Ism Allah, or science of
the name of God, and Mohammed the King; that consequently none
but Mohammedans can attain it; that it discovers what passes in
distant countries; that it familiarizes the possessors with the genii,
who are at the command of the initiated, and who instruct them;
that it places the winds and the seasons at their disposal; that it
heals the bite of serpents, the lame, the maimed, and the blind."
(Niebuhr, cited by Southey, Thalaba, vol. i., p. 198.)

[11] Vid. Asiat. Res., vol. i., p. 285.

[12] In the Oracles ascribed to Zoroaster is a passage which pronounces
the sacred *Names* used in the Mysteries to be ineffable, and not to be
changed, because revealed by God himself.

[13] Wilkins, notes on Bhagvat Geeta, p. 142. This mystic emblem
of the deity OM, is forbidden to be pronounced but in silence. It is
a syllable formed of the letters अ ă, उ ŏŏ, which in composition
coalesce, and make आ ŏ, and the nasal consonant म् m. The first
letter stands for the Creator, the second for the Preserver, and the
third for the Destroyer.

[14] Maur. Ind. Ant., vol. vii., p. 623. The perfections of God are
thus described in the last book of the Ramayan, translated by Sir W.
Jones. (Works, vol. vi.) "Vishnu is the being of beings; *one substance in three forms;* without mode, without quality, without passion;
immense, incomprehensible, infinite, indivisible, immutable, incorporeal,
irresistible. His operations no mind can conceive; and his will moves
all the inhabitants of the universe, as puppets are moved by strings."
It must be observed, however, that the same is also true of the other
two persons in the divine triad; for as these three are in fact but one
person, the above attributes were ascribed to him, under what name
soever he might be designated.

[15] Bhagvat Geeta, p. 74.

[16] Mr. Faber says, that this cipher graphically exhibits the divine
triad, Balrama, Subhadra, and Jagan-nath. In an old Purana, as we
learn from the Abbé Du Bois, the following passage is found, which
shows the veneration displayed by the ancient Indians for this tremendous word:—"All the rites ordained in the Vedas, the sacrifices

and even the angels of heaven to quake for fear. When it was thus perfectly communicated, the aspirant was directed to meditate upon it with the following associations, which are the mysterious names of the seven worlds, or manifestations of the power of OM, the solar fire. "OM!"[17] Earth, sky, heaven, middle region, place of births, mansion of the blessed, abode of truth."[18]

The Arch Brahmin, making a sign to the initiated to be silent and attentive, now entered on the explanation of the various emblems which were arranged around him; with the arcana of the hidden science enfolded under the holy gloom of their mysterious veil; the names and attributes of the several deities whose symbols were sculptured on the cavern walls; and an elucidation of the mythological figures which every where abounded; emblems of wisdom, strength, and beauty; temperance, fortitude, prudence, and justice, and every other commendable virtue.

The science of astronomy occupied a proportionate share of attention during this display; but its more abstruse problems were hid from common investigation by the enigmatical obscurity with which they were studiously invested. Thus a horned elephant's head symbolized the Sun, and a rabbit the Moon;[19] but the Sun and Moon were termed, in their sacred dialect, the two eyes of God; therefore the foregoing emblems were mystically the two eyes of God. Geometry was very early practised in India, as is evident from the true proportions of those stupendous caverns which have been already described.[20] The Brahmins were consequently acquainted with the science of arithmetic; they understood music, and Mr. Maurice thinks they were the inventors of algebra.

---

to the fire, and all other solemn purifications shall pass away; but that which shall never pass away is the word OM; for it is the symbol of the Lord of all things." Mr. Wilkins informs us, from the Bhagvat Geeta (p. 122), that in addition to the above cipher, which signifies Om, the combination of two others, *Tat*, and *Sat*, are necessary to compose the mysterious name of the deity. An elephant's head was the visible emblem of this awful name.

[17] OM is termed by Dara Shekoh, the seal by which secrets or mysteries are revealed. (Vid. Wait. Orient. Ant., p. 36.)

[18] Porph. de. Ant. Nymph., p. 268. Asiat. Res., vol. v., p. 348.

[19] Heetop., p. 177.   [20] Vid. ut supra, p. 21.

Their sylvan residence imparted a taste for the study of botany, which exemplified itself in the practice of medicine and surgery; nor were they ignorant of chemistry, mineralogy, metallurgy; and excelled in many other abstruse arts, as well as those domestic manufactures which are attendant on civilization, and contribute their aid to the refinements of social life.

An extensive system of symbolical instruction was used in the Mysteries, and the veil by which they were covered was too dense for the uninitiated to penetrate.[21] Eternity was symbolized equally by a serpent and a wheel; fire by a trident;[22] wisdom, strength, and beauty by a circle of horned heads; benevolence by the cow;[23] friendship by the buccinum or conch; wisdom by the chakram;[24] the lotos[25] was an emblem of the soul's free-

---

[21] "In truth," says Stukeley, " the first learning in the world consisted chiefly in symbols. The wisdom of the Chaldeans, Phenicians, Egyptians, Jews; of Zoroaster, Sanchoniathon, Pherecydes, Syrus, Pythagoras, Socrates, Plato, of all the ancients that is come to our hand, is symbolic. It was the mode, says Serranus on Plato's Symposium, of the ancient philosophers to represent truth by certain symbols and hidden images."

[22] Maur. Ind. Ant., vol. v., p. 857.

[23] The cow was also a symbol of the great mother (Herod., l. ii., c. 41, et Vid. Tobit i., 5); for this animal was usually identified with the Ark. Thus the great father is indifferently said to be born from a cow and from the Ark.

[24] Krishna is described in the Geeta (p. 91) as " of infinite shape; formed with abundant arms, and bellies, and mouths, and eyes; crowned, and armed with a club and Chakra; a mass of glory darting refulgent beams around." The Chakram is a round or circular machine, of which many devotees of Vishnu bear the emblem, imprinted on their shoulders with a hot iron. It is still used in some places as a weapon of war, and is nothing more than a large circular plate of iron, the outer edge of which is made very sharp. Through the centre a shaft passes, by means of which a rotatory motion is given to the plate, which whirls with great rapidity, and cuts whatever it approaches." (Dubois on the Inst. of Ind., p. 3, c. 11.) It is also used without the shaft, for Mr. Wilkins, in his notes on the Geeta (p. 96), describes it as "a kind of discus with a sharp edge hurled in battle from the point of the fore finger, for which there is a hole in the centre."

[25] This plant had the good fortune to be held sacred in most countries. In Egypt it was called the lily of the Nile; and Mr. Savary (vol. i., p. 8) says it still maintains its pristine veneration in that country. It was the great vegetable amulet which distinguished the eastern nations. Their gods were always represented as seated on the lotos; it was the sublime throne of oriental mythology, and referred indubitably to the ark of Noah.

dom when liberated from its earthly tabernacle, the body; for it takes root in the mud deposited at the bottom of a river, vegetates by degrees from the germ to a perfect plant, and afterwards rising proudly above the waves, it floats in air as if independent of any extraneous aid. The Bull was an emblem of religion, his four legs being representations of purity, compassion, penance, and truth; and the *triple* headband with which he was usually bound denoted that he was to be worshipped morning, noon, and night. A spear was a symbol of omnipotence, as rays of glory were of blessings emanating from the gods. A serpent, bearing a globe in its folds, represented the union of wisdom and eternity; and pointed to the great father and mother of the renovated world; the egg and lunette[26] symbolized the generative principle, in the persons of the same progenitors; for the moon and egg were equally symbols of the ark from which they issued when they became the parents of a new race.[27] The triangle within a circle referred to the Trimurti;[28] and the trident had a similar allusion. The ark of Noah, as a lunette, symbolized the female principle, with the linga, or male principle for a mast; for according to the Brahmins, it was under this form that the two principles of generation[29] were preserved at the universal Deluge.[30] Thus were religion and

[26] Siva is called "the god with the crescent." (Bhagvat Geeta' p 81.)

[27] "In memory of the Ark, the ancients were not only accustomed to carry about small navicular shrines, but sometimes even built their temples in the form of ships. Diodorus Siculus mentions, that Sesostris constructed a ship, which was 280 cubits long, and adds that it was made of cedar; that it was covered with plates of gold and silver; and that it was dedicated to Osiris or Noah, at the city of Theba or the Ark. It is sufficiently evident, both from the preceding description of this ship, from its being dedicated to Osiris, and from its being placed in the inland district of the Thebais, that it never was designed for a voyage at sea. It was, in fact, an immense navicular temple, built in imitation of the Ark, and destined for the solemn performance of the diluvian mysteries. Hence the Greeks designated a temple and a ship by the very same word, *Naus* or *Naos*; and hence what is, doubtless, a relic of the primeval arkite idolatry, we still call the body of a church, in contradistinction to the chancel, the nave or ship." (Fab. Cab., vol. i., p. 215.)

[28] Moor's Hind. Panth., p. 400.

[29] The fact is, that the entire worship of these idolaters was and still continues to be nothing less than a disgusting scene of lasciviousness, obscenity, and blood. (Vid. Buchanan, Researches in Asia, p. 129–141.) [30] Asiat. Res., vol. vi., p. 523.

philosophy veiled under the impervious shade of hiero
glyphical symbols; unintelligible to the profane, and
intended to lead them into a maze of error, from which
it was difficult to extract a single idea which bore any
resemblance to the original truth. These symbols were
publicly displayed in their temples, beaming streams of
light to the initiated; while to the profane they were
but an obscure mass of unintelligible darkness.

Here the initiation ended, and the candidate was
allowed to marry, and bring up his family. His third
probation, or *Banperisth*, commenced when his children
were all capable of providing for themselves, and he was
weary of the troubles and vexations of active life. He
returned with his wife into the recesses of the forest;
renounced all other society; lived in the open air; ate
only vegetables; practised every kind of ablution known
in his caste; used all the daily prayers without any
omission, and occupied himself principally in sacrificing
to the gods.[31] And from this point of time he was said
to be *twice born*,[32] and was considered as a being of a
superior order.[33]

The fourth degree was believed to impart an extreme
portion of merit to the intrepid sage who possessed
courage enough to undertake the performance of its
duties. After being formally installed by an assembly
of his caste, he was solemnly bound by oath to the
following observances: to rub his whole body every
morning with ashes; to avoid the company of women; to
wear heavy and inconvenient clogs, made of wood; to
subsist entirely on alms; to renounce the world and all
his former connections, and to exercise himself in incessant contemplation. This, added to an endless catalogue
of other duties, penances, and mortifications, was believed
capable of transforming the happy Sannyase[34] into the
divine nature,[35] and to secure him a residence amongst
the celestial gods.[36]

---

[31] Maur. Ind. Ant., vol. v., p. 977.
[32] Valmic. Ramayun, p. 90. This corresponds with the regeneration of the mysteries of Greece and Rome.   [33] Ibid., p. 95.
[34] The word Sannyase means a total abstraction from all worldly
things. (Bhagvat Geeta, p. 143.)
[35] Ordin. of Menu. Sir W. Jones. Works, vol. iii., p. 461.
[36] "Higher worlds," say the Ordinances of Menu, "are illuminated

In the initiations in India a lecture was delivered to the candidate, founded on the following principles. The first element and cause of all things was water, which existed amidst primordial darkness. Brahm was the creator of this globe, and by his spirit invigorates the seventy-four powers of nature; but the universe is without beginning, and without end.[37] He is the being who was, and is, and is to come; and his emblem was a perfect sphere, having neither commencement nor termination.[38] Endowed with the attributes of omnipotence, omnipresence, and omniscience.[39] And in the Asiatic Researches[40] we find him designated, "the great God, the great omnipotent and omniscient ONE; the greatest in the world; the Lord," &c., &c., &c.

This divine Being created the waters with a thought, and placed in them a seed, which soon became an egg, brilliant as the meridian sun. Out of this egg[41] Brahma

with the glory of that man, who passes from his house into the fourth order, giving exemption from fear to all animated beings, and pronouncing the mystic words of the Veda." (Sir W. Jones. Works, vol. iii., p. 230.)

[37] Bhagvat Geeta, p. 116.

[38] Holwell. Hist. Event. Capt. Seely (Wonders of Elora, p. 73) says, "there is no idol in front of the great altar in the Temple of Ekverah, or at Elora; the umbrella covering rises from a wooden pedestal out of the convexity of the altar. A Brahmin whom I questioned on the subject of the altar, exclaimed, in nearly the words of our-own poet, *Him first, Him last, Him midst, Him without end.* In alluding to the Almighty, he nearly spoke as above described, placing his hand on this *circular* solid mass. He rejected all idea of assimilating Buddha or Brahma with the Eternal God, who, he said, was One alone from beginning to end; and that the circular altar was his emblem."

[39] This Being was identified with LIGHT, for the Brahmins say, "because the Being who shines with *seven* rays, assuming the forms of time and fire, matures productions, is resplendent, illuminates, and finally destroys the universe, therefore, he who naturally shines with seven rays is called Light, or the effulgent power." (Colebrooke. Asiat. Res., vol. v., p. 350.) Thus Brahm is Light; and light is the principle of life in every created thing. "Light and darkness are esteemed the world's eternal ways; he who walketh in the former path returneth not; i. e., he goeth immediately to bliss; whilst he who walketh in the latter cometh back again upon the earth," or is subjected to further tedious transmigrations. (Bhagvat Geeta, p. 76.)

[40] Vol. viii., p. 325.

[41] The egg which contains the rudiments of life, and was hence esteemed no unimportant symbol of the resurrection, was no other

was produced,[42] after having remained a full year enclosed
in absolute absorption, who was hence termed the emanation of the deity. The egg was afterwards divided
into two equal parts, one of which formed the concave
and egg-like canopy of heaven, and the other the earth.[43]
Brahma, invested with power, created inferior gods and
men; the latter springing from his head, his arms, his
thighs, and his feet, were naturally divided into so many
distinct *castes*,[44] between which all communication was
strictly interdicted.

They taught the unity of the godhead;[45] the happiness
of the first created men;[46] the destruction occasioned by
the general Deluge;[47] the depravity of the human heart,
and the necessity of a mediator to atone for sin; the
instability of life;[48] the final dissolution of all created
things;[49] and the restoration of the world in a more per-

than the Ark; and the legend in the text corresponds exactly with the
belief of other nations Dionusus was fabled by the Greeks to be
born from an egg (Orph. Hymn, 5). And he and Noah were the
same person; therefore the birth of Brahma or Dionusus from an
egg was nothing more than the egress of Noah from the Ark. (Vid.
Fab. Pag. Idol., b. i., c. 4.)

[42] Here is a manifest confusion of terms. The creation of the
world, and its restoration after the Deluge are frequently identified in
the heathen cosmogonies; and. in the present case, although the
work of creation is intended to be exclusively illustrated, yet the year
which Brahma spent in the egg was evidently the confinement of
Noah in the Ark; for Brahma equally represented Adam and Noah.

[43] See Manava Sastra, translated by Sir William Jones, Asiat.
Res., vol. i., p. 244.

[44] These were called the Brahmins; the Cshatriya, the Vaisya, and
the Sudra; so named from Scripture, Protection, Wealth, and Labour.
(Ordin. of Menu. Sir W. Jones. Works, vol. iii., p. 69.)

[45] It is a question whether the Creator in India was esteemed to be
the true God, or an emanation, from their belief in a succession of
similar worlds; and, consequently, a personification of Adam and
Noah, who were equally worshipped under the name of Brahma, or
the creative power, because he was the parent of mankind; for
Brahma was only a created being. In truth, Brahma appears to have
been Adam or Noah; and Brahma, Vishnu, Siva, was either Abel,
Seth, Cain, or Shem, Japheth, Ham; and there exists considerable
doubt after all, whether the being to whom the rites of Hindoo worship are so devoutly paid, were not a mere deified mortal. See
Faber's Pagan Idolatry (b. i., c. 2), where many powerful arguments
are used to this effect.

[46] Signs and Symbols, Lect. 5.   [47] Ibid. Lect. 5.

[48] Hitopadesa, l. 4.

[49] The Indians believed that the duration of the world would cease,

fect and happy form.[50] They inculcated the eternity of
the soul and the metempsychosis, under the name of
regeneration, to account for the mysterious dispensations
of Providence; for this doctrine embodied and familiarized
the idea of man's personal responsibility. They held the
doctrine of a future state of rewards and punishments;[51]
and pressed on the initiated, with great earnestness, the
indispensable necessity of voluntary penances to atone
for sin, and appease the wrath of an avenging deity.

The Mysteries of China and its dependencies were

and its destruction be consummated when the zodiac had effected
one complete revolution. And as, by the precession of the equinoxes,
this was supposed to advance about one degree in something less
than a century, so the universal dissolution of the present system
would undoubtedly be accomplished 36,000 years from the creation.
Then the Calci, mounted triumphantly on a white horse, and armed
with a Scimeter which blazes like a comet, shall involve all things in
fire, and reduce the world to ashes. "Ruddery (Siva) shall, at that
period, summon up all the powers of destruction; the moon shall
look red, the sun shall shed his purling light like flaming brimstone;
the lightning shall flash with terror; the sky shall change into all
colours, but, especially, a fiery redness shall overspread the face of
heaven; the four elements of which the world at first was constituted,
shall be at opposition and variance, till, by this agony, she be turned
to her first confusion. Then shall Ruddery carry up the souls of all
people to heaven with him, to rest in God's bosom, but the bodies
shall perish." (Lord Ban. Rel., p. 91.)

[50] From the ruins of every world a new one was expected to arise,
where peace and harmony should prevail in a perfect and renewed
creation. From a firm persuasion that souls were subject to the
process of transmigration, they considered each period to be similar
and parallel in all its events. (Book of Abad. Desatir.) At the
commencement of each Manwantera, the first created man, corresponding with Adam, was supposed to triplicate himself; and the
three productions thus formed were the counterpart of Abel, Seth,
Cain, who were worshipped as a triad of Deity. The souls of these
persons were reanimated in Shem, Japheth, Ham, who were acknowledged in India, under the names of Brahma, Vishnu, Siva. This
system they believed to be eternal; and thus every individual who
lived in a former world, was supposed to be renewed, and act precisely the same part as he had done before. Hence might probably
originate the abominable custom of burning widows, that they might
accompany their deceased husbands into another state, and there
remain united in the nuptial tie. (See Fab. Pag. Idol., b. i., c. 2.)

[51] "As a man throweth away old garments and putteth on new, even
so the soul having quitted its old mortal frame, entereth into others
which are new.....Wise men, who have abandoned all thoughts of
the fruit which is produced from their actions, are freed from the
chains of birth, and go to the regions of eternal happiness." (Bhagvat Geeta, p. 37, 40.)

essentially similar to those of India, being derived from
the same source, and containing the same rites, founded
on the same general principles; for ancient India comprehended the whole of that vast continent. A recapitu-
lation of the ceremony of initiation will, therefore, be
unnecessary, and I shall confine my notices of China and
Japan to the detail of a few prominent facts, which constituted the shades of difference between them and other
Asiatic nations.

The Chinese practised Buddhism in its most simple
form, and worshipped an invisible God,[52] until a few
centuries before the Christian era, when visible objects
of adoration were introduced;[53] and so rapid was the
march of innovation, that in the course of a very short
period, China was as famous as any other idolatrous
nation for the number and variety of its objects of popular adoration.[54] It is true that many abuses had crept,

[52] Martinius. in Maur. Ind. Ant., vol. v., p. 797.
[53] Lao-Kium, who flourished about the year A. C. 600, introduced
a system which bore a striking resemblance to that of Epicurus, and
his followers styled themselves Immortals. (Maur. Ind. Ant., vol. v.,
p. 807.) They were materialists, but addicted, notwithstanding, to
the worship of idols.
[54] Confucius attempted to reform the abuses which had crept into
their religious mysteries: but licentiousness long indulged, could not
quietly submit to the mortifying castigation of austere and unbending
virtue. The Emperor and his grandees disregarded his admonitions;
the Mandarins hated him for projecting a reformation in those
abstruse mysteries, which, in their present state, were the chief
source of all their wealth and all their power; and one of them actually made an attempt upon his life. And the great philosopher, who
was afterwards adored as a god by his countrymen was obliged to
fly from civilized society to escape from the dreaded machinations of
his powerful opponents. He retired into the desert, and formed a
school of philosophy, to which he invited all who were inspired with
a love of virtue and science; and the genial effects of his improved
system were reserved for the enjoyment of posterity. One prominent misconception, however, counteracted the benefits which might
reasonably be expected to result from this great man's improvements.
On his death bed he predicted that there should arise in the western
part of the world a GREAT PROPHET (Couplet, p. 78), who should
deliver mankind from the bondage of error and superstition, and
establish an universal system of religion, which should be ultimately
embraced by all the nations of the earth. His followers erroneously
concluded that this great and powerful being was no other than
Buddha or Fo himself, who was, accordingly, installed into their
Temples in a visible form (Asiat. Res., vol. vii., p. 299), with solemn
pomp, as the chief deity of the Chinese empire. This proceeding

by gradual approaches, into their former system of worship; and the people, debased by superstition, were prepared for any novel scheme which might gratify their pride, or satiate their curiosity. The priests converted the profound veneration of the worshippers to their own aggrandizement; and successive changes tended, in the revolution of ages, greatly to deteriorate the primitive simplicity of their devotion.

The initiations were performed in a cavern; after which, processions were made round the *Tan* or altar,[55] and sacrifices offered to the celestial gods. The chief end of initiation was a fictious immortality, or absorption into the deity;[56] and to secure this admirable state of supreme and never changing felicity, amulets[57] were as usual delivered to the newly initiated candidates, accompanied by the magical words O-MI-TO FO,[58] which denoted the omnipotence of the divinity; and was considered as a most complete purification, and remission of every sin. Their morality was limited to five precepts. The first

opened a door to other idolatrous innovations; and ideal objects of worship, attended with indecent and unnatural rites (Martin. Sinic. Hist., p. 149), accumulated so rapidly, that China soon became celebrated for the practice of every impurity and abomination which characterized the most degraded nation of the heathen world.

[55] Bryant. Anal., vol. i., p. 94.

[56] Gros. Chin., vol. ii., c. 5.

[57] The most valuable amulet they can possess, is a small idol enfolded in a sheet of consecrated paper. To his neck and arms are appended bracelets composed of a hundred small beads and eight large ones; and in a conspicuous situation is placed a large bead in the shape of a gourd. The happy possessor of this trinket, on important occasions, counted the beads pronouncing the mysterious words O-mi-to Fo! accompanied by many genuflections. The performance of this ceremony is recorded by marking a red circle round the neck of the genius; and, at the death of the devotee, the aggregate number of these circles, as indisputable testimonials of the divine favour, or of deliverance from danger, are minutely attested and sealed by the officiating Bonze. The whole is then deposited in a small box and buried with the deceased as a passport to heaven, and a certain deliverance from the dreaded evil of successive transmigrations.

[58] *Omito* was derived, says Sir W. Jones (Asiat. Res., vol. ii., p. 374), from the Sanscrit Armida, *immeasurable;* and *Fo* was only another name for Buddha; or, more properly, the same name softened down by a diversity of language and pronunciation. See Faber's Pagan Idolatry (vol. ii., p. 342), where the grades are traced by which the one became transformed into the other.

forbids murder; the second, theft; the third, external impurity; the fourth, lying; and the fifth, drunkenness. They particularly recommended the candidate to afford protection to the bonzes,[59] that by the prayers of these holy men, they might be exempted from the fearful punishment of their transgressions; which, they were told, would otherwise consign their transmigrating souls to the purifying medium of a horse, a mule, a dog, a cat, a rat, or of a loathsome and insignificant reptile.

Much merit was attached to the possession of a consecrated symbol representing the great triad of the gentile world. This was an equilateral triangle, said to afford protection in all cases of personal danger and adversity. The mystical symbol Y was also much esteemed from its allusion to the same tri-une god;[60] the *three* distinct lines of which it is composed forming *one*, and the one is three.[61] This was in effect the ineffable name of the deity; the Tetractys of Pythagoras, and the Tetragrammaton of the Jews. A ring, supported by two serpents, was emblematical of the world protected by the power and wisdom of the Creator; and referred to the diluvian patriarch and his symbolical consort, the ark; and the ark itself was represented by a boat, a mouth, and the number eight.[62]

The Rainbow was a celebrated symbol in these mysteries, and doubtless originated in the history of the Deluge; for it was believed that the father of their radiant god Fo-hi was a rainbow,[63] which miraculously surrounded his mother while walking by a river's side. The aspi-

---

[59] These artful priests used magical ceremonies to delude the multitude, and to direct the tide of popular prejudice in their favour through the medium of superstition. They boasted of their power over the winds and elements, and proclaimed themselves the possessors of the philosophers' stone, which would transmute the baser metals to gold, and convey the blessing of immortality.

[60] Fab. Pag. Idol., vol. i., p. 248. "Tao, or reason, hath produced *one*; one hath produced *two*; two hath produced *three*; and three have produced all things." (Du Halde, China, vol. ii., p. 30. Le Comte. China, p. 318.)

[61] We find here again a superstitious veneration for odd numbers, as containing divine properties. Thus while the sum of the even numbers, $2+4+6+8+10=30$ designated the Number of *Earth*; the sum of the odd numbers, $1+3+5+7+9=25$ was dignified with the appellation of the Number of *Heaven*.

[62] Fab. Mys. Cab., vol i., p. 253.

[63] Vid. Signs and Symbols, Lect. 5.

ant, however, was the representative of Noah; and the ark, which was accounted his *mother* as well as his wife, was actually surrounded by a rainbow, at the time of his deliverance or new birth; and hence he was figuratively said to be the offspring of the rainbow.[64]

The Japanese held that the world was enclosed in an egg[65] before the creation, which floated on the surface of the waters.[66] At this period a prickle[67] appeared amongst

---

[64] The universal prevalence of this symbol in all the systems of which we have any knowledge, is very remarkable; and points out that the Spurious Freemasonry had a reference, in its original state, to the Deluge; and that the holy covenant of God was embodied in its system of hieroglyphical symbols.

[65] The Egg was always esteemed an emblem of the earth.

[66] The history is thus given in the Ceremonies and Religious Customs of various Nations. (p. 417.) "There is a pagoda at Micoa consecrated to a hieroglyphic Bull, which is placed on a large square altar, and composed of solid gold. His neck is adorned with a very costly collar; but that indeed is not the principal object that commands our attention. The most remarkable thing is the Egg, which he pushes with his horns, as he gripes it between his forefeet. This Bull is placed on the summit of a rock, and the Egg floats in some water, which is enclosed within the hollow space of it. The Egg represents the Chaos; and what follows is the illustration which the doctors of Japan have given of this hieroglyphic. The whole world at the time of the Chaos was enclosed within this Egg, which swam upon the surface of the waters. The Moon by virtue of her Light and her other influences, attracted from the bottom of these waters a terrestrial substance which was insensibly converted to a rock, and by that means the eggs rested upon it. The bull observing this egg, broke the shell of it, by goring it with his horns, and so created the world, and by his breath formed the human species. This fable may in some measure be reconciled with truth, by supposing that an ancient tradition had preserved amongst the Japanese some idea of the creation of the world; but that being led into an error, in process of time, by the ambiguous meaning of the name of the Bull, which in the Hebrew Language is attributed to the Deity, they ascribed the creation of the world to this animal, instead of the Supreme Being."

[67] To this source may be referred the Gothic idol Seater, which Verstegan, from Johannes Pomarius, thus describes. (Restitution of Decayed Intelligence, p. 78.) First, on a pillar was placed a *pearch on the sharp prickled back whereof stood this idol.* He was lean of visage, having long hair and a long beard; and was bareheaded and barefooted. In his left hand he held up a wheel; and in his right he carried a pail of water, wherein were flowers and fruits. His long coat was girded unto him with a towel of white linen. His standing on the sharp fins of this fish, was to signify that the Saxons for their serving him, should pass steadfastly and without harm in dangerous and difficult places, &c.

4

the waves which became spirit, and was called *Kunitoko-datsno-Mikotto;* from whence sprang six other spirits ;[68] who, with their wives, were the parents of a race of heroes, from whom proceeded the original inhabitants of Japan.[69] They worshipped a deity who was styled the son of the unknown god, and considered as the creator of the two great lights of heaven.[70]

The caverns[71] of initiation were in the immediate vicinity of their temples, because one of their old deities was said to be born from a cave ;[72] and generally in the midst of a grove, and near to a stream of water. They were furnished with large mirrors to signify that the imperfections of the heart are as plainly displayed to the sight of the gods, as the worshippers behold their own image in the glass. Hence the mirror was a significant emblem of the all-observing eye of the god Tensio Dai Sin. They were also decorated with a profusion of hieroglyphical designs cut in white paper, as striking symbols of the purity acquired by initiation.

The term of probation for the highest degrees was twenty years; and even the hierophant was not competent to perform the ceremony of initiation until he himself had been initiated the same period; and his five assistants must necessarily have had each ten years' experience from the date of their admission before they were competent to take this subordinate part in the initiations. The aspirant, during the term of his trial, learned to subdue his passions; devoted himself to the practice of austerities, and studiously abstained from every carnal indulgence.[73] In the closing ceremony of preparation he was

---

[68] The good deity was called Amidas; the evil, Jemma.

[69] Kæmpf. Japan, b. iii., c. 1.

[70] In some of the representations of this idol he was pourtrayed sitting on the Lotos, with four arms, referring to the four seasons of the year, each of which had its appropriate emblem. In others he had seven heads, symbolical of the seven days of the week, and thirty arms, which represented the period or cycle of thirty years. His image was made of solid gold, to denote his eternity and imperishable nature.

[71] Asiat. Res., vol. vii., p. 422.

[72] Kæmpf. Japan, p. 153.

[73] He was obliged to renounce the use of flesh, and to subsist wholly upon vegetable food; to use numerous ablutions daily ; and as it is expressed by Kæmpfer, kneeling down on the ground, with his but-

entombed within the Pastos or place of penance; the door of which was said to be guarded by a terrible divinity, armed· with a drawn sword, as the vindictive fury or god of punishment. During the course of his probation the aspirant sometimes acquired such a high degree of enthusiasm, as induced him to refuse to quit his confinement in the pastos ; and to remain there until he literally perished with famine. To this voluntary martyrdom was attached a promise of never-ending happiness in the paradise of Amidas. Indeed the merit of such a sacrifice was boundless. His memory was celebrated with annual rejoicings. The initiations,[74] however, were dignified with an assurance of a happy immortality to all who passed through the rites honourably and with becoming fortitude.

Amongst the amulets used on this occasion, two were the most venerated;[75] a ring or circle of gold, as an emblem

.ocks to his heels, and clapping his hands over his head, to lift himselt up seven hundred and fourscore times every day.

[74] Vid. Signs and Symbols. Lect. 10.

[75] The amulets within their dwellings were numerous ; every disease and misfortune having its appropriate charm. There was also one, says Kæmpfer, (Hist. Japan, b. v., c. 4) against poverty ; and this author quaintly remarks, "houses with this last mark must needs be very safe from thieves and housebreakers." But one of their mos efficacious amulets was the ofarrai, or indulgence, which was usually presented to the devout pilgrim who had performed his devotions at the Temple of the most high god Tensio Dai Sin, at Isge. "This Ofarrai is a small oblong square box, about a span and a half long, two inches broad, an inch and a half thick, made of small thin boards, and full of thin small sticks, some of which are wrapped up in a bit of white paper, in order to remind the pilgrim to be pure and humble, these two virtues being the most pleasing to the gods. The name of the Temple Tai Singu, that is, the Temple of the great God, printed in large characters, is pasted to the front of the box, and the name of the Canusi who gave the box, for there are great numbers that carry on this trade, to the opposite side, in a smaller character, with the noble title of Taiju, which is as much as to say, Messengers of the gods, a title which all the officers of Mias assume to themselves. This Ofarrai, the pilgrims receive with great tokens of respect and humility, and immediately tie it under their hats, in order to keep it from the rain. They wear it just under their forehead, and balance it with another box, or bundle of straw, much of the same weight, which they fasten to the opposite side of the hat. Those that travel on horseback have better conveniences to keep and to hide it. When the pilgrims are got safe home, they take especial care for the preservation of this Ofarrai, as being a relic of very great moment and consequence to them." (Kæmpf. Japan, b. iii., c. 4.)

of eternity, ritually consecrated, was supposed to convey
the blessing of a long and prosperous life; and a chaplet
of consecrated flowers or sacred plants and boughs of
trees; which being suspended about the doors of their
apartments, prevented the ingress of impure spirits; and
hence their dwellings were exempted from the visitations
of disease or calamity.

LECTURE IV.

THE Persian Mysteries were indebted to Zeradusht,[1] or Zoroaster, for much of the celebrity which they attained. This great reformer is said by Hyde[2] and Prideaux[3] to be a Jew by birth,[4] and to have received his education in the elements of the true worship amongst

---

[1] He was called by the Persians, Zeradusht, and by the Greeks, Zoroaster. The question of the identity of Zeradusht and Zoroaster will form no part of the present undertaking. Such a person, under one of these names did actually flourish in Persia, and reform its religion about the latter end of the Babylonish captivity, and I am little concerned in this much agitated question. The curious reader may profitably consult Hyde on the Religion of ancient Persia; Richardson's Dissertation, Sec. 2; Prideaux Connection, p. 1, b. iv.; and Faber's Pagan Idolatry, b. iii., c. 3.

[2] Hyde. Rel. vet. Pers., p. 314.   [3] Prid. Con., vol. i., p. 213.

[4] The Persian historians have shewn much anxiety to establish the supernatural perfection of this great prophet's birth. "A Persian author has declared," says Sir John Malcolm, (Hist. Pers., c. vii.,) "that the religious, among the followers of Zoroaster, believed that the soul of that holy person was created by God, and hung upon that tree, from which all that is celestial has been produced. . . . I have heard, this author observes, the wise and holy Mobud, Seeroosh declare, that the father of Zoroaster had a cow, which, after tasting some withered leaves that had fallen from the tree, never ate of any other: these leaves being her sole food, all the milk she produced was from them. The father of Zoroaster, whose name was Poorshasp, was entirely supported by this milk; and to it, in consequence, they refer the pregnancy of his mother, whose name was Daghda. Another account says, this cow ate the soul of Zoroaster as it hung to the tree, and that it passed, through her milk, to the father of that prophet. The apparent object of this statement is to prove that Zoroaster was born in innocence; and that not even vegetable life was destroyed to give him existence. When he was born, he burst into a loud laugh, like the prince of necromancers, Merlin, and such a light shone from his body as illuminated the whole room. This ancient tradition respecting Zoroaster, which we meet with in Persian books, is mentioned by Pliny." The phosphoric property here referred to was not confined to Zoroaster, but is recorded of many other eminent personages, Christian as well as heathen.

his countrymen in Babylon. He afterwards became an
attendant on the prophet Daniel, and from him received
initiation into all the mysteries of the Jewish doctrine
and practice. His abilities being of a superior cast, he
made a rapid progress in his studies, and became one of
the most learned men of his age. Perceiving that the
homage paid to his master was inspired by his extraordinary endowments, Zoroaster was desirous of converting
his own acquirements to the same purpose; and as he
was not enabled to prophesy by the aid of God's Holy
Spirit, he had recourse to the study of magic, which he
prosecuted under the Chaldean philosophers, who conferred upon him the privilege of initiation into their
Mysteries. This brought him into disgrace with Daniel,[5]
who banished him from the land, and prohibited his return on pain of death.[6] He fled to Ecbatana, and giving
out that he was a prophet, set about the arduous and
dangerous design of reforming[7] the Persian religion; the
character of which, by a series of gradual and impercep-
tible changes, had become subverted from its primitive
object; and the Sabian system had almost prevailed over
the ancient Magian form of worship. Professing to be a
rigid Magian, this plausible impostor, like other bold in-
novators of all ages and nations, soon found himself surrounded by followers in every rank of life, who entered
into his schemes with all the enthusiasm usually excited
by novelty, and gave their most strenuous support to his
projected plan of reformation.[8] He was openly patronised

[5] Hyde. Rel. vet. Pers., p. 114.
[6] I have given the above account of the early life of Zoroaster on
the authority of Hyde and Prideaux, although I myself entertain
some doubts of its probability. Whoever this extraordinary character might be, it is certain that he possessed an extensive knowledge
of all the science and philosophy then known in the world, and had
been initiated into the peculiar mysteries of every nation, to qualify
himself for the distinguished part he was now about to act on the
great theatre of the world. I think also it is highly probable that
two distinct personages of the same name flourished in Persia at
different eras, the former perhaps the inventor of a system which the
other improved. (Vid. Justin., l. i., c. 1. Plin., l. xxx., c. 1. Diog.
Laert., in Proem., &c. Prid. Con., vol. i., p. 212. Stanley on the
Chaldean Philosophy, c. 2; and Richardson's Dissertation, 2nd edi
tion, p. 230.)   [7] Pococke. Specim. Hist. Arab., p. 147.
[8] His object evidently was to restore the ancient system of worship
And he succeeded; and established a reputation which has asso.

by the monarch, Darius Hystaspes,[9] who accompanied him into Cashmere,[10] for the purpose of completing his preparatory studies by the instruction of the Brahmins, from whom he had previously received initiation.[11] After having obtained a complete knowledge of their theological, mathematical, and astronomical system, he returned into Bactria, and took up his residence with his royal patron at Balk.[12]

He began with their religion. Before his time the Persians worshipped in the open air, and resisted the innovation of covered temples,[13] long after they were adopted by other nations; for they thought that an immaterial Being could not be confined in buildings erected by the hand of man; and, therefore, they considered the broad expanse of heaven as the sublime covering of a temple consecrated to the Deity.[14] Their places of sacrifice were of an open and very simple nature, being elevated on hills,[15] and composed principally of irregular circles of unhewn stone, like those of the northern nations of Europe.[16] They abominated images,[17] and worshipped the Sun and Fire,[18] as representatives of the

ciated his name with those of Confucius, Mahomet, and other successful reformers of religious rites.

[9] Hyde. Rel. vet. Pers., p. 323.

[10] "Cashmere, which has often been called the terrestrial paradise, may indeed be justly denominated the holy land of superstition. In the Ayeen Akbery, forty-five places are stated to be dedicated to Mahadeo; sixty-four to Vishnu; twenty-two to Durga: and only three to Brahma." (Maur. Ind. Ant., vol. v.. p. 861.)

[11] Am. Marcell., l. xiii.

[12] Prid. Con., vol. i., p. 220.

[13] The Persians were not singular in this custom; for the early Egyptians, as well as the Druids and others, worshipped in uncovered temples. (Clem. Alex. Strom., 5. Lucian de Deâ Syria.)

[14] Vid. Cic. de. Leg., l. ii., c. 2.   [15] Strabo., l. xv.

[16] By some unexplained process in the human mind, huge stones were always objects of veneration with every people who had forsaken the true God.

[17] Herod. Clio., l. i. Yet, "according to the Zinat o'ttawarikh, idolatry first arose in Persia, from survivors preserving the busts and images of their deceased friends; which, in subsequent ages, were venerated with divine honours by their posterity." (Wait. Orient. Ant., p. 11.)

[18] Even the Jews in their idolatries were not exempt from the superstitious adoration of this element, a practice which they pretended to justify from their own Scriptures. God, say they, appeared in the Cherubim over the gate of Eden as a *flaming sword*, (Gen. iii.,

omnipresent Deity. Zoroaster succeeded in prevailing on them to preserve the Sacred Fire, which, by burning on the highest hills, was liable to be extinguished by storms and tempests, in covered fire towers,[19] which were circular buildings, with a dome, and a small orifice at the top to let out the smoke. In these the sacred flame, where God was supposed to reside, was kept perpetually alive.[20] Thus the building represented the universe; and the central fire which constantly blazed within it, was figurative of the great luminary, the Sun

He then proceeded to remodel the Mysteries;[21] and to accomplish with greater effect this design, he retired to a circular cave or grotto in the mountains of Bokhara,[22] which he ornamented with a profusion of symbolical and astronomical[23] decorations, and solemnly consecrated it to the middle god or Mediator,[24] Mithr-As, or as he was else-where denominated, the invisible Deity,[25] the parent of the universe, who was himself said to be born, or pro-

---

24,) and to Abraham as *a flame of fire*; (Gen. xv., 17,) and again to Moses as *a fire* at Horeb; (Exod. iii., 2,) and to the whole assembly of the people at Sinai, when he descended upon the mountain *in fire*; (Exod. xix., 18,) and they further urged that Moses himself had told them that their God was *a consuming fire*, (Deut. iv., 24,) which was reëchoed more than once; (Deut. ix., 3,) and thence the Jews were weak enough to worship the material substance, in lieu of the invisible and eternal God.

[19] Hyde. de Rel. vet. Pers., c. 8, et passim.

[20] "The Orientals make Nimrod the author of the sect of the Magi, or worshippers of fire; and tell us that accidentally seeing fire rise out of the earth at a great distance from him *in the East*, he worshipped it; and appointed one Andesham to attend the fire there, and throw frankincense into it." (Univ. Hist., vol. i., p. 90.)

[21] Pococke. Spec. Hist. Arab., p. 147.

[22] Porph. de Ant. Nymph., p. 254.

[23] There do not exist two opinions respecting the early knowledge of astronomy in this quarter of the globe. Indeed, Pliny says, (Nat. Hist., l. i., c. 26.) Belus, inventor fuit sideralis scientiæ; and Belus was the grandson of Ham.

[24] The Persians were so deeply impressed with this amiable characteristic of their god, that they denominated every person *who acted in the capacity of a mediator* between two contending parties; Mithras. (Plut. Isid. et Osir., p. 43.)

[25] Mithras, whether corporeal or incorporeal, was unquestionably taken by the Persians for the Supreme Deity, according to that of Hesychius, Μιθρας ὁ πρῶτος εν Περσαις θεός, Mithras the first god among the Persians; who was, therefore, called in the inscription, (Apud Gruter. Thesaur. Inscrip., p. 34,) Omnipotenti Deo Mithræ. (Cudw. Intell. Sys., l. i., c. 4.)

duced from a cave hewn out of a rock.[26]   Here the Sun [7] was represented by a splendid gem, which, with an insupportable lustre,[28] occupied a conspicuous situation in the centre of the roof; the planets were displayed in order round him, in studs of gold glittering on a ground of azure; the zodiac was richly chased in embossed gold,[2c] in which the constellations Leo,[30] and Taurus, with a Sun and Lunette emerging from their back[31] in beaten gold, were peculiarly resplendent.   The four ages of the world were represented by so many globes of gold, silver, brass, and iron.   The whole were decked with gems and precious stones, and knobs of burnished gold; and during the celebration of the mysteries, illuminated by innumerable lamps which reflected a thousand different colours and shades of colour,[32] like the enchanting vision of a celestial palace.[33]   In the centre of the cave was a marble fountain of water,[34] transparent as crystal, to supply the numerous basons with which the grotto was furnished for the purpose of ablutions and ceremonial purifications.[35] The cavern thus ornamented, furnished, and disposed, was an emblem of the widely extended universe,[36] supported by the three grand Pillars of Eternity, fecundity, and authority;[37] and the symbols with which it was profusely adorned referred to every element and principle in Nature.[38]

[26] Just. Mart. dial. cum Tryph., p. 296.

[27] Porph. de Ant. Nymph., p. 265.

[28] Maur. Ind. Ant., vol. ii., p. 28.

[29] The tomb of Osymandyas in Egypt, was surrounded with a broad circle of beaten gold, three hundred and sixty-five cubits in circumference, to represent the number of days in the year. (Diod. Sic., p. 44.)

[30] Maur. Ind. Ant., vol. v., p. 987.

[31] The bull and sun were emblematical of the great father or Noah riding in safety in the Ark; for Noah was the sun, and the bull was an acknowledged symbol of the Ark. (Porph. de Ant. Nymph., p. 265.) Hyde (de Rel. vet. Pers.,) says that the Mogul emperors use this device on their coins. Sometimes, however, Leo is substituted for Taurus.

[32] Maur. Ind. Ant., vol. v., p. 987.

[33] See the Story of the Second Calendar in the Arabian Nights Entertainments.   [34] Maur. Ind. Ant., vol. v., p. 990.

[35] Porph. de Ant. Nymph., p. 263.

[36] Ibid., p. 254.   [37] Signs and Symbols, Lect. 7.

[38] And let it not be thought that these riches and this refulgent splendour are inconsistent with probability, for the Persians of this age were a magnificent people, and possessed an abundance of wealth,

Every preparation being completed, Zoroaster caused a rumour to be propagated that he had been favoured with a celestial vision, received up into the abode of the Most High,[39] and permitted to converse with that awful Being face to face, who, he said, was encircled with a bright and ever living flame of fire; that a system of pure worship had been revealed to him,[40] which he was directed to communicate to those only who possessed sufficient virtue to resist the allurements of the world, and were willing to devote themselves to the study of philosophy, and the pure and unmixed contemplation of the Deity and his works.

In the most secret recesses of this hallowed cave,[41] he now commenced the celebration of those famous rites which exalted his name to the highest summit of celebrity. Every person who wished to attain a knowledge of the Persian philosophy resorted to the Mithratic cave for initiation. The fame of Zoroaster spread throughout the world. Numbers from the most distant regions[42]

which they used with great profusion. The palace of Ecbatana, the imperial residence, is thus described: "The walls and ceilings were overlaid with gold, ivory, and amber, exhibiting the noblest designs, wrought in the most exquisite taste. Its lofty throne of pure gold was raised on pillars refulgent with jewels of the richest lustre. The monarch's bed, also of pure gold, was shaded with a golden vine and palm tree, on whose branches hung clusters of emeralds and rubies. He reposed his head on a casket containing five thousand talents of gold, which was called the king's bolster; and his feet rested on another, containing three thousand talents of the same metal, &c., &c." (Maur. Ind. Ant., vol. vii., p. 481.)

[39] Prid. Con., vol. i., p. 216. This was in imitation of the Jewish legislator, who was with the Deity forty days in the mount which burned with fire. Zoroaster had become acquainted with this fact in Babylon.

[40] As the Jewish law was revealed to Moses. All these men, Zoroaster, Pythagoras, Plato, and others, drew alike from the sacred fountain of truth.

[41] Lucian, describing the Temple of the Syrian goddess, says: "The interior temple, or choir, has no gates, but is open in the front. Everybody may go into the outer temple, but to the inner none are admitted but the priests; and even amongst them, only those who are supposed, from their piety and virtue, most to resemble the deities; and to whom the care of all religious matters is entrusted. Here is the statue of the deity."

[42] The commentary on the book of Zeratûsht in the Desatir, contains many curious instances of these visits, which uniformly ended in conversion.

came to hear his Lectures; and, it is said, even Pythagoras travelled from Greece for initiation by this celebrated philosopher.[43] His doctrines, however, were a continued tissue of allegory, which none could understand but those who were qualified by initiation; and his system embraced all sciences, human and divine.

To prepare the candidate for initiation, numerous lustrations were performed with water, fire, and honey.[44] It is said by some that the aspirant went through *forty* degrees of probation,[45] by others *eighty*,[46] which ended with a fast of fifty days' continuance.[47] These intense and protracted trials were endured in the gloomy recesses of a subterranean cavern, where he was condemned to perpetual silence, wholly secluded from society, and confined amidst cold and nakedness, hunger and stripes,[48] accompanied with an extreme degree of refined and brutal torture.[49] The unbending severity of this stern novitiate was in some instances attended with fatal effects;[50] in others, the candidate suffered a partial derangement of intellect; but the few, whose robust nerves enabled them

[43] Sir W. Jones thinks "it is barely possible that Pythagoras knew him. The Grecian sage," says he, "must have been far advanced in years; and we have no certain evidence of an intercourse between the two Philosophers." (Asiat. Res., vol. ii.) On the other hand, Dean Prideaux observes, "that they who write of Pythagoras do almost all of them tell us, that he was the scholar of Zoroastres at Babylon, and learned of him most of that knowledge which afterwards rendered him so famous in the West. So saith Apuleius, and so say Jamblichus, Porphyry, and Clemens Alexandrinus." (Connect., v. i., p. 228.)

[44] Lucian in Necyom.   [45] Non. Dion., p. 297.

[46] Porph. de Abstin., p. 150.

[47] Nicætas cited by the Abbé Banier. Myth. Vid. Deut. ix., 18.

[48] Maur. Ind. Ant., vol. v., p. 992.

[49] "The *dark places* of the earth are full of the habitations of cruelty." (Psalm lxxiv., 20.)

[50] When a candidate died under the infliction of these rigid penances, an event by no means uncommon, his body was cast into an inner cavern, and he was never more heard of. In the fifth century of Christianity, according to the report of Socrates, a Christian writer, (Hist. Eccles., l. ii., c. 2.) "the Christians of Alexandria having discovered a cavern *that had been consecrated to Mithras*, but for a long period closed up, resolved to explore it, and examine what remnants of that superstition it contained; when to their astonishment, the principal thing they found in it was a great quantity of human skulls and other bones of men that had been thus sacrificed; which were brought out, publickly exposed, and excited the utmost horror in the inhabitants of that great city." (Maur. Ind. Ant., vol. v., p. 965.)

to rise superior to the most extreme suffering of a fully
extended probation, were eligible to the highest honours
and dignities; and received a degree of veneration equal
to that which was paid to the supernal deities.   But
the unhappy novice, who suffered his courage to forsake
him through excess of fatigue or torture, was rejected
with the strongest marks of infamy and contempt, and
for ever accounted profane and excluded from the rites.

The successful probationer, at the expiration of his
novitiate, was brought forth into the cavern of initiation,
where he entered on the point of a sword presented to
his naked left breast, by which he was slightly wounded,[51]
and then he was ritually prepared for the approaching
ceremony.   He was crowned with olive,[52] anointed with
oil of *ban*,[53] and armed with enchanted armour[54] by his
guide, who was the representative of Simorgh, a monstrous griffin,[55] and an important agent in the machinery

[51] Tertull. apud Maur. Ind. Ant., vol. v., p. 991.
[52] "The olive in the mysteries was commemorative of the olive
branch brought back to Noah by the dove; and it was the propitious
omen that the patriarch and his family would speedily emerge from the
gloom of the Ark to the light of day; that they would each soon be
able to exclaim, I have escaped an evil; I have found a better lot.
With a similar allusion to the history of the Deluge, the priests of
Mithras were styled Hierocoraces, or sacred *Ravens*; and the oracular
priestesses of Hammon, Peleiades, or *Doves*; while in consequence of
the close connection of the *dove* and the *olive*, a particular species of
that tree was denominated Columbas."   (Fab. Mys. Cab., c. 10, with
authorities.)
[53] Berhni Kattea.   The oil of ban is the balsam of Bezoin.   (Wait.
Orient. Ant., p. 194.)   [54] Rich. Dissert., p. 170.
[55] "The Simorgh," says Wait., (Orient. Ant., p. 155) "whose name
implies that it is of the size of thirty birds, appears to have been a
species of Eagle."   In Richardson's Dictionary it is thus described:
"It corresponds in some respects with the idea of the Phœnix, one
only of the species being supposed to exist, and like the Griffin in
shape and monstrous size.   It is fancied to be rational, to have the
gift of speech, and to have reigned as queen on the fabulous mountain
of Kàf.   The Caharmàn nàmah gives an account of a conversation which
that hero had with her, in which she informed him of her having
lived several ages before Adam, and seen many wonderful revolutions
of different species of beings that inhabited the globe before the creation of man.   It is described by naturalists as a creature whose
name is known, its body unknown;" and is probably but a duplicate
of the Arabian *Roc*, (Vid. Arabian Nights' Entertainments; Tales of
Sinbad) for the Arabian word for the Simorgh was Rakshi; (Rich.
Dissert., p. 174) the Egyptian *Phœnix* (Ovid Metam., l. xv, 392) or
the Indian *Garuda*. (Asiat. Res., vol. i., p. 248.)

of Persian mythology, and furnished with talismans[56] that he might be ready to encounter all the hideous monsters raised up by the Dives to impede his progress to perfection.[57] Introduced into an inner apartment he was purified with fire and water,[58] and solemnly put through the SEVEN[59] STAGES of initiation.[60] From the precipice where he stood, he beheld a deep and dangerous vault into which a single false step might precipitate him down to the "throne of dreadful necessity,"[61] which was an emblem of those infernal regions through which he was about to pass. Threading the circuitous mazes of the gloomy cavern, he was soon awakened from his trance of thought, by seeing the sacred fire, at intervals, flash through its recesses to illuminate his path; sometimes bursting from beneath his feet; sometimes descending on his head in a broad sheet of white and shadowy flame. Amidst the admiration thus inspired, his terror was excited by the distant yelling of ravenous beasts; the roaring of lions, the howling of wolves, the fierce and

[56] " The most famous talismans, which rendered the heroes of Persian romance proof against the arms and magic of the Dives, (or wicked genii) were *mohur Solimani*, or the seal of Solomon Jared, the fifth monarch of the world, which gave to its possessors the command of the elements, demons, and of every created thing;—the *Siper*, or buckler of Jan-ben-Jan, more famous in the east than the shield of Achilles among the Greeks;—the *Jebeh*, or the impenetrable cuirass;—and the *Tigh atish*, or the flaming sword." (Dissert., p. 272.)

[57] The preparation for these encounters consisted of spells as a defence against enchantment, accompanied with ceremonies differing little from those practised by our European knights errant, when setting out on their adventures to rescue distressed damsels from the power of necromancers or giants. (Vid. Rich. Dissert., 280.)

[58] Maur. Ind. Ant., vol. v., p. 991.

[59] This is represented as a high ladder with seven steps or gates. (Orig. con. Cels., l. iv. Vid. Signs and Symbols, Lect. 8.) The use of the number *Seven* forms an important feature in all the institutions of antiquity, whether their tendency be idolatrous or otherwise. The reference might probably be to the seven antediluvians who were saved with Noah in the ark. The conjecture bears strong marks of truth from the extraordinary fact, that almost every ancient idolatrous nation addressed the rites of divine worship to the seven hero-gods. This remarkable number will be copiously illustrated in Lect. 7.

[60] This part of the ceremony might probably bear some allusion to the soul toiling through the *metempsychosis* towards perfection and everlasting beatitude; for Hyde informs us, (De Rel. vet. Pers., p. 254) that this doctrine was *shadowed out* in the Persian mysteries.

[61] Celsus, cited by Maur. Ind. Ant., vol. iv., p. 645.

threatening bark of dogs.[62]   Enveloped in blackest darkness,[63] he was at a loss where to turn for safety; but was
impelled rapidly forward by his attendant, who maintained
an unbroken silence, towards the quarter from whence
the appalling sounds proceeded; and at the sudden
opening of a door he found himself in a den of wild
beasts,[64] dimly enlightened with a single lamp.   His
conductor exhorted him to courage,[65] and he was immediately attacked, amidst the most tremendous uproar, by
the initiated in the forms of lions,[66] tigers, wolves, grif-
fins,[67] and other monstrous beasts; fierce dogs appeared
to rise from the earth, and with dreadful howlings endeavoured to overwhelm the aspirant with alarm;[68] and how
bravely soever his courage might sustain him in this
unequal conflict, he seldom escaped unhurt.

Being hurried through this cavern into another, he
was once more shrouded in darkness.   A dead silence
succeeded, and he was obliged to proceed with deliberate
step, meditating on the danger he had just escaped, and
smarting under the wounds he had received.   His atten-

[62] In the Zoroastrian Oracles, these dogs are said to spring out of
the earth, and bay tremendously at the aspirant.

[63] Darkness was a symbol of secrecy, and hence it was adored, and
hailed with *three cheers*.   (Vid. Signs and Symbols, Lect. 6.)

[64] To such miserable expedients were the idolaters reduced to perpetuate their system, that even these farcical representations were
encouraged to give effect to the mysterious celebrations.

[65] Rich. Dissert., p. 170.

[66] Mr. Maurice thinks that real lions and other savage beasts were
introduced (Ind. Ant., vol. v., p. 997); but this terrible conjecture
must be admitted with great reluctance, from the imminent danger
with which it would have been accompanied.

[67] Vid. Signs and Symbols, Lect. 8.

[68] Pletho, in his notes on the magic oracles of Zoroaster, says Mons.
de Gebelin speaks also of the dogs which are mentioned by Virgil.
It was the custom, he adds, in the celebration of the Mysteries, to
place before the aspirant, phantoms in the figure of dogs, and other
monstrous spectres and apparitions. (Monde Primitif., tom. iv., p. 336.
Vid. also Warb. Div. Leg., vol. i., p. 203.)   Apollonius speaks of the
same thing:

> Brimo up rises from the land of shades:
> Snakes wreath'd in oaken boughs curl'd round their hair,
> And gleaming torches cast a dismal glare.
> To guard their queen, the hideous dogs of hell
> Rend the dark welkin with incessant yell;
> The heaving ground beneath her footsteps shakes,
> Loud shriek the Naiads of the neighboring lakes; &c.
>
> FAWKES.

tion, however, was soon roused from these reflections and directed to other dangers which appeared to threaten. An undefined rumbling noise was heard in a distant range of caverns, which became louder and louder as he advanced, until the pealing thunder[69] seemed to rend the solid rocks and burst the caverns around him ;[70] and the

[69] They were probably acquainted with a chemical process to imitate thunder and lightning. (Philostrat. Vita Apollon., l. 2, c. 33.)

[70] This was intended to represent the tremendous contests between the Peris and the Dives, which shook the earth to its foundation. These fabulous struggles for preeminence ran through the whole system of Persian romance, which indeed derives its principle attraction from the use of this machinery. In general the Peris or good genii have the superiority, but "when they are in danger of being overpowered by their foes, they solicit the assistance of some mortal hero; and to put them on a footing of prowess with the gigantic dives, or evil genii, he is armed with enchanted talismans, and mounted on some tremendous monster. One of the most famous adventurers in fairy land is Tahmuras, an ancient Persian king. The Peris honour him with a splendid embassy; and the Dives, who dread him, send also another. He consults the griffin Simorgh; she speaks all languages and knows future events. She counsels him to aid the Peris; informs him of the dangers he will encounter, and gives him instructions how to proceed. She offers her assistance to conduct him to Jinnistan; and as a token of friendship, pulls some feathers from her breast, with which he ornaments his helmet. He then mounts the Simorgh, and armed with the buckler of Jan-ben-Jan, *crosses the dark abyss* which mortals cannot pass without supernatural assistance. He arrives at Kaf; he defeats Arzshenk; and also another Dive still more fierce, called Demrush; whose residence is described as a gloomy cavern, where he is surrounded with vast piles of wealth amassed by plunder. Here Tahmuras, amongst other rich spoils, finds a fair captive, the Peri Merjan, whom the Dives had carried off, and her brothers had long searched for in vain. He chains the vanquished demons in the centre of the mountain; sets Merjan at liberty; and then in the true spirit of knight errantry, flies. at the Peris request. to the attack of another powerful Dive, called Houdkonz; but here Tahmuras falls. In the Shah namé the celebrated Rostam, many ages afterwards, engages the Dive Arzshenk, who had escaped from the chains of Tahmuras, and kills him after a fierce battle. Arzshenk is there painted with a body somewhat human. and the head of a bull, which Rostam strikes off at a blow. The Dive Munheras is wounded with an arrow in the mouth by Gershab, the last king of the Pishdadian dynasty; and he is afterwards put to death by Sohrab, the son of Rostam. In the first encounter he has the head of a hog; but in the next he is pictured as a bifrons; one side resembling the head of a lion, the other that of a wild boar. Rostam, who is considered as the Hercules of Persia, among many other Dives, dragons, and enchanters whom he destroys, kills a demon called the Dive Sepid; and Father Angelo mentions having seen a stupendous monument in the midst of a plain, near the

vivid and continued flashes of lightning,[71] in streaming
sheets of fire, rendered visible the flitting shades[72] of
avenging genii, who, frowning displeasure, appeared to
threaten with summary destruction these daring intruders
into the privacy of their hallowed abodes.[73]   Scenes like
these were multiplied with increasing horror, until nature
could no longer endure the trial; and when the aspirant
was ready to sink under the effects of exhaustion and
mental agony, he was conveyed into another apartment
to recruit his strength.   Here, a vivid illumination was
suddenly introduced, and his outraged feelings were
soothed by the sound of melodious music,[74] and the
flavour of grateful perfumes.   Seated at rest in this
apartment, his guide explained the elements of those
invaluable secrets which were more fully developed when
his initiation was complete.

Having pronounced himself disposed to proceed through
the remaining ceremonies, a signal was given by his conductor, and three priests immediately made their appearance; one of whom, after a long and solemn pause, cast
a living serpent[75] into his bosom as a token of regeneration;[76] and a private door being opened, there issued
forth such howlings and cries of lamentation and despair,
as struck him with new and indescribable emotions of
terror.   He turned his eyes with an involuntary motion
to the place from whence these bewailings appeared to
proceed, and beheld in every appalling form, the tor-

city of Fehelion, between Shuster and Shiraz, supposed to be commemorative of this combat; which was cut into a quadrangular fortifi-
cation, with such regularity, that it had the appearance of being formed
of one entire stone." (Rich. Diss., p. 170, 171, 172, and see Signs and
Symbols, Lect. 8.)

[71] Maur. Ind. Ant., vol. v., p. 996.

[72] It has been thought that these illusions gave the first impulse to
the practice of magic. (Wait. Orient Ant., p. 135.)

[73] This was the emblematical FIERY GATE of heaven through which
souls descended in transmigration, under the conduct of Mercury, the
celestial messenger of the gods. (Hom. Odyss., l. 24. Virg. Æn., l. 4.
Lucian. dial. Mai. et Merc.)

[74] Zoroaster introduced music into the Persian Mysteries, which
gave them a more imposing effect. (Strabo., l. 17.)

[75] Sometimes a serpent of ductile gold was used; but I am inclined to think from the analogy of other nations, that the snake was
generally alive. Compare Maur. Ind. Ant., vol. v., p. 992, with vol
vi., p. 209.   [76] See the Sixth Lect.

ments of the wicked in Hades.[77]   Turning from this scene
of woe, he was passed through some other dark caverns
and passages;[78] until, having successfully threaded the
labyrinth, consisting of six[79] spacious vaults,[80] connected
by winding galleries,[81] each opening with a narrow stone
portal, the scene of some perilous adventure ; and having,
by the exercise of fortitude and perseverance, been triumphantly borne through this accumulated mass of
difficulty and danger; the doors of the seventh vault, or
Sacellum, were thrown open, and his darkness was
changed into light.[82]   He was admitted into the spa-

---

[77] Maur. Ind. Ant., vol. vii., p. 675.
[78] Tale of Rustam, in Fab. Pag. Idol., vol. iii., p. 328.
[79] In conformity with these *seven* subterranean caverns, the Persians held the doctine of *seven* classes of demons.   First, Ahriman,
their chief; second, the spirits who inhabit the most distant regions
of the air; third, those who traverse the dense and stormy regions
which are nearer the earth, but still at an immeasurable distance;
fourth, the malignant and unclean spirits who hover over the surface
of the earth; fifth, the spirits of the "vasty deep," which they
agitate with storms and tempests; sixth, the subterranean demons
who dwell in charnel vaults and caverns, termed Ghools, who devour
the corrupted tenants of the grave, and excite earthquakes and con-
vulsions in the globe; and seventh, the spirits who hold a solemn
reign of darkness in the centre of the earth.   (Vid. Maur. Ind. Ant.,
vol. iv., p. 642.)   From this doctrine probably emanated the Maho-
metan belief of *seven* hells, or stages of punishment in the infernal
regions, (Vid. Signs and Symbols, p. 153,) and *seven* heavens, in the
highest of which the Table of Fate is suspended, and "guarded from
demons, lest they should change or corrupt anything thereon.   Its
length is so great, as is the space between heaven and earth; its
breadth equal to the distance from the east to the west; and it
is made of one pearl.   The divine pen was created by the finger of
God; that is also of pearls, and of such length and breadth that a
swift horse could scarcely gallop round it in five hundred years!   It
is so endowed, that, self-moved, it writes all things, past, present,
and to come.   Light is its ink; and the language which it uses, only
the angels can understand."   (Maracci, in Southey's Thalaba, vol. ii.,
p. 247.)   The *seven* hells of the Jewish Rabbies were founded on the
seven names of hell contained in their Scriptures.   (Basnage, Hist.
Jews, p. 389.)   All these fancies might safely date their origin from
the hebdomadal division of time observed by the Creator, and enjoined
on man by divine authority.
[80] Signs and Symbols, Lect. 8.   [81] Porph. de Ant. Nymph., p. 262.
[82] Ibid., p. 253.   The progress of the candidate through the seven
stages of initiation being in a circle, referred to the course of the planets
round the sun; or more probably, the apparent motion of the sun himself, which is accomplished by a movement from east to west by the
south.

cious and lofty cavern already described, which was
denominated the sacred grotto of Elysium. This consecrated place was brilliantly illuminated,[83] and sparkled
with gold and precious stones. A splendid sun[84] and
starry system emitted their dazzling radiance, and moved
in order to the symphonies of heavenly music.[85] Here
sat the Archimagus in the East, elevated on a throne
of burnished gold, crowned with a rich diadem decorated
with myrtle boughs,[86] and habited in a flowing tunic of
a bright cerulean tincture;[87] round him were arranged
in solemn order the Presules,[88] and dispensers of the mysteries; forming altogether a reverend assembly, which
covered the awe-struck aspirant with a profound feeling
of veneration; and, by an involuntary impulse, frequently produced an act of worship. Here he was
received with congratulations; and after having entered
into the usual engagements for keeping secret the sacred
rites of Mithras, the sacred WORDS were entrusted to
him, of which the ineffable TETRACTYS, or Name of God
was the chief.

The aspirant, having surmounted the dangers of initiation, now claimed investiture[89] and instruction. An
abundance of amulets and talismans were delivered to
him; and he was even taught the secret of constructing
them, that he might be exempt from all assailing dangers, both in his person and property.[90] Every emblem

---

[83] The radiance which illuminates the celestial abodes, gave rise to
many superstitions in different nations. I quote one from D'Ohson
as a specimen :—"The night Leileth-ul-cadr, is considered as being
particularly consecrated to ineffable mysteries. There is a prevailing opinion, that a thousand secret and invisible prodigies are performed on this night; and that all inanimate beings then pay their
adoration to God. It has not, however, pleased him (says the legend)
to reveal it to the faithful; but it is universally agreed, that sometimes on this night, *the firmament opens for a moment or two, and the
glory of God appears visible to the eyes of those who are so happy as
to behold it;* at which juncture, whatever is asked of God by the fortunate beholders of the mysteries of that critical moment, is infallibly
granted." Southey has a long note on this subject. (Thalaba,
book ii.)

[84] Apul. Metam., l. 1.   [85] Strabo, l. 17.   [86] Herod. l. 1.
[87] Maur. Ind. Ant., vol v., p. 1004.
[88] Hyde de Rel. vet. Pers., p. 380.
[89] The ceremony of investiture is described in Signs and Symbols,
Lect. 10.
[90] These potent auxiliaries were very numerous, and applied to

displayed to his view by the *divine lights*[91] in this vast
and diversified cavern,[92] every incident which excited his

every transaction in life, how trivial soever. I subjoin an enumeration
of many of them from Richardson. (Dissert., p. 275.) "*Nushret*
was an amulet for preventing or curing insanity, or other malady.
Keble, a philtre by which necromancers pretended to reconcile enemies. *Ghezshghaw* were tufts made of the hair of sea-cows, and
hung round the necks of horses to defend them from fascination.
Shebarik, a tree of which they make amulets for the same purpose.
Azimet, an amulet, incantation, or spell against serpents, disease, or
other evil. *Sulwanet*, shells, rings, or beads used as amulets. *Sul-
wan* denotes water taken from the grave of a dead man, poured from
a kind of shell upon the earth, which they drink to the health of a person as a cure for love, or any severe affliction. *Atfet* or *Antefet*, small
beads hung by women round their necks, as a charm to gain the affection of lovers. *Akret*, a spherical amulet worn by some women round
their waists to prevent pregnancy; and by others to favour a conception. *Akhzet*, an amulet in form of a knot, which women wear to
keep their husbands faithful. *Nirenk, nirek, hemail tawiz, mikad,
mutemmim, gezz, kherez, kehal, wejihet, rab, kyrzehlet, mawiz, berim,*
signify amulets made of shells, beads, tufts of wool or hair, dead
men's bones, &c. *Neju, ferhest, reki, shuh, latet, nezret, &c.*, imply
fascination or malignant eyes. *Kherchare* is an ass's head placed on
a pole in a garden, &c., to guard against fascination. *Bazur* and
bazubend signify amulets or any kind of ligatures used in enchantment, because they are in general fastened round the arm, which the
latter word implies. *Cheshm benam*, an amulet for averting the fascination of malignant eyes." Thus far Richardson, but I beg leave
to quote a very curious passage on this subject from Odoricus, in Hak-
luyt, cited by Southey, in his fine poem of Thalaba, (vol. i., p. 114,)
although the note is already somewhat too much extended. " In the
country called Panten or Tathalamasin, there be canes called Cas-
san, which overspread the earth like grasse, and out of every knot of
them spring foorthe certaine branches, which are continued upon the
ground almost for the space of a mile. In the sayd canes there are
found certaine stones, one of which stones whosoever carryeth about
with him, cannot be wounded with any yron; and therefore the men
of that country, for the most part, carry such stones with them,
whithersoever they goe. Many also cause one of the armes of their
children while they are young, to be launced, putting one of the
sayd stones into the wound, healing also and closing up the sayd
wound with the powder of a certain fish, (the name whereof I do not
know,) which powder doth immediately consolidate and cure the sayd
wound. And by the vertue of these stones, the people aforesaid doe,
for the most part, triumph both on sea and land."

[91] This display was denominated Ἀυτοψία, as we learn from Psellus
in his Notes on the Oracles of Zoroaster.

[92] He was taught the hieroglyphical *character*, or sacred cipher, in
which their mysterious dogmata were perpetuated; specimens of
which, according to Sir W. Jones, (Asiat. Res., vol. ii., p. 57,) still
remain.

astonishment during the tedious process of initiation, was now converted to a moral purpose, and explained in a series of disquisitions, calculated to inspire an irrevocable attachment, alike to the mysteries, and to the persons of their administrators.

The candidate was taught that the benign influence of the superior light derived from initiation, irradiates the mind with some rays of the divinity ; and inspires it with a degree of knowledge which is unattainable without this distinguished privilege. He was instructed to adore[93] the consecrated fire, the gift of thè deity,[94] as his visible residence.[95] He was taught the existence of two independent and equally powerful principles, the one essentially good, the other irreclaimably evil ;[96] and the cosmogony was this : Ormisda, the supreme source of light and truth,[97] created the world at six different periods.[98] First, he made the heavens; second, the waters; third, the earth; fourth, trees and plants; fifth,

[93] Ramsay on the Theology of the Pagans, p. 276.

[94] Hyde, Rel. vet. Pers., p. 160.

[95] The throne of the deity was believed to be in the Sun, (Hyde ut supra, p. 161,) which was the Persian paradise ; but he was equally supposed to be resident in the Fire. In the Bhagvat Geeta, (p. 54,) Krishna says, " *God is in the fire of the altar ;* and some of the devout, with their offerings, *direct their worship unto god in the fire.*" The priest alone was allowed to appear in the presence of this Shekinah ; and he was obliged first to purify himself by washing from head to foot, and being clothed in *a white garment,* as an emblem of ceremonial cleanness. He then approached the sacred element with the utmost veneration ; was careful not to pollute it by the use of any *metal tool,* but used an instrument made of the purest wood divested of its bark. Even his breath was supposed to convey pollution ; (Vallancey, Anc. Hist. Irel., p. 203,) and, therefore, while offering up his petitions for the public good, he covered his mouth with a linen cloth to prevent the possibility of profanation. The veneration of the Persians for Fire was so unbounded, that its pollution was strictly forbidden, even in private dwellings ; the richest noble, equally with the meanest slave, would not dare so much as to spit in the fire ; and if his dwelling, and every thing it contained were perishing by this devouring element, he was prohibited from controlling its progress by the use of water, which was also held sacred by the people, and was allowed merely to smother it by throwing earth, stones, or any other similar anticombustible substance on it. The Parsis of Guzerat still practise the same superstition. (Strabo, l. 15. Perron's Zendavesta, vol. ii., p. 567. Notes on Richardson's Dissertation, p. 277.)

[96] Vid. Berhani Kattea, cited by Wait. Orient. Aut., p. 85.

[97] Porph. in vit. Pyth.

[98] Perron. Zendavesta, vol. iii., p. 384. Prid. Con., vol. i., p. 225

animals; and sixth, man,[99] or rather a being compounded of a man and a bull. This newly created being lived in a state of purity and happiness for many ages, but was at last *poisoned* by the temptations of a subtle serpent-genius, named Ahriman,[100] who inhabited the regions of darkness, and was the author of evil;[101] and his ascendency upon earth became at length so great as to create a powerful rebellion against the creator, Ormisda; by whom, however, he was at length subdued. To counteract the effect of this renunciation of virtue, another pure being was created, compounded, as before, of a man and a bull, called Taschter, or Mithras,[102] by whose intervention, with the assistance of three associates,[103] a flood of waters was produced to purify the earth, by prodigious showers of rain, each drop as large as the head of an ox, which produced a general lustration. A tempestuous wind, which blew for three successive days from the same quarter, dried the waters from the face of the earth; and when they were completely subsided, a new germ was introduced, from which sprang the present race of mankind.[104]

This theogony was also inculcated. Ormisda created six benevolent gods, and Ahriman formed the same number of malignant spirits, who were always engaged in a violent contention for pre-eminence. The evil spirits at length succeeded in gaining the dominion over one half of the year, which the celestials deities were contented to resign to their superintendence;[105] which was explained by a reference to the change and variety of the seasons;

---

[99] "Mezdam," says the prophet, "separated man from the other animals, by the distinction of a soul, which is a free and independent substance, without a body or any thing material, indivisible and without position, by which he obtaineth the glory of the angels. The Lord of Being created his servant *free; if he doeth good he gaineth heaven; if evil, he becometh an inhabitant of hell.*" (Desatir. Book of Abad. [100] Diog. Laert. in Prœm.

[101] This Persian doctrine was the foundation of the Manichean heresy, which vexed the Christian Church from the fifth to the ninth century. (Vid. Bower. Hist. of Popes, vol. ii., p. 19.)

[102] This being was denominated Μεσιτος Θεος, and referred to the sun.

[103] Here we find another evident duplicate of Noah and his triple offspring.

[104] Vid. Perron's Zendavesta. vol. iii. Hyde, Rel. vet. Pers., p. 160. Bryant Annal., vol. iii., and Fab. Pag. Idol., b. iii., c. 3.

[105] Plut. de. Isid. et Osir., p. 63.

and represented the manner in which the year was governed by the successive recurrence of summer and winter, or light and darkness; the six summer, and the like number of winter months,[106] pointing also to the twelve signs of the zodiac, which were emblazoned on the roof of the Mithratic cavern. The mysterious emblem which served to typify these perpetual contests for superiority was, *two serpents*[107] *contending for an egg*,[108] the former being symbolical of the powers of light and darkness, and the latter of the world.[109]

On these legends many wild and improbable fictions were engrafted. The Archimagus related to the initiated how the world had been seven times created and destroyed;[110] how Simorgh, the omniscient griffin,[111] who had

[106] Thus every month was under the peculiar guardianship of a genius, from whom it received its name; (Rich. Dissert., p. 183,) and a particular day of each month was dedicated to him by festal rites and ceremonies.

[107] The deity was frequently represented as involved in the folds of a serpent, (Mont. Ant. Supplem., p. 211,) in reference to the solar superstition, for the serpent was a symbol of the sun, and hence it was often depicted in the form of a ring with its tail in its mouth, as a striking emblem of the immortality of the deity, for whom this reptile was often substituted. Much may be seen on this subject in Signs and Symbols, Lect. 2.

[108] Vid. Montfauc. l'Antiq. Expl., tom. ii., p. 2, where is a plate of this emblem, which has been copied by Maurice into the fourth volume of his Indian Antiquities.

[109] Calmet says, that the Persians "offered sacrifices of thanksgiving to Oromazes; and to Ahrimanes, sacrifices to avert misfortunes. They took an herb called Omomi, which they bruised in a mortar, invoking at the same time the god of hell and darkness; they mingled with it the blood of a wolf which they had killed, and carried this composition to a place where the rays of the sun never entered, here they threw it down and left it." (Dict. in v. Demons.)

[110] Orient. Coll., vol. i., p. 119. This doctrine is set forth in an ancient Persian book, called the Desatir, which has been recently discovered and translated into English. "In the beginning of each Grand Period, a new order of things commenceth in the lower world. And, not, indeed, the very forms, and knowledge and events of the Grand Period that hath elapsed, but others precisely similar to them will again be produced. And every grand period that cometh, resembleth from beginning to end the grand period that is past. At the conclusion of a grand period, only two persons are left in the world, one man and one woman; all the rest of mankind perish: and hence mankind derive their origin from the woman and man who survive, and from whose loins numbers issue in the new grand period." (Book of Abad, and Commentary.)

[111] Rich. Dissert., p. 170. "In Mr. Fox's collection of Persio

existed through all these revolutions of ages, revealed to a hero, called Caherman,[112] that the first inhabitants were the Peris, or good beings, and the Dives, or wicked ones,[113] who waged eternal war with each other,[114] and though the former were the most powerful,[115] their contests for superiority were sometimes so violent as to throw nature into convulsion,[116] and cover the universe with dismay.[117]   Then succeeded an animated account of

books, says Southey in a note on Thalaba, (B. 11.) is an illuminated copy of Ferdusi, containing a picture of the Simorgh, who is there represented as an ugly dragon-looking sort of bird.   I should be loth to believe that she has so bad a physiognomy ; and as, in the same volume, there are blue and yellow horses, there is good reason to conclude that this is not a genuine portrait.   When the genius of the lamp is ordered by Aladin to bring a roc's egg and hang it up in the hall; he is violently enraged. and exclaims, Wretch, wouldst thou have me hang up my master ?   From the manner in which rocs are usually mentioned in the Arabian Tales, the reader feels as much surprised at this indignation as Aladin was himself.   Perhaps the original may have been Simorgh instead of roc.   To think, indeed, of robbing the Simorgh's nest, either for the sake of drilling the eggs, or of poaching them, would in a believer, whether Shiah or Sunni, be the height of human impiety."

[112] Vid. Caherman namè.

[113] "Those who wish for success to their works of this life, worship the Devatas" (Dives.)   (Bhagvat Geeta, p. 52.)

[114] D'Herbelot in voc. Peri.   Rich. Dissert., p. 169.

[115] The following description of meeting between two of these imaginary beings, from the Arabian Night's Entertainments, will show this fact.   "As Maimoune mounted high to the middle region of the air, she heard a great flapping of wings, which made her fly that way ; and when she approached, she knew it was a genie who made the noise ; but it was one of those that are rebellious against God. As for Maimoune, she belonged to that class whom the great Solomon compelled to acknowledge him.   This genie, whose name was Danhasch, knew Maimoune, and was seized with fear, being sensible how much power she had over him by her submission to the Almighty. He would fain have avoided her, but she was so near, he must either fight or yield."   (Amours of Carmaralzaman and Badoura.)

[116] There is a good account of these Peris and Dives in Calmet's Historical Dictionary under the word Dæmons, but too diffuse for insertion here.

[117] "The Peris are described as beautiful and benevolent, and though guilty of errors which had offended Omnipotence, they are supposed, in consequence of their penitence, still to enjoy distin-guished marks of divine favour.   The Dives, on the contrary, are depicted as hideous in form, and malignant in mind; differing only from the infernal demons in not being confined to hell; but roaming for ever around the world to scatter discord and wretchedness among the sons of Adam.   In the Peris we find a wonderful resemblance to

the valour and prowess of certain Persian heroes, who dissolved enchantments, vanquished giants, destroyed the power of magicians, and made hostile fairies obedient to their will.   And at the conclusion of the ceremony or initiation; as a last, great secret, the initiated were taught that important prophecy of Zoroaster, which he had learned in his travels through India and Egypt; that, in future times, a great prophet should appear in the world, the desire of all nations, who should be the son of a pure virgin, and whose advent should be proclaimed to the world, by a new and brilliant star in the heavens, shining with celestial brightness at mid-day. The newly initiated candidate was strictly enjoined to follow the direction of this supernatural appearance, if it should happen in his day, until he had found the new born babe, to whom he was commanded to offer rich gifts and sacrifices, and to fall prostrate before him with devout humility as the Creator of the world.[118]

This celebrated system, like all others which have not the revealed Word of God for their basis, branched out into numerous abominable rites, to sanction the vicious practices of potent individuals, whose countenance was found necessary or useful to aid the extension of its schemes; and thus the initiations gradually became so corrupt as to serve as a cloak for licentious indulgences. The mysteries being connected with the services of religion,[119] the miserable jugglers who profited by magnifying the absurd fears of superstition, carried on the deception to its utmost extent, and to the latest moment

the fairies of the European nations; and the Dives or Genies differ little from the giants and savages of the middle ages; the adventures of the eastern heroes breathe all the wildness of achievement recorded of the knights in Gothic romance; and the doctrine of enchantments in both, seem to claim one common source." (Rich. Dissert., p. 167.)

[118] Abulfarag. Hyst. Dynast., p. 54. Hyde, Rel. vet. Pers., p. 382.

[119] In the concluding period of the Jewish history, we find the Temple at Jerusalem profaned by these abominations, even to the preliminary ceremony of public prostitution in the holy porch. (2 Mac. vi., 4.)   The Jews were compelled to participate in the rites of the Dionysiaca, and to appear in the public processions of the Bacchantes as Periphallia, bearing ivy branches; for which, indeed, they had been prepared by their own custom of the οσχοφορια, or carrying vine branches at the feast of tabernacles.

of their powers. Here the phallus was a consecrated symbol, which led to the grossest obscenities. To conciliate the Persian monarchs and nobility, who were much addicted to incestuous connexions;[120] these were at length sanctioned, and even encouraged in the mysteries;[121] and it became an axiom in religion, that the produce of a son and a mother was the best calculated for the office of a priest.[122]

[120] Vid. Fab. Mys. Cab., vol. i., p. 182.

[121] "The Persians marry their mothers, the Egyptians their sisters; and Chrysippus, in his treatise of Policy, asserts, that the father may lie with the daughter, the mother with the son, and the brother with the sister; but Plato more universally saith, that all wives ought to be in common." (Stanley's Lives, vol. iii., p. 94.)

[122] Strabo, l. 15. Diog. Laert. in Prœem. A most appalling description of the abominations necessarily resulting from such pernicious tenets is displayed in the Apocryphal Book, called the Wisdom of Solomon. (xiv. 22–27.)

LECTURE V.

HISTORY OF INITIATION IN GREECE.

THE mysteries formed an important feature in the system of religion practised amongst the Greeks. In the institutions of polytheism the gods were worshipped openly by prayer and sacrifice; and to these rites the people of every rank were admitted without distinction, because they formed the beaten track of duty which mortal man was supposed to owe to the immortal deities. But the highest ceremonies of religion were of a nature too sublime to be exposed to public view; and were, therefore, only celebrated in the presence of that distinguished portion of the community which had bound themselves by voluntary vows to preserve the solemn rites inviolably secret from the rest of the world.[1] These rites were known under the high and significant appellation of The Mysteries;[2] and even in them a subdivision had been made, because it was thought dangerous to entrust the ineffable secrets[3] to any but a select and chosen few,[4] who were prepared for a new accession of knowledge by processes, at once seductive and austere, and bound to secrecy by fearful oaths, and penalties of the most sanguinary character.[5] The former were denominated *the Lesser*, and these *the Greater* Mysteries.

In Greece the mysteries were celebrated in honour of various deities, but the ceremonial did not vary in any essential points. The Eleusinian mysteries were per-

Warb. Div. Leg., vol. i., p. 142.
[2] These Mysteries were divided into three degrees, which were styled το καθαρσια; τα μικρα Μυστηρια; and τα εποπτικα.
[3] Clem. Alex., Strom. 5.
[4] No foreigner is to be initiated into the holy Mysteries. (Aristoph. Schol. Plut.)
[5] Death shall be his penalty who divulges the Mysteries. (Sopat. in divis. quæst.)

formed by the Athenians at Eleusis,[6] a town in Attica,[7] every fifth year, and were subsequently translated to Rome by Adrian.[8] The Bacchic mysteries were equally celebrated, and consisted of the Lenea and the Dionysiaca, instituted in honour of the Bromian Dionusus; the former, so named from Lenos (Δηνος)[9] a wine press, were a preparation for the latter, which received their designation from Dionysus, (Διοννσος) one of the names of Bacchus.[10] At Athens they obtained the most distinguished popularity, and were consequently invested with a proportionate degree of splendour and magnificence.

Under the fostering care of Pythagoras and Plato, the

[6] "No woman shall go in her chariot to Eleusis," says Plutarch, (In Lycurg. Rhet.) "and whoever commits theft during the feast kept at that place, shall be fined 6000 drachms."

[7] The statue of the Eleusinian Ceres by Phidias is now in the public library at Cambridge.

[8] This festival was of nine days' continuance, and was celebrated with much imposing splendour, heightened by the charms of music, both vocal and instrumental. (Diod. Sic., l. v., c. 3.) The first day was usually consumed in assembling together, and in making the requisite preparations for the solemnity; the second was employed in ceremonial purifications and ablutions in the sea; the third was appropriated to sacrifice; the fourth to public processions; the fifth to an illumination with torches; the sixth to songs accompanied with the music of flutes and brazen kettles; the seventh to public games; the eighth to the solemn purpose of initiation, and the performance of sacred rites; and the ninth to the final ceremonies of libation. (Potter. Archæol. Grec., vol. i., p. 383.)

[9] Wait (Orient. Ant., p. 216,) thinks it probable that Lenos was derived from the Sancrit Linga, the Phallus.

[10] The arcane narration of these mysteries is thus related by Mr. Taylor. (On the Eleus. and Bacch. Mys., in Pamphleteer, vol. viii.) "Dionysus or Bacchus, while he was yet a boy, was engaged by the Titans, through the stratagems of Juno, in a variety of sports with which that period of life is so vehemently allured; and among the rest he was particularly captivated with beholding his image in a mirror; during his admiration of which he was miserably torn in pieces by the Titans; who, not content with this cruelty, first boiled his members in water, and afterwards roasted them by the fire. But while they were tasting his flesh, thus dressed, Jupiter, excited by the steam, and perceiving the cruelty of the deed, hurled his thunder at the Titans; but committed his members to Apollo, the brother of Bacchus, that they might be properly interred. And this being properly performed, Dionysus, whose heart, during laceration, was snatched away by Pallas and preserved, by a new regeneration, again emerged, and being restored to his pristine life and integrity, he afterwards filled up the number of the gods. But, in the mean time, from the exhalations formed from the ashes of the burning bodies of the Titans, mankind were produced."

Mysteries were greatly improved. The former received the rudiments of that knowledge which afterwards elevated him to such a distinguished rank, from Anaximander the Milesian. His first initiation took place at Sidon; and he was so impressed with the idea that something more was intended to be conveyed by this solemnity, than the priests were able or willing to explain, that he resolved to devote his life to the discovery. He travelled over the world for knowledge, and was initiated into the mysteries of all nations, that by analysing the peculiarities of each system, he might discover the source of truth. Hence his improved mysteries were the most perfect approximation to the original science which could be accomplished by an idolatrous philosopher bereft of the aid of revelation. Some parts of his scheme would have been unaccountable, but from the fact of his Jewish initiation, and instruction in sacred things by Ezekiel the prophet.[11]

He enjoined upon his candidates a probation of five years abstinence and silence;[12] for he esteemed the latter virtue as an unobjectionable proof of wisdom.[13] This extended trial, called a quinquennial silence, was intended to abstract their minds from sensible things, that they might be enabled to reflect on the nature of the deity with a pure and undivided attention.[14] This probation embraced many important particulars. The candidate was rejected if found passionate or intemperate, conten-

[11] "Nazaratus the Assyrian, one of Pythagoras' masters, was by some supposed to be the prophet Ezekiel; which opinion Clemens (Strom. 1.) oppugns; nevertheless, as Mr. Selden observes, the most accurate chronology teacheth that Ezekiel and Pythagoras flourished together, betwixt the 50th and 52nd Olympiad; and, therefore, the account hinders not but this Nazaratus might be Ezekiel." (Stanley, Life of Pyth., p. 7.

[12] Diog. Laert. in vit. Pyth.

[13] Apul. Florid., l. ii. Hence the English proverb, a *still tongue* marks a wise head.

[14] Clem. Alex., Strom. 5. This probationary silence differed essentially from that which was denominated $\pi\alpha\nu\tau\epsilon\lambda\dot{\eta}s$ $\dot{\epsilon}\chi\epsilon\mu\nu\vartheta\epsilon\dot{\iota}\alpha$, which implied that the initiated were bound to conceal from all the world the secrets of the institution. The former was peculiar to the *exotericks*, the latter to the *esotericks*. The probation of five years was sometimes partly remitted to those who, by their age and well-known prudence, were supposed to possess the requisite qualifications. With these, two years were deemed a sufficient trial.

tious or ambitious of worldly honours and distinctions.[15]
Pythagoras made particular enquiry as to the kind of
society in which the aspirant had passed his time;[16] he
tried his fortitude and constancy by the infliction of
bodily wounds with an iron instrument heated red hot,
or with the point of a sword, or other sharp weapon.[17]
And if he endured these torments without shrinking;
and proved in other respects worthy of admission, he was
allowed to receive the first degree, conformably to the
system of Grecian initiation;[18] and as an exoterick, was
ranked among the *Acousmatici*.[19] After the lapse of
another considerable space of time, they were admitted
to the second degree, and were termed *Mathematici*:[20]
and afterwards, on receiving the third degree, they were

[15] Jambl., c. 20. This rejection was attended with circumstances
so galling to the mind, that the unfortunate person frequently expired
under its infliction. See Theocr. Phil. of Freem., p. 246.

[16] Ibid. c. 17.

[17] Notwithstanding this rigid probation, Pythagoras had no sooner
established his system at Crotona, than in a very short time he had
six hundred candidates for initiation. (Jambl., c. 6.) And " soon all
Italy was filled with his disciples; and though before obscure, it was
afterwards, in compliment to Pythagoras, denominated Magna Grecia."
(Ibid. c. 29.)

[18] The Oath propounded to the aspirant was made on the number
FOUR or Tetractys, which was expressed by *ten* commas or Jods,
(supposing it to be derived from the Tetragrammaton of the Jews,)
disposed in form of a triangle, each side containing *four*; as follows:

Monad, Fire, or the active principle.
Duad, the passive principle.
Triad, the world proceeding from their union.
Quaternary, the liberal Sciences.

This triangle, some authors suppose, bore a reference to the triune
God, whence it was termed, Trigonon mysticum. (Jennings, Jewish
Ant., b. i., c. 12.) Jamblichus gives us the words of this oath. (De
vit. Pyth., c. 29.) *Ου μα τον αμετερη,* &c. By the Great Tetractys,
or name Jao, who hath communicated the fountain of eternity to our
souls, &c. [19] Jambl., c. 17.

[20] The doctrine of Aristotle, says Lucian, was of two kinds, exoteric
and acroatic. Under the first were ranked rhetoric, meditation, nice
disputes on the knowledge of civil things; under the other, the more
remote and subtle philosophy, the contemplation of nature and dialec-
tive disceptations.

clothed in white garments as emblematical of purity;[21] were entitled to all the privileges of esotericks, and admitted within the screen, or into the sanctum sanctorum of the philosopher; and from henceforth received the appellation of *Pythagoreans*, as having had perfect initiation into the mysteries of Pythagoras, and fully instructed in the abstruse principles of his philosophy.[22]

In his Lectures, Pythagoras defines his system, the true method of obtaining a knowledge of divine and human laws,[23] by meditation on death,[24] by purifying the soul of its imperfections, and by the discovery of truth, and the practice of virtue; thus imitating the perfections of God, as far as is possible in a human being.[25] He taught the mathematics as a medium whereby to prove the existence of God from the results of reason and observation, and to convey happiness to man; grammar, rhetoric, and logic were taught to cultivate and improve the human reason; and arithmetic, because he conceived that the ultimate benefit of man consisted in the science of numbers.[26] He thought the creation of the world was

[21] Persius, Sat. 2, v. 40.

[22] "Pythagoras went to Phlius, and made a great display of his learning before Leo, the prince of the Phliasians. The prince, charmed with his discourse. asked him what art he professed. He answered, that he knew no art, but was a *Philosopher*. Leo, surprised at this new name, asked, what are *Philosophers*, and wherein do they differ from others? Pythagoras answered, that human life is like the Olympic Games, some attend for glory, some for profit, and some to observe curiously what is there performed. These despise both glory and profit, and employ themselves studiously to inquire into the causes of all things. These are inquirers after wisdom, or Philosophers." (Cicero Tuscul. quæst., 5.) Valerius Maximus relates also, that when Pythagoras founded his school, he was asked what was the name of his system, and answered, I am not *Sophos*, wise; but *Philo-sophos*, a lover of wisdom; and my followers shall be called Philosophers.

[23] Psell. compend. de 5000.   [24] Hieron. ad Rufin.

[25] Stobæus. Serm.

[26] The Pythagorean system of numbers may be found in Signs and Symbols, Lect. 9; and the Theocr. Phil. of Freemas., Lect. 6; to which I may add, that the great Pythagoric Symbol was ONE and TWO, which were used as the names of propagation. *one* being the father, *two* the mother. The multiplication of *unity* and *duity* (once twice two) make FOUR, the Tetractys, the idea of all things, which are consummated in the number TEN. (Stanley, Lives, p. 106.)

effected by the harmony of numbers,[27] and that they existed in the regions of the blessed before the world began.[28] Odd numbers he assigned to the celestial gods, and hence all sacrifices to those beings ought to be in odd numbers. Even numbers were for the infernal deities.[29] Geometry, music, and astronomy were inculcated, because he conceived that man is indebted to these sciences for a knowledge of what is really good and useful. He accounted his system vain if it did not contribute to expel vice, and introduce virtue into the mind;[30] and he taught that the two most excellent things for man, were theoretic and practical virtue; i. e. to speak the truth; and to render benefits to each other. The several heads to which he reduced these virtues[31] were institution,

[27] Stob. Physic., l. ii.   [28] Nicom. Arith., c. 5.
[29] Serv. in Æn., 3. How did Pythagoras reconcile this doctrine of *odd* and *even* numbers, with his known axiom, that the numbers *four* and *ten* were the Tetractys, or sacred name of God?   [30] Stob. Serm.
[31] One of the methods which Pythagoras used to enforce on his disciples the practice of moral virtue, was by the use of short and pithy sentences, which were symbolical of some great moral duty. The following is a specimen of this mode of instruction:—*Sit not upon a Chænix*, means, live not without initiation; and be not initiated without contemplation and discipline; for initiation, without previous preparation and subsequent diligence, is but to enjoy a faint shadow of Light, and is worse than total darkness.—*Travelling from home, turn not back, for the furies go back with you.* A greater than Pythagoras hath said, "no man having put his hand to the plough and looking back, is fit for the kingdom of God." (Luke ix., 62.) Pythagoras meant the same thing applied to an inferior purpose. It was an exhortation to his followers to pass honourably through every degree of his system, that they might attain to perfection.—*Turn away from thyself every edge.* Use prudence, and abstain from ungovernable passion.—*Take off thy right shoe first.* This also denoted prudence.—*Pass not over a balance*, referred to justice and equality.—*Wear not a ring.* Bind not your soul about with the chain of ignorance as the finger is bound with a ring, but be initiated into philosophy, which separates the mind from terrestrial considerations, and fits it for the contemplation of high and immortal things.—*Look not in a glass by candlelight.* Beware of that state of twilight which consists in superficial knowledge; for this is worse than absolute ignorance; but search for the true light, that you may be enabled to find out the nature of the Deity, and estimate his infinite perfections. —*Lay not hold of every one readily with the right hand.* Try and prove every one before you admit him into your society as a friend and brother.—*Eat not the heart. Eat not the brain.* Do not rend asunder the social bond which unites your society, by unnecessary disputes or useless divisions.—*Put not meat in a chamber-pot.* Com-

silence, temperance, fortitude, prudence, and justice. He
proceeded to inculcate the omnipresence of God, the
immortality of the soul, and the necessity of personal
holiness to qualify man for admission into the society of
the gods; and declared his opinion that no man could be
accounted happy or miserable till the day of his death
because, in his most exalted moments he is not able to
pry into futurity, or to divine to-day what evils to-morrow
may bring upon him.

He taught that man is endowed with eight organs of
knowledge to which symbolical institution might be
usefully applied;[32] and these were, sense, phantasy, art,

---

municate not your mysteries to an idle or foolish person, for such an
one will disgrace and betray you.—*Sleep not at noon.* Shut not your
eyes against the Light of knowledge at a time when its hidden stores
are most clearly displayed before you, lest the remainder of your life
be passed amidst the uncertain glimmering of twilight, or the shades of
midnight darkness; the mists of imperfect information, or the dark
clouds of total ignorance.—The curious reader who wishes to pursue
this subject further, may find all the symbolical sentences of Pythagoras
in Stanley's Lives of the Philosophers, from which celebrated work the
above have been extracted.

[32] The following are some of the symbols of Pythagoras:—The
equilateral triangle, a perfect figure, refers to God, the principle and
author of all sublunary things; who, in his body, resembles *Light*,
and in his soul *Truth*. He was, and is, and shall be.—The *right
angle or square* comprehends the union of the celestial and terrestrial
capacities; and was an emblem of Morality and Justice.—*The perfect
square* represents the divine mind, as has already been explained of
the Tetractys.—The *cube* was a symbol of the mind of man after a
well spent life in acts of piety and devotion; which is thus perfectly
prepared by virtue for translation into the society of the celestial
gods.—*A point within a circle.* A symbol of the universe. Mesou-
raneo, because the most excellent body ought to have the most
excellent place, viz., the centre. The central fire was esteemed by
Pythagoras, the mansion of Jove.—*The Dodecaedron* was also a
symbol of the universe.—The *triple triangle* formed of five lines
returning into itself, was a symbol of health, and was called Hygeia.
—The *forty-seventh proposition of Euclid* was invented by Pythagoras, and is so extensively useful that it has been adopted in all lodges
since his time, as a significant symbol of Masonry. It is said by
Apollodorus and other authors, that Pythagoras sacrificed a Heca-
tomb on the discovery of this useful problem. This, however, is
exceedingly doubtful, because Pythagoras abhorred bloody sacrifices,
and directed his followers to offer nothing but cakes and wine, herbs,
flowers, and fruit.—*The letter Y.* This symbolical character represented the course of human life. Youth, arriving at manhood, sees
two ways before him, and deliberates which he shall pursue. If he

opinion, prudence, science, wisdom, and mind. He arranged his assemblies due East and West, because he said that motion began in the East or right side of the world and proceeded towards the West or left side. In a word, though his Institution was the most perfect system ever practised amongst idolaters, yet when he endeavoured to enter the Holy of Holies, and began to speculate on the knowledge of God and a future state, he was bewildered with childish notions and idle conjectures, instead of enjoying the brilliant beams of divine truth.

Plato was deeply versed in all the mysteries of antiquity,[33] which he believed capable of restoring the soul to its primitive purity.[34] He adopted the division of three degrees, because *three* was a mystical number, dedicated to the celestial deities. These degrees were progressive, the ceremonial being in accordance with the Greek mode; and no candidate was admitted to them without an elementary course of study and privation, during which he was subjected to the Pastos, by being placed in a well for a specified period, as the medium of regeneration.[35] The first degree was mathematical; and embraced arithmetic, geometry, music, and astronomy; the instruction of the second degree was confined to physics; and the third, in which the brows of the candidate were encircled with a crown or tiara, to intimate

meet with a guide that directs him to pursue philosophy, and he procures initiation, his life shall be honourable and his death happy. But if he omits to do this, and takes the left hand path, which appears broader and better, it will lead to sloth and luxury; will waste his estate, impair his health, and bring on an old age of infamy and misery. (Porph. vit. Pyth. Stob. Serm. Persius. Sat. iii., v. 56. Stanley. Lives of Philos., &c.) See also the Theocr. Phil. of Freemas., where the system of Pythagoras is elaborately explained.

[33] Proclus says that Plato derived his theology from Orpheus. (Cudw. Intell. Syst., p. 547.)

[34] In Phædone.

[35] "It was in allusion to such rites that Plato," says Faber (Pag. Idol., vol. iii., p. 188), "whose philosophy was largely tinged with the doctrines of the Mysteries, was wont to say, that *Truth must be sought for at the bottom of a well.* By *truth* he meant the speculations revealed to the initiated, who were henceforth styled Epopts, or persons who see things truly as they are; and by *the well*, he meant the sacred pit or cavern where the mysteries were so frequently celebrated."

5*

that he had now received the inestimable gift of superior endowments, and a power of instructing others, was confined to theology. His doctrines embraced disquisitions on the nature of God, and the creation and ultimate destruction of the world. His opinion of the divine nature was, that it contained three hypostases, which he termed Tagathon—Nous—Psyche, or Goodness, Wisdom, and Spirit, the second of which emanated from the first, and the third from both. But he taught that all good men, after death, became demons, and were, therefore, entitled to the homage of divine worship; that the governor of the world had committed all things to their superintendence; and that they were the authorized mediators between the gods and men, and appointed to convey sacrifices and supplications from earth to heaven, and blessings and rewards from heaven to earth. He taught that God created the world, but held, from the deductions of human reason, that, as something could not have been formed from nothing, the materials must have descended from some pre-existent state.[36] He believed that the universe was doomed to be ultimately destroyed by fire, in verification of the fable of Phaeton;[37] and preserved in his system a tradition of the first created beings in Paradise; how they conversed with angels in a state of nature and unclothed; how the earth brought forth its fruits spontaneously to provide these favourites of heaven with food; how they spent their time in innocence and unoffending simplicity; and how at length, *by the suggestions of a serpent*, they fell from their purity, became ashamed of their nakedness, and were cast forth into a world of sorrow, grief, and despair.[38] These traces

[36] De Repub., l. v. [37] In Timæo.

[38] An obscure tradition of this event had been propagated in every nation of the heathen world from the dispersion; but it had been studiously disguised by fable to keep it secret from the vulgar and uninitiated, until, in process of time, the true intent and meaning of the symbols and allegory in which it had been enveloped, were almost entirely lost. "Origen thinks that Plato, by his converse with the Jews in Egypt, did understand the history of the Fall of Man; which he, after his way, enigmatically describes in his Symposiacks. Where he brings in Porus the god of plenty feasting with the rest of the gods; after supper, Penia comes a begging to the door; Porus being drunk with nectar, goes into Jupiter's garden, and there falls asleep. Penia observing it, steals to him, and by this deceit con

of truth fully prove the source whence the mysteries in general proceeded, because they bear undoubted marks that at their institution they were commemorative rites pointing to events which actually took place at the commencement of the world.[39] He taught the history of the Deluge, and wrote a book professedly on the subject, which he called Atlanticus; and he inculcated the metempsychosis, and the important doctrine of man's personal responsibility.

The chief hierophant or dispenser of the mysteries, represented the Demiurgus, or Creator of the universe,[40] and led a retired life of perpetual celibacy, that he might be entirely at liberty to devote himself to the study and contemplation of celestial things, and thus become a perfect master of every science embraced by the Institution of which he was the despotic head.[41] The next

---

ceives by him. In this fable of Plato, Origen takes notice what a near resemblance the garden of Jupiter hath to Paradise, Penia to the Serpent which circumvented Adam, and Porus to the man who was deceived by the Serpent. Which he conceives to be the more probable, because of Plato his custom to wrap up those excellent things he knew under some fables because of the vulgar; for which he after speaks of his custom in altering and disguising what he had from the Jews, lest he should too much displease the fabulous Greeks, if he should adhere too close to the Jews, who were so infamous among them." (Stillingfleet. Orig. Sacr., p. 518.)

[39] The truth is, that though Plato professed to have received his knowledge from an ancient tradition, he had it in reality from the Jews, as Origen has truly testified (see also Clem. Alex. Strom. 1); but the facts were unaccompanied by the key; and, therefore, he inculcated on his disciples, the unimportant nature of the information, unless some future philosopher should rise up among them, who should be capable of revealing the true interpretation.

[40] Euseb. Præp. Evan., l. iii., c. 12.

[41] To accomplish this abstraction with the greater certainty, it was customary for these dignified priests, in the earlier periods of their history, to mortify the flesh by the use of certain herbs which were reputed to possess the virtue of repelling all venereal excitements. Nay, some were so rigid in this respect, as literally to proceed to the expedient of emasculating themselves, that all inclination to illicit pleasures might be effectually subdued. This practice was esteemed highly meritorious. It was an axiom that what is most valuable to man should be offered in sacrifice to the gods; and, hence, castration was invested with a high degree of supererogatory merit. Hence we are told by Lucian (de Dea Syria.), that in Syria, during the celebration of their most solemn rites, the priests would suffer themselves to be attired in female habiliments, and submit to the castigating knife, in the presence of the assembled crowd! Such is the power of enthusiasm!

superior officers were the torch-bearer, (Daduchus,) the herald, (Ceryx,) and the attendant on the altar, (O Epiboma.)[42]   Three other officers represented the Sun, the Moon, and the planet Mercury; besides whom there were four inferior attendants to whose care the less important departments of these mysterious celebrations were committed.   They were denominated Epimelitæ.[43] The aspirant was required to possess a character of irreproachable morality;[44] for as the system was reputed to be without stain of impurity, so a dissolute candidate was uniformly rejected with contempt, as calculated to bring disgrace on the Institution, and involve it in all the opprobrium of public scorn.   The probationary tests were strict and solemn.   The most minute colloquial examination of the aspirant was instituted to corroborate the testimony of others; so that it would require all the arts of successful imposture to elude the mystagogue's investigations into his former life, character, and conduct.[45]

The initiations were preceded by a public festival; and the candidates, whether male or female,[46] were carefully purified in the pellucid waters of a running stream, and endured the rigours of a nine days preparation; after which the ceremonies commenced with prayer and sacrifice.   During the continuance of these preliminary rites, the aspirants were exhorted to abstract their attention from every light and worldly subject, and to fix their minds intensely on the high and supernal celebrations which were performed under the actual inspection of the immortal gods,[47] to an intimate union and communion with whom. they were now about to be admitted.[48] The priests then proceeded to invoke a blessing by prayer; for the petitionary sacrifices (Αιτητίκά) of heathen nations were used at the commencement of every important undertaking; and success was anticipated in proportion with the degree of sincerity that was used in supplicating the favour of the gods, and the sterling value of

---

[42] Signs and Symbols, Lect. 11.   [43] Meurs. Eleusin., c. 15.
[44] Hence they were habited in *white*, because white was an emblem of innocence.   (Cic. de Leg. et Vid. Pers., Sat. ii., v. 40.)
[45] Plut. in Apopth. et Lacon.
[46] Apul. Metam., l. 11.
[47] Arrian. Dissert., l. iii., c. 20.   Cic. de Leg., l. ii., c. 14.
[48] Procl. in Ramp. Plat., l. i,

the accompanying offerings.[49]   The ceremonies were opened by the officiating priest, who asked publicly, "Who is fit to be present at this ceremony?" To which it was answered, "Honest, good, and harmless men." He then rejoined, "Holy things are for holy people;"[50] crying with a loud voice, "Let us pray;"[51] and proceeded in due form to make the requests of the attendant aspirants known to the benevolent deities.   Then the sacrifice was offered with the customary formalities, seasoned with salt, because salt was an emblem of hospitality and friendship: and the priest augured[52] from the entrails of the victim, whether the gods were propitious to their prayers. If the response were favourable, the rites of initiation were forthwith celebrated.

[49] Plat. Timæo.   [50] Kellet. Tricæn. Christ., p 548.

[51] At the commencement of these services amongst the Romans, proclamation was made, *ut faverent linguis,* that the people should govern their tongues: and, at the conclusion, before they were suffered to depart, they were enjoined *litibus et jurgiis abstinere,* to abstain from brawls and quarrels.   During the whole continuance of the festival, the strictest equality was observed, and a heavy fine was imposed on any opulent person who endeavoured to distinguish himself by an equipage.   But, when the celebration was ended, and every person resumed his ordinary station in life, the gradations of rank were defined and observed with their accustomed regularity. (Plin. Nat. Hist., l. xxviii., c. 2.   Hor., l. iii., Od. 1.   Juvenal., Sat. 12.)

[52] "The most ancient oracles in the heathen world were unquestionably dictated by the spirit of truth; for God never left himself unwitnessed by his extraordinary interpositions, as well as by the ordinary dispensations of his providence.   But, in process of time, the oracle degenerated and basely sanctioned the introduction of Egyptian Polytheism, with the rites of the Lingam or Priapus &c., celebrated at Samothrace likewise; as we learn from the candid and honest report of Herodotus, who was ashamed of their impurities." (Male's Anal., vol. 4, p. 465.)

LECTURE VI.

CEREMONIES OF INITIATION INTO THE MYSTERIES OF BACCHUS.

THE place of initiation was a gloomy cave,[1] or rather a connected range of caverns,[2] fitted up with machinery that might display, with full effect, all the terrors of the process. Streams of water ran through various parts of its dismal area; which served equally for the purpose of lustration, and to shadow out the diluvian waters pervading the material world. The cavern was ritually consecrated[3] and secreted from vulgar observation by being

---

[1] The Nympheum, or place of initiation in Greece, is thus briefly described by Homer·

> " High at the head a branching olive grows,
> And crowns the pointed cliffs with shady boughs,
> Beneath a gloomy grotto's cool recess,
> Delights the Nereids of the neighbouring seas;
> Where bowls and urns were form'd of living stone,
> And massy beams in native marble shone:
> On which the labours of the Nymphs were roll'd,
> Their webs divine of purple mix'd with gold.
> Within the cave *the clust' ring bees* attend
> Their waxen works, or from the roof depend.
> *Perpetual waters o'er the pavement glide;*
> Two marble doors unfold on either side;
> Sacred the south, by which the gods descend;
> But mortals enter at the northern end."
>
> Pope, Od., l. xiii., v. 122.

The gate of entrance for the aspirant was from the north; but when purged from his corruptions, he was termed indifferently, new-born, or immortal, and the sacred south door was from thence accessible to his steps.

[2] Vid. ut supra, p. 16. Plut. de Isid. et Osir., p. 639. The most celebrated of these Greek caverns were the caves of Eleusis, Athens, the grotto of Trophonius at Lebadea in Beotia, and the horrid subterraneous dens of Samothrace.

[3] In Egypt and other nations, the place of initiation was a pyramid erected over a subterraneous cavern. It appears to have been dedicated to that purpose with an intensity of labour that produced the solidity which bids defiance to the ravages of time. The Arabians have a tradition, says Greaves, in his Pyramidographia, that the Egyptian pyramids were built by Saurid Ibn Salhouk, king of Egypt·

the reputed residence of the vindictive deities, whose vengeance, it was believed, would undoubtedly descend on the unfortunate intruder, who, by accident or design, should penetrate unbidden within the sacred precincts.[4]

who lived three hundred years before the Flood ! The pyramidal form of building was adopted alike for its firmness and durability ; and its symbolical reference to the Sun from an imitation of the spiral flame. And what are the spires of our present churches but an imitation of this primitive system of pyramidal architecture ?

[4] Maundrell has accurately described one of these places of initiation near Tortosa, which, however, he erroneously conceives to be a double sepulchral monument. "The first antiquity that we observed," says he, " was a large dyke, thirty yards over at top, cut into the firm rock Its sides went sloping down with stairs formed out of the natural rock, descending gradually from the top to the bottom. The dyke stretched in a direct line from east to west, more than a furlong, bearing still the same figure of stairs running in right lines all along its sides. This dyke was on the north side of the *Serpent Fountain*." (Pinkert. Collect. of Travels, vol. x., p. 315.) Mr. Maundrell then describes a spacious court cut in the rock containing an altar or cromlech, and two pyramidal towers at the distance of about half a mile from it. "Each of these towers," says he, "has under it several sepulchres, the entrances into which are on the south side. It cost us some time and pains to get into them, the avenues being obstructed first with briars and weeds, and then with dirt, but we removed both these obstacles. Going down seven or eight steps, you come to the mouth of the sepulchre, when, crawling in, you arrive in a chamber which is nine feet two inches broad, and eleven feet long. Turning to the right hand, *and going through a narrow passage*, you come to a second room, which is eight feet broad and ten long. *In this chamber are* SEVEN *cells* for corpses, two over against the entrance, four on the left hand, and one *unfinished* on the right. These cells were hewn directly into the firm rock. We measured several of them, and found them eight feet and a half in length, and three feet three inches square. I would not infer from hence that the corpses deposited there were of such a gigantic size as to fill up such large coffins ; though, at the same time, why should any men be so prodigal of their labour as to cut these caverns into so hard a rock as this was, much farther than necessity required ?" (The fact is, they were never intended for corpses, but as conveniences for the terrific machinery of initiation.) "On the south side of the first chamber was a narrow passage of seven feet long, leading into a third room, whose dimensions were nine feet in breadth, and twelve in length. *It had eleven cells*, of somewhat a less size than the former, lying at equal distance all round about it. Passing out of the first room foreright, you have *two narrow entrances*, each seven feet long, into a fourth room. This apartment was nine feet square ; it had no cells in it like the others, nor anything remarkable but only a bench cut all along its side on the left hand." This was the sacellum. (Maundrell, ut supra, p. 316.) Several other similar ranges of subterraneous caverns are found in the same neighbourhood, which might be, and probably were, connected together.

Here the priests, crowned with serpents—the symbols
of initiation—performed their dreadful and unhallowed
rites. Their incantations commenced with the consecration of an egg,[5] to commemorate equally the creation of
all things, which were traditionally believed to have
sprung from an egg[6] formed by the deity; and the renovation of mankind by the great father.

The first actual ceremony among the Greeks was to
purify the aspirant with water, and to crown him with
myrtle,[7] because the myrtle tree was sacred to Proserpine;[8] after which he was free from arrest during the
celebrations.[9] He was then introduced into a small cave
or vestibule to be invested with the sacred habiliments;[10]

[5] Plat. Sympos., l. ii., q. 3.   "Hyginus has preserved a curious
tradition respecting the Assyrian Venus, in which the arkite dove, and
the mundane *egg*, make a very conspicuous appearance.   An egg of
wonderful magnitude was reported to have fallen from heaven into the
river Euphrates, and to have been rolled by fishes to the bank.   Upon
it sat doves; and out of it was at length produced that Venus, who
was afterwards styled the Syrian goddess."   (Fab. Mys. Cab., vol. i.,
p. 81, with authorities.)   Nigidius and other authors have recorded
the same thing.

[6] Vid. Grot. De Verit., i., s. 16, in nota *k*.

[7] Schol. Aristoph. Ranis.

[8] The machinery of these mysteries is thus described by Psellus in
a Greek MS. quoted by Taylor in his dissertation on the Eleusinian
and Bacchic mysteries. (Pamphleteer, vol. viii.)   "The Eleusinian
mysteries consisted in representing the fabulous narration of Jupiter
mingling with Ceres and her daughter Proserpine.   But as venereal
connections take place along with the initiations, a marine Venus is
represented as arising from certain fictitious genital parts; afterwards
the celebrated marriage of Proserpine with Pluto takes place, and
those who are initiated sing, 'I have eat out of the drum, I have drank
out of the cymbal, I have borne the mystic cup, *I have entered into the
bed.*'"   (This is evidently the Pastos of the mysteries, in which the
aspirant for the higher degrees was immured during the period of his
probation.)   "But the pregnant throes likewise of Ceres are represented."   (Here Ceres is the ark; and her pregnant throes refer to
the dismemberment of that sacred vessel, and the egress of the hero
gods.)   "Hence the supplications of Ceres are exhibited; her drinking
of bile, and the pains of the heart. . . . . . After all this, the honours of
Bacchus succeed; the cista, and the cakes with many bosses like those
of a shield; likewise the mysteries of Sabazius, divinations of the
priestesses of Bacchus; a certain sound of the Thesprotian kettle, the
Dodonœan brass; another Corybas, and another Prosperine, who are
resemblances of Demons," &c., &c.

[9] "No one shall be arrested or apprehended during the celebration
of the mysteries."   (Demosth. in Mediam.)

[10] Chrys., Orat. 12.

after which his conductor delivered him over to the mystagogue, who then commenced the initiation with the prescribed formula, Εκας, Εκας, εστε βεβηλοι, Depart hence, all ye profane; and the guide addressed the aspirant by exhorting him to call forth all his courage and fortitude, as the process on which he was now about to enter was of the most appalling nature. And being led forward through a series of dark passages and dismal caverns, to represent the erratic state of the Ark while floating on the troubled surface of the diluvian waters,[11] the machinery opens upon him. He first hears the distant thunder pealing through the vault of heaven,[12] accompanied by the howling of dogs[13] and wild beasts—an apt representation of the confusion which prevailed amongst the multiplicity of domestic and ferocious animals during the period of Noah's confinement in the Ark. These terrific noises rapidly approach, and the din becomes tremendous, reverberated, as it doubtless was, in endless repetitions, from the echoing vaults and lofty caverns within whose inextricable mazes he was now immured. Flashes of vivid light now broke in upon him, and rendered the prevailing darkness more visible; and by the momentary illumination he beheld the appearances by which he was surrounded. Monstrous shapes and apparitions,[14] demoniacal figures, grinning defiance at the intruder; mystical visions and flitting shadows, unreal phantoms of a dog-like form,[15] overwhelm him with

[11] It was a rude and fearful march through night and darkness. (Stobæus. apud Warb. Div. Leg., vol. i., p. 235.)

[12] It has been asserted that the Egyptians, and hence probably the Greeks, were acquainted with some chemical process to produce an explosion like gunpowder. (Maur. Ind. Ant., vol. vii., p. 671.) If this be correct, the imitative thunder is easily accounted for.

[13] St. Paul admonishes the heathen converts to *beware of dogs* (Phil. iii., 2.) They were symbols of the κακοδαιμων, or evil genius and were used and worshipped in the way of propitiation.

[14] Monstrum, horrendum, informe, ingens cui lumen ademptum (Æn., l. vi.)

[15] Pletho. Schol. in Orac. Zoroast., p. 131. The celebrated *Barker* Anubis (latratorem, semicanem deum. Æn., l. viii.) was exhibited. Cerberus, the infernal monster, was here represented in mimic show with his three heads, which are said by Porphyry to have referred to the rising, southing, and setting of the Sun (Apud Euseb. præp. Evan., l. iii.); and hence it is a reasonable conjecture that this noisy latratory porter of hell was nothing more than an emblem of the solar orb.

terror.[16]   In this state of horrible apprehension and
darkness, he was kept *three days and nights.*[17]

With passions thus excited, the aspirant was now made
to perform the *aphanism*, or ceremonies commemorative of
the mystical death of Bacchus.[18] He was covered with
the pastos or bed; or in other words he was subjected to
confinement in a close cell, that he might reflect seriously,
in solitude and darkness, on the business he was engaged
in; and be reduced to a proper state of mind for the
reception of sublime and mysterious truths.[19] This was
the symbolical death of the mysteries;[20] and the deliverance from confinement was the act of regeneration or
new-birth; and hence the renovated aspirant was termed
διφνης or twice born; once from the womb of his natural
mother and again from the pastos of initiation. During
the period of his imprisonment in the cell, he was

[16] Proclus. in Plat. Theol., l. iii., c. 18.   Dion. Chrys., Orat. 12.
Orig. cont. Cels., l. iv.

[17] Fab. Pag. Idol., vol. iii., p. 156.   This ceremony had a particular
and intimate connection with the Egyptian plague of *darkness*, says
Faber. "The scriptural account of it is very brief, yet it sets forth
one circumstance of high importance. There was a thick darkness in
all the land of Egypt *three days;* they saw not one another, neither
rose any from his place for *three days.* It appears, then, that the duration of the preternatural darkness was precisely equal to that of the
darkness of the Mysteries." (Fab. ut supra.)

[18] Or Osiris; for Bacchus and Osiris were one and the same mythological personage, (Auson, Epig. 30,) as were also Ceres and Isis;
(Diod. Sic., l. i.,) and as such they will be considered throughout this
description of the mysteries of Greece. (See on this point, Fab.
Mys. Cab., vol. i., p. 155.)   The same rites were also celebrated by
the Phrygians and Byblians in honour of Attis and Adonis or Thammuz. (Lucian de deâ Syriâ., s. 6, 7. Vid. Ant. of Masonry, p. 104.)
The death and resurrection of Osiris or Adonis has been made an emblem of the sowing and sprouting of corn; (Vid. Voss. de Idol.,) but
I think this idea is of modern date, and was borrowed from St. Paul.
(1 Cor. xv., 36, et seq.)

[19] In some of the mysteries a statue resembling a dead body, (Jul.
Firm. de error Prof. Rel., p. 45,) was enclosed within an ark, (Plut. de
Isid. et Osir., p 378,) shaped like a cresent; to represent the mystical
death of Noah when enclosed in that sacred vessel. (Apuleius, l. ii.)
In Egypt the symbol in which Osiris was feigned to be incarcerated
was sometimes *a wooden cow*, because that animal was emblematical of
the ark. (Fab. Pag. Idol., vol. i., p. 34, and refer to plate 42 of
Pococke's Description of the East, vol. i., p. 108.)   An oration was
pronounced *over the body* by the hierophant, relating most probably
to the Deluge. (Diod. Sic., l. i.)

[20] Orph. Argon., v. 28.

alarmed by a crash resembling the rush of waters bursting with sudden impetuosity from a deep abyss or the
deafening fall of a tremendous cataract; for now was the
representation displayed of the waters of the Deluge
breaking forth from Hades to inundate the globe. The
monstrous Typhon,[21] raging in quest of Osiris,[22] discovered the ark in which he had been secreted, and violently
rending it asunder,[23] scattered the limbs of his victim
over the face of the earth amidst the din of dissolving
nature.[24] The aspirant heard the lamentations which
were instituted for the death of their god, whose representative he was, accompanied with doleful cries and
howlings of men, women, and animals, to symbolise the
death-shrieks and exclamations of terror, consternation,
and despair, which prevailed throughout the world at the
universal destruction of animated nature, and which would
unquestionably salute the ears of Noah while enclosed
within the vessel of safety. Then commenced the wanderings of Rhea in search of the remains of Bacchus,
her body begirt with a serpent, and a flaming torch in
her hand,[25] with lamentations[26] for the loss; accompanied
with frantic shrieks and furious gesticulations; which
continued, accompanied by many minute ceremonies,[27]

[21] Typhon was a personification of the sea, (Plut. de Isid. and Osir.,
p. 363,) or the Deluge, as Osiris was of the patriarch Noah (Fab. Mys.
Cab., vol. i., p. 151,) and hence the propriety of the fable, however enveloped in mystery by the ritual of initiation.

[22] Jambl. de Myst., s. vi., c. 5.   [23] Plut. ut supra, p. 354.

[24] In this allegory we must view Osiris as the ark itself rather than
the diluvian patriarch, and his scattered limbs, its contents, which
supplied the whole earth with men and animals after the waters had
subsided. The ceremonies, however, were, in many respects, so con-
tradictory to each other, that there exists much difficulty in reducing
them to order.

[25] Minuc. Fel., p. 158. A torch was a symbol of Diana. *Upright*,
of the Sun in the east;—*reversed*, of the same luminary in the west.

[26] These lamentations were figuratively said to continue forty days,
in commemoration, probably, of the period in which the waters of the
Deluge actually increased upon the earth. (Gen. vii., 12.)

[27] The following account of a disgusting ceremony, quoted by Mr.
Taylor from Arnobius, will show one of the practices used both in
Egypt and Greece, at the period of initiation. "The goddess Ceres,
when searching through the earth for her daughter, in the course of
her wanderings arrived at the boundaries of Eleusis, in the Attic
region, a place which was then inhabited by a race of people called
autochthenes, or descended from the earth, whose names were as follows; Baubo and Triptolemus; Dysaules, a goatherd; Eubulus, a

for a considerable period.   The initiated, whether males
or females, some habited in splendid attire, with crowns
or mitres on their heads ; some bearing the thyrsis ;[28]
some the sacred vessels,[29] while others, covered with very
little clothing,[30] mixed promiscuously, and danced to the
sound of musical instruments played by the Corybantes ;[31]

keeper of swine ; and Eumolpus, a shepherd, from whom the race of
the Eumolpidæ descended, and the illustrious name of Cecropidæ was
derived, and who afterwards flourished as bearers of the Caduceus,
Hierophants, and Cryers belonging to the sacred rites.   Baubo,
therefore, who was of the female sex, received Ceres, wearied with
complicated evils. as her guest, and endeavoured to soothe her sorrows by obsequious and flattering attendance.   For this purpose she
entreated her to pay attention to the refreshment of her body, and
placed before her a miscellaneous potion to assuage the vehemence
of her thirst.   But the sorrowful goddess was averse to her
solicitations, and rejected the friendly officiousness of the hospitable
dame.   The matron, however, who was not easily repulsed, still continued her entreaties, which were as obstinately resisted by Ceres,
who persevered in her refusal with unshaken constancy and invincible
rigour.   But when Baubo had thus often exerted her endeavours to
appease the sorrows of Ceres, but without any effect, she at length
changed her arts, and determined to try if she could not exhilarate
by prodigies a mind which she was not able to allure by serious at-
tempts."   And in this she succeeded by an expedient too obscene to
be detailed here, which was imitated in the initiations, (Pamphleteer,
vol. viii.)

[28] The Thyrsis was a long pole adorned with garlands and ribbons,
intermixed with sprigs of the vine and leaves of ivy (Eurip. Bacch.,
v. 176, et passim,) and having at the end a conical fruit like a pomegranate or pine.   It represented the phallus.   Vid. Bishop Cumberland's Treatise on Sanchoniatho's Phenician History, p. 68.   The
phallus amongst the Egyptians was the symbol of fertility.   (Savary's
Letters on Egypt, vol. ii., p. 40.)   Athenæus (l., i.,) states distinctly
that Priapus and Dionysus were one and same person ; which accounts
for the gross obscenity of these rites.

[29] Plut. de. Isid. et Osir., p. 336.

[30] Ovid (Metam., l. iv., v. 6,) says that they had the skins of beasts
thrown over their naked bodies.   The bacchantes are generally depicted on gems, either naked, or merely covered with a thin transparent
garment.   Sometimes the sexes exchanged clothes, an abomination
expressly forbidden to the Israelites in the law of Moses, which points
out the very early date of a custom which was the source of many
licentious pollutions.   (Deut. xxii., 5.)   "The woman shall not wear
that which pertaineth unto a man, neither shall a man put on a
woman's garment, for all that do so are abomination unto the Lord
thy God."

[31] Wait. Orient. Ant., p. 218.   Sophocles addresses Bacchus as
the

" Immortal leader of the maddening choir,
    Whose torches blaze with unextinguish'd fire ;

blended with the howlings of despair for the dismemberment of their god. The dance progressively increasing in rapidity and wildness, soon degenerated into a scene of confusion. The whole party, as if under the influence of some supernatural fervour, incontinently threw off the remaining articles of their apparel, rushed amongst each other as if they were distracted; and vociferating[32] that their god had been murdered by the Titans,[33] threw themselves into lascivious postures,[34] and practised the most abominable filthiness.[35]

In the midst of all this confusion, a signal from the hierophant gave a sudden turn to the feelings and expressions of the mystæ; their mourning was changed into joy, and the aspirant was emancipated from his confinement amidst peals of laughter and deafening shouts of *Ευρηκαμεν, Ευγχαιρομεν,* we have found it! let us rejoice together![36] for now the Euresis, or discovery, was celebrated, and it was announced that the mangled corpse was found, and restored from the darkness of death to life and hope. A living serpent was inserted into the bosom of the affrighted candidate,[37] which passing through his garments

> Great son of Jove, who guid'st the tuneful throng,
> Thou who presidest o'er the nightly song;
> Come with thy Naxian maids, a festive train,
> Who, *wild with joy and raging o'er the plain,*
> For thee the dance prepare, to thee devote the strain."
>
> FRANCKLIN.

[32] The cry was Evoe! Sabai! Bacchi! Hues! Attes! Hues! all of which were names of Bacchus. (Clem. Alex. Protrept. Diod. Sic., l. iv., c. 3.) These exclamations are said by Strabo to have originated in the east; and hence Dr. Wait, (Orient. Ant., p. 214,) thus writes the passage in the Sanscrit;

Åhō! Sīvǡ! Īsǡ; Åd'hīsǡ! Ādyē sēvǡ!

which is thus translated; "Hail! O Siva! Lord! Supreme Lord! Salutation to the first existent!"—It is more probable, however, that this species of invocation was borrowed from the patriarchal worship. See Exodus, (xxxiv., 6, 7,) where God himself announces his divinity by eleven appellations.

[33] It was of this period of initiation that David speaks, when lamenting that the Israelites ate the offerings of the dead, during the disgraceful worship of Baal Peor. (Psalm cvi., 28. Signs and Symbols. p. 178.) [34] August. de Civ. Dei, l. vi., c. 9.

[35] Clem. Alex. Cohort. ad Gent., p. 17.

[36] Athen. Legat., p. 88; et vide etiam Plut. de Isid. et Osir., p. 366.

[37] Clem Alex. Cohort. ad Gentes. p. 11. Some say that a serpent of ductile gold was used. (Fab. Pag. Idol., vol. iii., p. 116.)

was taken out at the skirts of his robe;[38] and being conducted onwards, without time to reflect, the descent into
the infernal regions[39] was the next adventure he was to
accomplish.   On the banks of a sluggish stream he was
shewn a multitude of disembodied spirits, thronging to
procure a passage over the river, and clamorous at being
refused; which represented the turbulent race of antediluvians who perished in the Flood.[40]   Then the aspirant,
having crossed the river in a boat, was shewn the torments of those miserable wretches, who, for their vices,
had been condemned to everlasting punishment.[41]   Here,
during the intervals of howling and lamentation, and the
shrieks of woe by which those lost creatures vented the
unavailing sorrows of repentance, his attendant explained
the nature of the crimes which led to this dreadful termination; amongst which, the highest degree of punishment was assigned to the impious race who either refused
initiation, or betrayed the mysteries.[42]   But he was not
allowed to ask any questions, or even to speak during
the ceremonies.[43]   Leaving this place of horror and despair, the aspirant was conducted forward to the sound of
heavenly music, and soon entered on the plains of ravish-
ing delight, which are the reward of the virtuous initiated.[44]   The perturbation of his spirits was here allayed

---

[38] This ceremony was said to be commemorative of the ravishment
of Proserpine by Jupiter in the form of a serpent; (Euseb. præp.
evan.) or more properly to signify that as the parent of the present
race of men was regenerated by his confinement in the ark, symbolized by a serpent, which possesses the power of self-regeneration by
emerging periodically from its old skin and coming forth in all the
beauty and vigour of youth; so the aspirant was purified and born
anew by the sympathetic efficacy of the same animal brought into
close contact with his naked body, when delivered from the Pastos.
[39] Thus Hercules, before his descent into hell, was initiated into
the mysteries of Ceres.   (Apollod. Bibl., l. ii., c. 5.)
[40] Fab. Mys. Cab., vol. i., p. 278.   [41] Æn., l. vi., v. 752, 838.
[42] Warb. Div. Leg., vol. i., p. 225.
[43] "Let no petitionary address be made at the mysteries." (Andoc.
de Myst.)
[44] "The first stage of initiation," says an ancient writer, preserved
by Stobæus, "is nothing but errors and uncertainties; laborious
wanderings; a rude and fearful march through night and darkness.
And now arrived on the verge of death and initiation, everything wears
a dreadful aspect.   It is all horror, trembling, sweating, and affright-
ment.   But this scene once past, a miraculous and divine light dis-
closes itself; and shining plains and flowery meads open on all hands

by scenes in which were depicted the ever-verdant plains of Elysium ; and the souls of the just were exhibited in the enjoyment of those pure delights which constitute the reward of piety and virtue. The hero-gods passed in review before him, and he enjoyed the exhilarating vision, animated further by a hymn which was chanted on the subject of the prevailing mythology.

At this stage of the initiation the hierophant delivered a lecture on the nature and design of the mysteries ; accompanied by certain significant tests, the insignia of the Order, which served to distinguish the initiated from the rest of the world. The aspirant then underwent a lustration,[45] and having been purified, he was introduced into the sacellum, brilliantly illuminated and shining with a divine splendour,[46] as a striking symbol of the mind of the initiated, now emerged from pristine darkness into a full scientific and moral illumination ;[47] for he was greeted by the envied appellation of Epopt, being fully instructed in the nature and attributes of the divinity[48] and the doctrine

before them. Here they are entertained with hymns and dances, with the sublime doctrines of sacred knowledge, and with reverend and holy visions. And now become perfect and initiated, they are FREE, and no longer under restraints : but crowned and triumphant, they walk up and down the regions of the blessed, converse with pure and holy men, and celebrate the sacred mysteries at pleasure." (Warb. Div. Leg., vol. i., p. 235.)

[45] Sopat. in divis. Quæst.

[46] Apuleius, (Metam., p. 273,) says that at the close of his initiation *he saw the sun at midnight shining with a glorious brightness*, (nocte medio vidi Solem candido coruscantem lumine). Even Plato denominates the illuminated sacellum, μακαριαν οψιν, a beatific vision. (Phæd., p. 1224.)

[47] Themist. Orat. in Patrem. apud Warb. Div. Leg., vol. i., p. 231.

[48] "Augustine in the eighth book, de Civitate Dei, (c. 5,) tells us that Alexander wrote to his mother, *that even the gods of the higher rank, Jupiter, Juno, Saturn, &c., were men ;* and that this secret was laid open to him by Leo the great priest of Egyptian sacred things ; requiring the letter to be burnt after it had revealed this to her. The like Cyprian affirms, only he saith it was written to his mother *insigni volumine,* in a famous volume, that the memory of their greater kings was preserved, and hence arose the custom of sacrificing ; the priest confessing to him this secret. And, that we may not suspect these Christian writers, Tully, in his Tusculan Questions, not far from the beginning, owns that those who are initiated must know that they worshipped men's souls departed from their bodies into heaven ; and that *majorum gentium dii* were such ; and that almost all heaven was filled with men. I doubt not but Alexander, Cicero, and Atticus, and

of a future state. The unity of the godhead was inculcated ;[49] and during the process of celebration the following truth was repeatedly proclaimed: "Jupiter is King;
he is the primitive source of all things; there is ONE God;
ONE power, and ONE Ruler over all !"[50] These disquisitions were mixed up with the rhapsodies of Homer,[51] the
doctrines of purgatory, transmigration, and a series of
mythological allegories that darkly shadowed out the
events of the Deluge,[52] accompanied with diffuse and mys-

Sanchoniatho also, were admitted to be acquainted with the Greatest
Mysteries, in the religious initiations of the heathens; and that they
have truly told us that this worship of such great men as were the
founders of arts and civil government, was the grand secret of it; which
was not communicated even to those that were initiated into the
Lesser Mysteries." (Cumb. Sanch., p. 348.)

[49] Euseb. præp. evan., l. xiii.   Cudw. Intell. Syst., c. iv., s. 18.

[50] Proclus (in Tim., p. 95.) mentions a gem of Serapis, which bears
an inscription to the same purport, $E\iota\varsigma$ $Z\varepsilon\upsilon\varsigma$ $\Sigma\alpha\rho\alpha\pi\iota\varsigma$, ONE Jupiter
Serapis.   Many testimonies to this effect may be seen in Grotius. de
Veritate, l. i., s. 10.

[51] " It is enacted that at the celebration of the Panathenæa majora,
Homer's rhapsodies be repeated." (Lycurg. in Leocr. Elian.)

[52] To enumerate these legends would require a volume.   The fable
of the Titans making war on Jupiter was an instance of the allegoriz-
ing spirit of idolatry, for the rebellious Titans were no other than the
whole antediluvian race of mankind, except eight persons, who were
hence sometimes distinguished by the appellation of the *just* Titans;
Hesiod terms them gods. (Theog., v. 838.)   The former by their impiety set at defiance the divine power and justice, and were lost in
the Flood.   To the same effect was the tradition of the contest between
Jupiter and the giants, in which the latter were destroyed. (Apollod.
Bibl., l. i., c. 6.)   The overthrow of Typhon was but a representation
of the return of the diluvian waters into their subterranean recesses.
(Ovid. Metam., l. v.)   The wanderings of Io, Isis, Rhea, Ceres, &c., as
we have already seen, were but figurative allegories of the erratic
and desultory voyage of the ark; and the same event is referred to in
the fable of the wanderings of Lysippa, Iphinoe, and Iphianassa, the
three daughters of Pretus or Minyas, who were struck with madness
for having despised the Bacchic mysteries.   The murder of one of the
Cabiri by one of his brothers, like the death of Osiris and Bacchus,
related to the symbolical death of Noah.   The expedition of the
Argonauts might have a reference to the Deluge, as Mr. Bryant and
Mr. Faber are decidedly of opinion; the story of the birth of Bacchus
amidst the thunder and lightning which destroyed his mother Semele;
(Ovid. Metam., l. iii.) and his being enclosed in the thigh of Jupiter,
was only the fable of the Deluge, and the preservation of Noah in the
ark, for *Arech*, an ark, and *Yarech*, a thigh, might easily, by the fanciful genius of polytheism, be substituted the one for the other. (Vid.
Diod. Bibl., p. 123.)   The descent of Hercules to hell, and the restoration of Hyppolitus to life, were derived from the regeneration of

terious strictures on the abstruse points of human generation, of which the visible symbols were Phalli, described as emblems of the mystical regeneration and new birth attained by the aspirant from the divine qualities of the process of initiation.[53] He was then crowned and enthroned; clad in a purple vest with golden zones; and pronounced in a state of pure and ineffable light, and safe from henceforth under the protection of the celestial deities. Amulets were then delivered to him as preservatives against personal danger,[54] and he was instructed

Noah in the ark, as was also the descent of Orpheus in search of his wife; and in like manner, as the animals spontaneously followed Noah into the ark, so Orpheus is said to have drawn after him the brute creation by the force of Harmony. (Apol. Argon., l. i.) The fable of the rape of Europa affords another view of the same transaction; for a bull was the symbol of Noah, or the god of the ark, (Fab. Mys. Cab., vol. i., p. 177,) as a cow was an emblem of the ark itself; the legend of Hercules sailing over the world in a golden cup bears a decided reference to the Deluge, for Hercules was the arkite god, and the cup was the ark; and the submersion of the island of Atlantis is a plain description of the same event. The account of the deluge of Deucalion, however, is less impregnated with mystery than any of the preceding. During the reign of this prince over the kingdom of Thessaly, a general deluge inundated the earth, and destroyed the whole race of men except himself and Pyrrha his wife, who were preserved in a ship which finally rested on the summit of Parnassus. When the waters had subsided, this insulated pair were commanded by an oracle to restore the human race by casting behind them the bones of their mother, which referred to the loose stones which lay scattered on the surface of the earth. Losing no time to provide the renovated globe with inhabitants, they cast behind them a multitude of stones, and were astonished to behold the crowds of men and women by whom they were speedily surrounded. (Ovid, Metam., l. i.) It requires little ingenuity to interpret this fable; and accordingly it was delivered without disguise to the Epopt, or perfectly initiated candidate.

[53] This emblem was one of the abominations which defiled the mysteries, and, as we have already seen, (ut supra, p. 100,) was exhibited, with shameless impudence, even in public processions. Its origin has been variously explained; but it certainly sprang, either from the sin of Ham, or the mysterious doctrine that the ark was the common mother of the human race; and Noah, by what name soever he might be distinguished, the father.

[54] With this superstitious people, a relic, ritually consecrated, was believed to insure the special favour and protection of the deity, with whom the priests were reputed to hold an intercourse. Thus if sickness were inflicted by a hostile god, an amulet consecrated to a superior deity, and suspended from the afflicted person's neck, would speedily remove the disease. Young persons wore enchanted girdles to excite love towards them in the other sex. The garments which

6

in emblematical knowledge; for the morality of the
mysteries was involved in a series of visible symbols, for
the purpose of directing the enquiries of the uninitiated
into a mistaken channel, and leading them to conclusions
widely distant from the truth. Thus the figure of a hawk
was used to represent the Sun ; a crescent typified the
Moon; the omniscience of the deity was symbolized by
an eye placed in the centre of an endless serpent; an
obligated aspirant by a grasshopper ; knowledge by an
ant ; impossibility by two naked feet walking on the sea.[55]
The dove was a conspicuous symbol, and had been introduced with great propriety, for this bird was the diluvian
messenger of peace, and hovered over the retreating
waters like a celestial harbinger of safety.   Hence a
lunette floating on the surface of the ocean, attended by
a dove,[56] with an olive branch in its mouth, and encircled
by a rainbow, formed a striking and expressive symbol,
which needs no explanation.[57] After these and other

had been worn during initiation were accounted sacred, and able to
protect the wearer in every emergency.   It was even commanded that
" the initiated should dedicate the garments in which they were initiated at the temple of Ceres." (Aristoph. Schol. in Plut.)   These invaluable relics were therefore used by the fortunate possessor until
they were resolved to rags; and afterwards children were invested
with the tattered remnants, as undoubted preservatives from the
malign effect of all diseases to which their tender age is by nature
exposed.   It was also accounted lucky to collect remnants of the
sacrifices, which were denominated ὑγείαί, because they were thought
conducive to health.   The emblem of ὑγείαί Health, amongst the
Pythagoreans was a triple triangle, because being alternately conjoined
within itself, it constitutes a figure of five lines, ⛤ (Lucian pro. laps.

in sal. admiss. apud Stanley, Lives, vol. iii., p. 62.)   In India, the
Saivas use this figure to signify emblematically, Savi uniting in himself
the three great attributes. (Asiat. Res., vol. viii., p. 77.)
    [55] Hence the incident of Christ walking on the sea is a striking proof
of his divinity ; (Matt. xiv., 25,) for what is impossible with man, is
possible with God ; (Mark x, 27,) and Job says that God alone treadeth
on the waves of the sea. (Job ix., 8.)
    [56] The white dove was much esteemed by the Jews, and held in
sacred reverence, because they believed that Noah's dove was of that
colour.
    [57] From the circumstance of the patriarch reaching out his hand to
seize the dove, and bring it into the ark before the waters had subsided,
(Gen. viii., 9,) the Greeks invented many fictions, which subsequently
became established principles in their system of mythology.   The
fable of Ixion bore this reference.   He is said to have attempted to
deflower Juno, but embraced in her stead, a cloud, for which offence

illustrations of the like tendency,[58] the aspirant was dismissed through *the beautiful gate* of the Temple[59] with the two barbarous words Κογξ and Ομπαξ, which are said to mean, WATCH and ABSTAIN FROM EVIL,[60] as a person mysteriously regenerated, and placed in future under the protection of the celestial gods.

It is admitted by many learned writers that the Grecian mysteries contained many facts in the life of the Jewish lawgiver. Thus Bacchus is described as having been taken from a chest or ark; and as being the son of two mothers; because Pharaoh's daughter was like a second mother to Moses. The deliverance of the Israelites from their bondage in Egypt is another remarkable coincidence. In the Dionysiaca, the thyrsis or Rod of Bacchus was elevated, to perpetuate the remembrance of two remarkable miracles which were reputed to have been performed with this all-powerful instrument. On one occasion[61] he cast his rod upon the ground and it became a serpent;[62] and afterwards he struck the two rivers Orontes and Hydaspes[63] with it, and the waters immediately re-

he was cast into hell. Now Juno is *Juneh*, the dove, (Fab. Mys. Cab., vol. i., p. 83,) which was seized by Noah; and his punishment on *a revolving wheel* in hell, merely referred to his descent into the Hades of the mysteries, and his circumambulating progress through the caverns of initiation.

[58] A profusion of symbols which adorned these mysteries may be found in the "Signs and Symbols," and "Theocr. Phil. of Freemasonry."

[59] The caverns of initiation had two gates; one called the *descent* to hell, the other the *ascent* of the just; which, in the passage already cited from Homer, are inaccurately described. Mr. Pope has inverted the sense of the original, where he makes the gods, or in other words the Epoptæ, *descend* instead of *ascend*, and mortals *enter* instead of *descend*. Thus, corrected, the reference is perfectly easy to the destruction of the antediluvians and the safety of the eight just persons, who hence have been dignified with the name of immortals. (Vid. ut supra, p. 72.)

[60] Vid. Bibl. Univ., tom. vi., p. 86. Warb. Div. Leg., vol. i., p. 156. "When the rites of the east were imported into Greece," says Mr. Faber, "a strong charge was given that barbaric names should never be changed; concerning which injunction it is observed by Psellus, that there are sacred names of ineffable import, preserved in the mysteries of every nation, and delivered to them immediately by the gods; a circumstance which makes it unlawful to translate them into the Greek language." (Mys. Cab., vol. i., p. 116.)

[61] Non. in Dionys., l. 25.   [62] Vid. Exod. iv. 3.

[63] Non. in Dionys., l. 23.

ceded,[64] and he passed over dry-shod.[65]   The assembly
which celebrated these orgies was composed of men,
women, and children of all ranks, amongst whom, during
the continuance of the festival, distinction was unknown.[66]
This was intended to commemorate the manner of Israel's
departing out of Egypt, accompanied by a mixed multitude from all the neighbouring nations.[67]   During the
initiations, the purifying element was sometimes obtained
by striking a rock with the magical rod.[68]   The Bacchæ
crowned their heads with serpents, and carried serpents
in vases[69] and baskets, in allusion, it is said, to the plague
of fiery serpents[70] inflicted on the Israelites in the wilderness.[71]   And it was asserted by the hierophant that all
mankind were in *darkness*[72] except the initiated, who
alone were irradiated with the beams of true and scientific
light; referring, as some say, to the cloudy pillar which
enlightened and directed the Israelites, while it involved
the Egyptian army in the shades of impenetrable darkness ;[73] and, according to others, the doctrine was symbolical of the superior privileges enjoyed by the Israelites
in the immediate presence, and under the protection of
the divine Shekinah, while the nations around them were
involved in the hideous darkness of idolatry.   Nothing,
therefore, can be more clear than that a series of original
traditions of the fundamental truths of religion, were
scattered abroad at the dispersion of mankind; and adapted by each people to the peculiar character of their own
superstitions.

Such was the splendid importance attached to these

[64] Vid. Exod. xiv., 16.

[65] Speaking of the miraculous passage over the Red Sea, Diodorus
Siculus has this remarkable observation. "The Troglodytes, the in-
digenous inhabitants of this very spot, had a tradition from father to
son, from the very earliest times, that this division of the Red Sea did
once happen there ; and that after leaving its bottom some time dry,
the sea again came back with great fury, and covered the land."

[66] Diod. Bibl., l. 4.   [67] Exod. xii., 38.

[68] Eurip. et. vid. Numb. xx., 11.

[69] Atheneus, apud Fab. Pag. Idol., vol. iii., p. 171.   Mr. Faber conceives that the vases alluded to the ark, and the libation to the Deluge ,
and hence the emptying of them properly concludes the mystic festival, and represents the retiring of the diluvian waters.

[70] Vid. Signs and Symbols, Lect. iii.   [71] Numb. xxi., 6.

[72] Non. apud Boch. Can.

[73] Exod. xiv. 20.

deteriorated mysteries, which were under the protection of the civil magistrate.[74] They were places of assignation to the lustful,[75] and consequently fatal to the cause of virtue and morality.[76] And yet, strange to tell, no woman was qualified for the honour of officiating at the celebration of this miserable apology for religion, except she were able to testify on oath that she was free from all manner of pollution.[77] Several eminent men in different ages endeavoured to purge these orgies of their indecency, but without success. Orpheus and Pentheus[78] are mythologically[79] said to have been torn in pieces by the Bacchantes, for their exertions to stem the torrent of depravity and licentiousness which pervaded every rank and description of people who were engaged in these celebra-

[74] "An assembly of the senate shall convene in the Eleusinian temple on the day after the festival," say the laws of Solon, "to inquire whether every thing has been done decently and according to order."

[75] Vid. Eph. iv., 19.   [76] Clem. Alex. Cohort. ad Gentes, p. 19.

[77] The idea which these worthies entertained of personal purity may be correctly deduced from the following custom, preserved by Herodotus. This writer tells us, (l. i.,) that all the female votaries of Mylitta, who was the same with Ceres and Isis, without excepting the most dignified virgins, were obliged to prostitute themselves, at least once in their lives, in the porch of the temple, as an indispensable act of devotion! without which they were accounted polluted or unclean. "Amongst the Egyptians it is honourable for women to prostitute themselves; and those who have lain with many men used to wear a bracelet about their ankles as a badge of honour! Moreover, amongst them virgins before marriage used to gain a dower by prostituting themselves." (Stanley's Lives, vol. iii., p. 94.) It was in allusion to these and still more unnatural practices that induced St. Paul to exclaim with indignation: "It is a shame even to speak of those things which are done of them in secret!" (Eph. v., 12.) And the same intrepid Apostle enumerates these abominable sins in his Epistle to the Romans, (i., 26 to end).

[78] Virg. Æn., l. iv. Ov. Metam., l. xi. The most outrageous excesses were frequently committed by the female Bacchantes when inflamed with wine, lust, and enthusiastic fury, (Eurip. in Bacch.,) which they mistook for the inspiration of the jolly god. It is recorded that the daughters of Minya, under the furious impetus of this diabolical fervour, slew a young man named Hippasus, and served up his body as a banquet to the company. (Anton. Metam., l. x.)

[79] I say *mythologically*, for the fact appears doubtful respecting the violent death of Orpheus, notwithstanding the above authorities. It rather appears that he was killed by lightning; a death, esteemed by the ancients, as being fraught with a peculiar felicity. (Diog. Laert. Prooem.)

tions.[80] The rites passed, however, with all their con
taminations, from Greece to Rome, and remained a
lasting stain to the empire, long after the establishment of
Christianity.   At length the bold and frequent censures
of the Christian fathers roused the people to a sense of
shame;—by a public edict the excesses sanctioned by
the mysteries were restrained within more decent bounds;
and soon afterwards they were altogether suppressed
under heavy penalties.

[80] Plato, speaking of the abomination of the Dionysiaca, says that
he was present at one of these celebrations, and *saw the whole city
of Athens in a state of beastly drunkenness.* (De Leg., l. i.)   Hence
the prophetical figure used in the threatened destruction of Babylon.
"In their heat I will make their feasts, and *I will make them drunken,*
that they may rejoice, and sleep a perpetual sleep, and not awake,
saith the Lord. (Jerem. li., 39.)

LECTURE VII.

IN attempting to reduce the Celtic Mysteries to orde. and regularity, the inquiry will be confined almost exclusively to Druidism as practised in Britain, which contains the essence and perfection of the system; for Cesar informs us that the principles of Druidism were better understood in Britain than in Gaul; and that it was customary for the inhabitants of the latter country, who wished for more perfect information on the intricate subject of their mysterious doctrines and practies, to pass over into Britain, where accurate instruction was alone to be obtained.[1]

The name of these extraordinary priests[2] has been variously derived. The most commonly received opinion is, that its origin must be ascribed to the Greek *Δρῦς*, an oak, because this tree was esteemed peculiarly sacred by the Druids;[3] and from its spontaneous production of the sacred misletoe,[4] they believed that the deity had selected

---

[1] Ces. de bel. Gal., l. vi., c. 12.

[2] Mr. Reuben Barrow, in the second volume of the Asiatic Researches, (p. 489,) says, "That the Druids of Britain were Brahmins is beyond the least shadow of a doubt; but that they were all murdered and their sciences lost, is out of all bounds of probability; it is much more likely that they turned schoolmasters, *Freemasons*, and fortunetellers, and, in this way, part of their sciences might easily descend to posterity, as we find they have done." With what feeling towards Masonry Mr. Barrow said this, I have not the means of determining, nor does it in the least alter the character of his assertion. I shall consider the opinion as tending to illustrate the antiquity of the science. The Druids were schoolmasters, fortunetellers, and Freemasons also, though the name was not known in the ages when they flourished. They certainly did practise a science derived from Freemasonry, and applied to the same object, the worship of the deity; but deteriorated, as all institutions must necessarily be, when the vital principle is wholly discarded.

[3] Plin. Nat. Hist., l. xvi., c. 4.

[4] The misletoe was invested with a character so holy, that it was accounted a profanation to touch it with the finger. The ceremonies

it from all the trees of the grove as his own peculiar residence.   In the ancient British dialect, an oak was termed
Derw;[5] in the Armorican, *Deru* ; and hence the priests of
the oak are said to have been denominated *Derwydden*.
Some authors have, however, referred to other tongues
for the etymology of this title.   One says it was derived
from the German *Trowis*, which signified a revealer of
truth ;[6] another thinks it sprang from *Trutis*, an old
British name for the deity, and that his first priests were
hence called *Truti*.[7]   Mr. Smith, in his Gaelic antiquities,
concurs with Major Vallancey in deriving Druid from
Druidh, which in their own language signifies wise men,
and is still the Gaelic term for philosophers or magicians.
It seems, he says, to have the same import with the
name of the eastern magi, who, like the Druids and
many other religious sects, united the characters of the
philosopher, the magistrate, and the divine, making each
of these services one and the same profession.[8]

The system of Druidism embraced every religious and
philosophical pursuit which was then known in the
island ; and had a further tendency to spread liberty,
peace, and happiness amongst mankind.[9]   The rites bore
an undoubted reference to the salvation of Noah and his
seven companions in the Ark ;[10] and were celebrated first

---

used in gathering this mysterious plant were of a nature calculated to
infuse a sacred reverence deeply into the mind; and when plucked
and ritually consecrated, it was reputed to possess every sanative
virtue ; and was hence dignified with the appellation of All Heal.

[5] Owen's Dict. v. Derw.   [6] Gerop. Becan.

[7] Sammes. Brit., vol. i., p. 104.

[8] Hutchinson, Cumb., vol. i., p. 248.

[9] Meyrick, Hist. Cardigan, Introduction.

[10] It is a most remarkable fact, that we find in every system of antiquity a frequent reference to the number *seven*, which, from its
nature, can scarcely be ascribed to any event save that named in the
text, except it be to the institution of the Sabbath.   Thus the *seven*
score Ogyrvens, or mystical personages, which, according to Taliesin,
pertain to the British muse ; the *seven* score knobs in the collar of the
ox, (Dav. Dru., p. 523, 524,) the *seven* persons who returned from
Caer Sidi, in the spoils of the deep; (Ibid., p. 515.) the *seven* Pleiades ; (Ovid. Fast. 5,) the *seven* Hyades; (Aratus. Astron.) the *seven*
Titans and Titanides ; the *seven* Heliades of the Greeks ; (Diod. Bibl.,
l. v.) the *seven* Cabiri of the Phenicians ; the *seven* Amschaspands of
the Parsees ; and the *seven* pieces into which the body of Bacchus
was torn by the Titans, (Plut. de Isid. and Osir., p. 368,) were equally
the *seven* hero-gods who accompanied Noah in the Ark ; and these

by the Pheryllt, who correspond with the Telchines, the Curetes, or the Idei Dactyli of other nations. The ceremonies of initiation and worship also bore a character similar to those of the people whence they were derived, accommodated to the peculiar genius of the people, and amditting of various minute modifications, arising from the accidental circumstances of local situation, and the temporary revolutions of manners and government.

corresponded with the *seven* Menus, the *seven* Pitris or Rishis, and the *seven* Brahmadicas of Hindoo mythology; and for the same reason, perhaps, as these persons were *the whole* of mankind then living in the world, the septenary number, amongst the Cabalists, denoted *universality,* and was termed by the Pythagoreans *ϑλομελεια.* To one of the above causes may be ascribed the origin of the *seven* vases in the temple of the sun near the ruins of Babian, in Upper Egypt. (Savary, Letters on Egypt,) the *seven* altars which burned continually before the god Mithras in many of his temples: (Montf. Ant., tom. ʳii., l. 7.) the *seven* holy temples of the ancient Arabians; (Sale, Koran, Prelim. Disc., p. 22,) the *seven* bobuns of perfection exhibited in the Hindoo code; (Holwell, in Maur. Ind. Ant., vol. ii., p. 331,) with the defective knowledge of the same people which circumscribed the whole earth within the compass of *seven* peninsulas, or dwipas; (Sacontala. Sir W. Jones. Works, vol. vi.) the *seven* planets of antiquity; the Jewish Sephiroth consisting of seven splendours; the *seven* Gothic deities; commensurate with the hebdomadal division of time; the *seven* worlds of the Indians and Chaldeans; and the *seven* virtues cardinal and theological. (Vid. Signs and Symbols, p. 159.) In a word, *seven* was always considered as a number possessed of many mysterious properties; and divine sacrifices were considered most efficacious when composed of this number.

> *Seven* bullocks yet unyoked for Phœbus chuse,
> And for Diana, *seven* unspotted ewes.
> DRYDEN.

And even our own Scriptures abound with innumerable instances of the authorized use of this number. At the Deluge, Noah received *seven* days notice of its commencement, (Gen. vii., 4,) and was commanded to select *clean* beasts and fowls by *sevens,* while the unclean were only admitted by pairs, (Gen. vii., 2.) On the *seventh* month the Ark rested on Ararat, (Gen. viii., 4,) and Noah despatched his dove at the distance of *seven* days each time. (Gen. viii., 10, 12.) Job and Balaam each offered sacrifices by the express command of God, consisting of *seven* bullocks and *seven* rams; (Job xlii., 8. Numb. xxiii., 1,) and this was undoubtedly conformable with the usual practice of Jewish antiquity. The destruction of Jericho was miraculously effected by the use of this number; for *seven* priests bearing *seven* rams' horns for trumpets, were directed by the Almighty to compass the city *seven* days, and on the *seventh* to proceed round it *seven* times, when the walls should fall into ruin. (Josh. vi., 4, 5.) Solomon was *seven* years building the Temple; (1 Kings vi., 38,) which was dedicated in the *seventh* month, (1 Kings

6*

Respecting these ceremonies, the ancient historians are
not wholly silent; although we shall gather more information from the bardic than the classical writings on this
abstruse subject. Strabo informs us that the Druids
practised the rites of Samothrace.[11] Mr. Faber adduces
other authorities in support of the same hypothesis
" With regard to the devotion of the Hyperboreans,'
says this author, "to the arkite mysteries, we ar

viii., 2,) and the public festival lasted *seven* days. The whole machinery of the Apocalypse is conducted on precisely the same principle
The Iconisms are almost all *septenary.* Here the FIRST PERSON in
the sacred Trinity is represented under the figure of a glorious being
clothed with surpassing brilliancy, seated on a throne encircled by a
rainbow, (Rev. iv., 3, 4,) and receiving from the assembly of saints a
most profound adoration, in which they ascribe to Him *seven* degrees
of beatitude. (Ib. vii., 12.) He is attended by FOUR beasts full of
eyes, emblematical of their perfect knowledge of ALL things, past,
present, and to come. Now the number *four* was esteemed to possess similar properties with the number *seven.* It signified *universality* amongst the Cabalists and Pythagoreans, probably because the
whole of the *male* kind in the Ark consisted of *four* persons, and it
formed the holy Tetragrammaton of the Jews. (Vid. More's Apocalypsis Apocalypsios, p. 92, 148.) The SECOND PERSON is described
as a majestic and venerable personage standing in the midst of *seven*
golden candlesticks, and holding in his hand *seven* stars, the emblems
of Light and Revelation; (Rev. ii., 1,) and in another place as a
Lamb that had been slain having *seven* horns and *seven* eyes, symbols
of universal power and knowledge; and receiving from the heavenly
host a loud acknowledgment of *seven* potencies. (Ib. v., 6, 12.) And
the THIRD PERSON is described as *seven* lamps of fire, which are the
seven Spirits of God. (Ib. iv., 5.) Again, the Apocalypse contains *seven* Synchronisms, which were preceded by a succession
of woes addressed to *seven* churches, (Ib. i., 4,) recorded in a book
with *seven* seals, (Ib. v., 1,) denounced by *seven* angels to the sound
of *seven* trumpets, (Ib. viii., 2,) and revealed by *seven* thunders or oracular voices. (Ib. x., 3.) The wrath of God against the idolatrous
world, is let loose by *seven* angels having *seven* plagues inclosed in
seven golden vials. (Ib. xv., 1, 7.) Idolatry is represented under the
figure of a scarlet-coloured beast having *seven* heads, to represent
probably the *seven* mountains on which Rome and Constantinople, the
two capital cities of " the mistress of the world" were respectively
founded; (Ib. xvii., 9,) and *seven* idolatrous kings, or *seven* forms of
polytheism are pointed out for destruction. (Ib. xvii., 10.) This
very extraordinary and universal application of the number *seven,* as
I have already observed, must have originated either in a tradition
borne away from Shinar by every tribe who wandered in search of a
new settlement, respecting the institution of the Sabbath; and it
must be observed that almost all idolatrous nations kept holy the
seventh day; (Vid. Usher on the Sabbath, p. 73,) or the *seven* hero-
gods who were saved with Noah in the Ark.
    [11] Strabo. Geogr., l. iv.

plainly informed by Dionysius, that the rites of Bacchus and Noah were duly celebrated in Britain. Hence arose their veneration for the bull, the constant symbol of the deity of the Ark. . . . . . To the testimony of Dionysius, I shall add the authority of Artemidorus concerning those (mysteries) of two other Cabiric deities. In an island, says he, close to Britain, (by which, in all probability, he meant Anglesey, the chosen seat of superstition,) Ceres and Proserpine are venerated with rites similar to the Orgies of Samothrace. This island was dedicated, as we learn from Mnaseas, to the Cabiri; and he further informs us that Ceres, Proserpine, and Bacchus were reckoned in the number of these deities. Hence it evidently appears, that the gods of Britain were the same as the Cabiri of Samothrace; and, consequently, whatever observations are applicable to the latter are no less applicable to the former."[12]

" Dr. Borlase has traced a surprising uniformity in the temples, priests, doctrines, and worship of the Persian magi and the British Druids. This conformity, indeed, is so striking and extraordinary, that Pelloutier, in his history of the Celts, will have it that the Persians and the Celts were originally one and the same people.[13] Major Vallancey is of the same opinion; adding that the Druids first flourished in the east; in Hindoostan as Brahmins; in Babylon and Syria as Chaldeans; and in Persia as Magi;[14] and from thence came hither with that

[12] Fab. Mys. Cab., vol. i., p. 210, 214, with authorities.
[13] And both were derived from the same common source. "A celebrated grammarian has remarked, Nec modo Indicam, Persicam Syram, Arabicam, Hebræ junctissimas linguas; sed et Gothicam, seu Celticam, linguam; and Roland, in his Mona, asserts, that no less than three hundred Hebrew *radices* are to be found in the British tongue alone. From this list I shall select a few only which must carry conviction of their primæval derivation. For instance, who can doubt of the British word *Booth*, a cottage, being derived from the Hebrew *Beth*, a house; the earth from *Eretz;* to babble, from *Babel*, alluding to the confusion of tongues; *Cist*, from Cis, a chest; *Dagger*, from *Dakar*, a short sword; the British *Kern*, or Corn, a horn, from *Keren ;* Cromlech, a sacrificial stone of the Druids, from *Ceremluach* a burying-stone; and *Sarph*, an old British word for serpent, from the Hebrew *Saraph*." (Maur. Ind. Ant., vol. vi., p. 37.)
[14] The Druid and the Dervise possessed many qualities in common "Sacerdotum," says Keysler, "genus apud Turcas ab antiquissimus, temporibus conservatum Dervis, et nomine et re Druidis." (Antiq Septentr., p. 36.)

great body of Persian Scythians, whom the Greeks call Phenicians." These opinions, collected by Mr. Hutchinson,[15] can only prove that the nations agreed as to the practice of similar rites and ceremonies in the administration of religious worship; for the Druids flourished in Gaul and Britain, at least coeval with the planting of many other nations, from which theorists have conjectured they might derive their original.[16] Besides, these several people paid their devotions to different objects of worship; some were Sabians, and worshipped the host of heaven; others were magians, and confined their adoration to the solar fire; two sects which always entertained the utmost contempt and hatred for each other's principles.[17] The testimonies, however, are amply sufficient to point out the analogy which subsisted in early times between the mysterious institutions of those

[15] Hist. Cumb., vol. i., 247.

[16] The first people who settled in Britain are said to have been led hither by Gomer, or some of his immediate descendants. (Turn. Angl. Sax., vol. i., p. 14.) If this be true, Britain received its population very soon after the Dispersion. The continent of Europe was peopled by the children of Dodanim, the grandson of Japheth; and by the operation of some or all of the causes resulting from a redundant population, the surplus being pressed to the sea coast of Gaul, our island was discovered in the distance, and a wandering tribe called the Hord Gaeli, who, on a casual visit, named it the Watergirt Green Plot, according to the testimony of the Welsh Bards—having been tempted to take possession of it, found it so rich and beautiful that they changed the name to the Honey Island. I have the authority of Sammes for saying that this took place about A. M. 1910, the exact period when Ninus founded the kingdom of Assyria, or a little before Abraham first went into the land of Canaan. This tribe was subsequently dispossessed by a stronger party, under the command of Prydain, the son of Aedd the Great, who, collecting together some scattered tribes of the Cymri who were friendly to his interests, made an inroad upon the island, and took an undisputed possession. Its name was once more changed to Prydain or Britain; and he subdivided it into three parts, and placed in them as viceroys three of his most distinguished followers, at the head of their respective tribes. First the Cymri, who came with Hu the mighty. These introduced arts and civilization, and inhabited Wales. The second tribe who settled in the island were the Lloegrians. They came from Gwasgwyn, and were descended from the primitive nation of the Cymri, and took possession of England. The Brython, descended from the same stock, came from the land of Llydaw, and peopled Scotland. Hence the Britons adopted the ternary division of the island which it has ever since retained; and called the several portions Lloeger, Cymru, and Alban, corresponding with England, Wales, and Scotland.

[17] Vid. Prid. Connect., vol. i., p. 226.

countries, which were formed by the migration of the first descendants of Noah and his family.[18]

The Druids did not worship idols in the human shape, because they held that the divinity, being invisible, ought to be adored without being seen. But we are told that they did occasionally erect, like the primitive Buddhists of the east,[19] in retired places, statues of Isis[20] or Ceridwen; which must have been gigantic stones,[21] rough as when taken from the quarry,[22] the *Betulia* of the eastern nations,[23] which are ritually consecrated, and invested with peculiar and distinctive properties. These stones, so highly venerated,[24] so enthusiastically adored, were the representations of the great British deities, whose abundant merits have been so extravagantly eulogized by the bards. These deities, by what variety of names soever they may have been designated, all melt into two, a male and a female, the great father and mother,[25] who were worshipped under the appellation of Hu and Ceridwen, and bore the same conspicuous character with the Egyptian Osiris and Isis; the Grecian Bacchus and Rhea, or any other supreme god and goddess who represented the great father and mother of mankind in the mysteries of idolatrous antiquity.

---

[18] Vid. ut supra, l. i.   [19] Fab. Pag. Idol., vol. ii., p. 340.

[20] The Scandinavians had a goddess of this name. (Ol. Rudbeck. Atlant., vol. ii., p. 212.)

[21] "Several of the idols of the old Arabs," says Sale, in his Preliminary Discourse to the Koran, "were no more than large, rude stones, the worship of which the posterity of Ishmael first introduced. . . . . These stones they at first only compassed out of devotion; but at last it ended in rank idolatry; the Ishmaelites forgetting the religion left them by their father so far as to pay divine worship to any stone they met with." Captain Hamilton describes one of the idols in the Indian Temple of Jagan-nath, as being "a huge black stone of a pyramidal form;" or, in other words, a stone pillar.   [22] Bryant. Anal., vol. i., p. 13.

[23]   "The mighty pile of magic planted *rock*
        Thus rang'd in mystic order, marks the place
        Where, but at times of holiest festival
        The Druid leads his train."   MASON.

[24] Dr. Gordon informs us that the Irish peasants still pay these stones an awful respect. (Hutch. Cumb., vol. i., p. 243.)

[25] We find Pindar (Nem. Od. 6,) asserting the dignity of the great mother, where he says that all the gods as well as men sprang from her fruitful womb.

All rocks containing an aperture, whether natural or artificial,[26] were thought to convey purification, because they equally shadowed out the door of the Ark through which the favoured few issued into a renovated world; and it is worthy of remark, that the same belief distinguished every ancient nation; for all practised the helio-arkite superstition, and all alike admitted the regenerating properties of the consecrated orifice.[27] They varied, however, in proportion with the supposed sanctity of the petræ, arising from the solemnity of the rites of consecration. Thus a natural cavity in a rock unhallowed by the sacred ceremonial, was of inferior virtue to an artificial pastos, erected ritually, consecrated with holy oil, and dedicated to a religious use; and as soon as a pastos was thus anointed, it acquired the distinguishing name of *lapis ambrosius*.[28]

A considerable degree of sanctity was attached to small islands in the centre of a consecrated lake. Floating islands, considered as the residence of a happy and

[26] On the estate of the Right Hon. C. T. D'Eyncourt, M. P., at Bayon's Manor, near Market Rasen, in Lincolnshire, is a *petra ambrosiæ* consisting of a gigantic upright stone, resting on a slender basis, at the foot of which another stone has been placed, hollowed out so as to form an aperture of sufficient dimensions for a man to creep through. It stands in a commanding situation, on the bold brow of a hill, and has, doubtless, been used by the Druids in the performance of their sacred rites.

[27] This was the abomination referred to by the prophet Isaiah, where he denounces *the holes of the rocks*, and the caves of the earth, as insufficient to avert the indignation of the Almighty. (Isai. ii 19.) Borlase (Ant. Cornw., p. 167) thus explains the probable use of these Tolmen: he says, "It is not improbable but the holed stone served for libations; to initiate and dedicate children to the offices of rock-worship by drawing them through this hole, and also to purify the victim before it was sacrificed; and, considering the many lucrative juggles of the Druids. it is not wholly improbable that some miraculous restoration to health might be promised to the people for themselves and children, upon proper pecuniary gratifications, provided that at a certain season of the moon, and whilst a priest officiated at one of the stones adjoining, with prayers adapted to the occasion, they would draw their children through the hole."

[28] The city of Tyre, according to Stukeley, was built by Hercules on a spot where a petra ambrosiæ stood, which were two hollow rocks, shaded by an olive tree; and, accordingly, on the ancient Tyrian coins we find these ambrosial petræ represented overshadowed by an olive tree; and on the reverse, Hercules offering a sacrifice of dedication.

perfect people, bore an allusion to the garden of Eden, where Adam dwelt in a state of absolute felicity; and, perhaps, also to the then known world, which was in reality an immense island; and, therefore, the places of mysterious celebration were frequently constructed in such situations.[29] They bore a reference also to the Ark,

[29] The interior recesses of the insular sanctuary were considered as the seat of every supernal delight. Here the heavens had exhausted their stores to confer gifts on their favoured and chosen residence. Mr. Davies has given a description of these distinguished privileges in the translation of a Mabinogion, which I shall transcribe, after remarking that its contents are corroborated by a testimony from a quarter the least expected. The Hindoos have a tradition current amongst them, that the gardens of the Hesperides are situated in the British Isles; and the beauties of this imaginary paradise, as we are told by Mr. Wilford, are described in strains of the most exaggerated panegyric; greatly exceeding even the legend here subjoined.—" In ancient times, it is said, a door in a rock near this lake, was found open upon a certain day every year. I think it was May day. Those who had the curiosity and resolution to enter, were conducted by a secret passage, which terminated in a small island, in the centre of the lake. Here the visitors were surprised with the prospect of a most enchanting garden, stored with the choicest fruits and flowers, and inhabited by the Tylwyth Teg, or fair family, a kind of fairies, whose beauty could be equalled only by the courtesy and affability which they exhibited to those who pleased them. They gathered fruit and flowers for each of their guests, entertained them with the most exquisite music, disclosed to them many events of futurity, and invited them to stay as long as they should find their situation agreeable. But the island was sacred, and nothing of its produce must be carried away. The whole of this scene was invisible to those who stood without the margin of the lake. Only an indistinct mass was seen in the middle; and it was observed that no bird would fly over the water, and that a soft strain of music, at times, breathed with rapturous sweetness in the breeze of the mountain.—It happened upon one of these annual visits, that a sacrilegious wretch, when he was about to leave the garden, put a flower, with which he had been presented, into his pocket; but the theft boded him no good. As soon as he had touched unhallowed ground, the flower vanished, and he lost his senses.—Of this injury the fair family took no notice at the time. They dismissed their guests with their accustomed courtesy, and the door was closed as usual. But their resentment ran high. For though, as the tale goes, the Tylwyth Teg and their garden undoubtedly occupy the spot to this day—though the birds still keep at a respectful distance from the lake, and some broken strains of music are still heard at times, yet the door which led to the island has never re-appeared; and, from the date of this sacrilegious act, the Cymri have been unfortunate." It is added, that "Some time after this, an adventurous person attempted to draw off the water, in order to discover its contents, when a terrific form arose from the midst of the lake, commanding him to desist, or otherwise he would drown the country." (Dav. Dru., p. 155.)

which, at the time of the Deluge, was the sole existing
place of habitation, and contained the whole human
race. Each of these islands bore the mysterious name of
Avanc, and drawing it out of the lake with a yoke of
oxen, attended by many mystical ceremonies, formed one
of the principal rites of the Druidical religion.[30] In every
nation of the world, water was profusely used during the
initiations; and hence the propriety of the British custom
of performing their celebrations in the centre of a lake.
It had a twofold reference; first, to the diluvian waters
which cleansed the earth from its impurities by a general
lustration;[31] and secondly, as the external medium of
purification by which the Mystæ were ritually regenerated.[32] It was a maxim with the Druids, that water
was the first principle of all things, and existed before
the Creation in unsullied purity; but that its perfect
qualities were diminished when it became blended with
the earth at its original formation out of chaos; and
hence it was believed that water lost some portions of
its purifying qualities by contact with the earth, which
was considered the very principle of contamination; and,

---

[30] Vid. Signs and Symbols, Lect. 5. Hist. of Beverley, pp. 14, 41.
[31] 1 Pet. iii., 20, 21. Grot. in Matt. iii., 6.
[32] Nothing could be more universal than this practice. The Jewish
religion and all the systems of Paganism, however diversified in other
respects, held equally the necessity of repeated ablutions to cleanse
the soul from moral defilement. From the plains of India to the
utmost regions of the West, this doctrine was implicitly received;
originating, most probably, from some uniform practice which accompanied the patriarchal performance of religious rites anterior to the
general dispersion from Babel. It was believed by the Druids that
the earth was the great principle of contamination, and that every
thing was polluted, in a greater or less degree, which had communication with it. Even the stone deities were superincumbent on other
stones, lest they should be subject to defilement; but when the
Mediator of the Christian covenant came into the world to restore the
true religion, and to show that ritual pollutions and purifications were
at an end, he clothed his divinity with earthly flesh, by being born of
a woman, and yet received no contamination. for he was free from
every imputation of sin; and in his doctrine strongly and constantly
inculcated that man's defilement was not derived from anything
external, but that it proceeded from the heart. The Pharisees used
many ablutions to cleanse ceremonial impurity. They taught that
to perform even the common offices of life without washing, was
sinful. This doctrine was condemned by Him who knoweth the most
secret thoughts of every heart; and he openly proclaimed that their
frequent washings could never atone for sin.

therefore, to secure to themselves a certain supply of this element unpolluted with any impure alloy, they used to scoop hollows or cavities on the upper surface of certain elevated stones to catch the waters of heaven before they reached the ground.[33] Rain was preferred to river water, snow to rain, and ice to snow. These rock basons were hence invested with a peculiar degree of sanctity, and were always attached to their temples, or places of initiation, when not situated on a lake[34] or river of water.

The Britons had the utmost veneration for a grove of oaks,[35] and here the most sacred places of religious celebration were constructed;[36] particularly if hills or moun-

---

[33] Borl. Ant. Corn., b. iii., c. 11, p. 225.

[34] Sir Walter Scott has woven this superstition into a most beautiful Poem (Lady of the Lake), attended with all the machinery of initiation. The island in the lake called Loch Katrine (Ketturin), which signifies the *Gate of Hell*, and in India and some other countries was but another name for the Pastos; and Brownie's cavern (Coir Uriskin), for the whole superstition of the brownies was but a remnant o the stories of initiation; the Lady in the boat, and the range of caverns which the island contained, are all indications of this fact. Mr. Stuart, the guide to this lake island, and scenery, says, "In the bosom of a rock south of the Pass, there was a cave where an outlaw named Fletcher resided many years; but, though tradition is so particular with regard to its situation, as to describe minutely the different views which it commanded, he said he had entirely lost the entrance of it, though he had searched for it with the utmost care." (Hogg's Tales, vol. i., p. 150.) The island is called Rough Island, and the attendant spirit is like a satyr or goat. (Lady of the Lake, Notes p. 355.) [35] Lucan. Pharsal., l. iii.

[36] The sacred grove was a primitive place of devotional celebration. Abraham planted a grove of trees as a retreat of silence, solitude, and prayer; but the same practice having been subsequently used by idolaters, and their groves converted to the most horrible and revolting purposes, the denunciations of heaven were launched against consecrated groves in general. The Israelites were not only forbidden to plant them, but their destruction was enjoined in every country which they conquered. It was accounted sin in the Hebrew monarchs if they presumed to sacrifice in groves; and it is said of Ahab, that he did more to provoke the Lord to anger than any of his predecessors because, amongst other acts of iniquity, he made a consecrated grove. The first patriarchs also worshipped in groves of oak (Gen. xviii., 1, 4, 8. xxi., 33. Josh. xxiv., 26); but the custom was subsequently condemned, because it led to disorder and prostitution. (Deut. xvi. 21. Isai. i. 29. Hosea iv., 12, 13, 14.) In the idolatrous nations a grove was essential to divine worship. (Diod. Sic., l. xvii. Quint. Curt., l. iv., c. 7. Strabo. Geogr., l. viii.) Pindar (Olymp. x., 52,) introduces Hercules as planting a sacred grove; and in India, groves of olive were planted in the most venerated situations. (Asiat. Res., vol. vi., p. 524.) In a word, as I have many times observed, idolatry was nothing but a perversion of the patriarchal rites.

tains were found within the compass of the inclosure;
for it is well known that these eminences were highly
venerated by the Druids in common with the rest of
mankind; partly from an idea that the tops of hills made
a nearer approach to the heavens, from whence the deity
could more perfectly hear their prayers; and partly from
a faint remembrance of an old tradition of the Deluge,
and probably of the burning bush, which induced a belief
that mountains were the consecrated residence of the
deity;[37] but principally because the conical mountain,
variously diversified, was considered an apt representation of the union of the two great generative principles
personified at the Deluge.[38]   The mountain with one

[37] It may be here remarked, that mountain-worship was common
with the antediluvian patriarchs, and was followed by Noah (Gen.
viii., 20) on the mount where the Ark rested, and where the parents
of mankind resided after their deliverance from danger; by Abraham
(Gen. xii., 8), who performed an act of worship on Mount Moriah, at
the express command of God (Gen. xxii., 2); and again by Moses on
Mounts Horeb (Ex. iii., 1) and Sinai (ib. xix.)   This custom was
soon imitated by those nations which had renounced the true God.
(Numb. xxii., 41. xxiii., 14, 27, 28.)   When Philip II. made war
against the Spartans, he sacrificed on the two mountains of Olympus
and Eva. (Polyb., l. v.) Cyrus sacrificed to the gods on a mountain
just before his death. (Cyrop., l. viii.) So in the Iliad Hector does
the same. (Il. xxii., 171.)   The Persians worshipped on mountains
(Strabo., l. xv.); and 2300 years before our era, sacrifices were offered
in China to the supreme god Chan-Ti, on four great mountains, called
the four Yo. The sovereigns, finding it inconvenient to go thither in
person, caused eminences representing these mountains to be erected
by the hands of men, near their habitations. (Voyage of Macartney,
vol. i., p. 58.)   The American savages used the same custom. (Humboldt's Research. in Amer., vol. ii., p. 244.) "In short, every towering
hill was reckoned holy; and we are assured by Melanthes, that it was
the universal practice of the ancients to offer sacrifice on the highest
mountains, to him who was accounted the highest god." (Nat. Corn.,
l. i., c. 10, apud Fab Pag. Idol., vol. iii., p. 200.)   The Israelites,
too, when they fell into idolatry, adopted the same custom, and worshipped the host of heaven on mountains (2 Kings xiv., 4. Jerem. ii.,
20. Ezek. vi., 2, 3), though it was absolutely forbidden in the law of
Moses (Deut. xii., 2).

[38] This system of veneration was not peculiar to Britain, but was
common to all the idolatrous nations of the earth. When the Ark, or
female principle, with the whole human race in her womb, floated on
the surface of the diluvian waters; the male principle, or the great
father, was placed in the centre of the lunette as a mast; and thus
the two principles united floated in safety over the earth (Wilf. on M
Cauc. in Asiat. Res., vol. vi., p. 521); and when the waters had sub
sided, they remained firmly fixed on a rock, which the superstition o

peak only, represented the male principle; with two peaks, the figurative lunette or Ark, symbolized the female principle; and with three, the two principles united.[39]

each nation feigned to be within its own boundaries. When a mountain was adorned with three peaks, therefore, it was accounted perfect, and worthy of superior veneration, from its apt representation of this union of the sexes, which furnished the natural means by which the world was repeopled. (Vid. Signs and Symbols, Lect. 9.) Perfect specimens of all these varieties of mountains are frequent in the counties of Lancaster, Cumberland, and Westmoreland; and I cannot but think that this part of the island was a favourite resort of the druids; for they contained every requisite in vast abundance for the practice of their religious rites. The rivers and lakes; the many natural caverns and excavations; the numerous specimens of the holy mountain in every possible variety; afforded such a combination of natural facilities for the exercise of their mysterious celebrations, that they could not be overlooked by that acute and politic order of men. Accordingly, we find, in the stupendous monuments with which these counties still abound, the most positive traces of Druidical ingenuity in all its several forms; whether consisting of stone or earthen temples, the cromlech or the kistvaen, the logan or the tumulus, the seat of justice or the sacred grove: all being unquestionable evidences of Druidical habitation. A learned and indefatigable writer, whose opinions claim every attention and respect, says the same thing of some of the southern counties. "Numerous remains of stone circles, cromlechs, rocking stones and tumuli still exist in the Scilly islands, and are continued along the coast of Cornwall and Dorset, to the widely-extended plains of Wiltshire; all, from their rudeness, bespeaking a very ancient, and, I may pronounce, a Celtic origin; and corresponding in a very striking degree with those on the opposite shores of our mother country Gaul." (Hoare's Ancient Wilts., vol. i., p. 12.)

[39] We are indebted to Capt. Wilford for bringing to light a recorded tradition of the Hindoos, that the British Druids held mountains and lakes in superior veneration from the causes just enumerated. "Britain," says this author, "was termed by the Indians, Tricatachel, or the mountain with three peaks; and was hence considered as a place of peculiar sanctity. England was denominated, Rajata-Dweep; Scotland, Scuteya-Dweep; and Ireland, Suvarna-Dweep. The pitris, or primitive fathers, were said to reside in Suvarna; and their place of abode was either on the summit of a mountain, or in a cave called Maha Dewa, in an island situate in the midst of a lake, whose waters were reputed bitter. From this cave issued a long passage into the infernal regions. Here the souls of their deceased ancestors were invoked." This is a correct account of a place of initiation, and is thought to have a reference to the celebrated Purgatory of St. Patrick, in Lough Derg, in Ireland, into which no person was allowed to enter without first undergoing all the ceremonies of purification and preparation. This purgatory, according to the opinion of Mr. Faber (Myst. Cab., vol. ii., p. 392), was, doubtless, a place appropriated to the performance of the rites of Druidism. It will be remembered that the

The places of initiation and worship were generally
either circular, because a circle was a significant emblem
of the universe, governed and preserved by an omnipresent deity, who is described in the writings of Hermes
Trismegistus, as a circle[40] whose centre is every where,
and whose circumference is no where; and pointed out
the unity of the godhead; a doctrine distinctly asserted
by the Druids;[41] or oval,[42] in allusion to the mundane

holy mountain was considered the sacred ascent to Elysium; and the
cave or womb led downwards to Hades. The most ancient monument of British antiquity at Abury, in Wiltshire, was constructed on
two eminences; and to complete the allusion, a gigantic mound, called
Silbury hill, was thrown up, so as to form a triangle with the other
two, thus constituting the sacred three-peaked temple. The hill at
Karn-bre, in Cornwall, is furnished by Nature with three distinct and
beautiful peaks, and hence became an early object of superstitious
reverence, which the Druids appear to have exhausted all their ingenuity in adorning with a profusion of sacred embellishments. Here
was a consecrated grove of oaks, furnished with solar temples, caverns
of initiation, thrones, phalli, altars, adyta, inclosures, rock basons for
the water of purification, and every requisite for public worship and
the celebration of the mysteries on a grand scale; for the whole
extent of this magnificent establishment comprehended an area of more
than four miles in circumference. (Borl. Ant. Corn., p. 113.)   It
may be here observed, that the grove was sacred to the celestial, the
altar to the terrestrial, and the cell to the infernal deities. (Maur.
Ind. Ant., vol. ii., p. 317.)

[40] The usual appellation given by the bards to the sacred inclosure
of an open temple, was the mundane circle; and Faber says that the
Ark was called, the circle of the world; it follows, therefore, the open
circular temple was a representation of the Ark.

[41] Specimens of the circular temple are common in this country; but
the most stupendous specimen is exhibited at Stonehenge, on Salis-
bury Plain, which was anciently denominated Caer Gaur, or the Great
Cathedral, or the mundane ark, and was intended probably as a place
of general assembly for the detached communities throughout the
kingdom at their grand triennial meetings. Surrounded by a deep
ditch and lofty mounds, the interior space was divided, like most other
difices of peculiar sanctity, into three seperate inclosures; an outer
and inner court, and an adytum; the first for the people, the second
for the priests, and the third for the chief Druid alone. The entrance
to this wonderful temple was by an avenue towards the north-east,
which to this day is accurately defined by a bank of earth on each side
extending to a considerable distance from the temple, and forming at
the end a double avenue; one branch of which communicated with
what is now termed the Cursus; but I should think that this space is
probably the site of the sacred buildings. At a short distance from
the circle was a huge stone, sixteen feet in height, which was doubtless
the presiding deity of the place; a vestige of the Buddhic superstition; (Hesych. Lex. apud. Fab. Pag. Idol., vol. ii., p. 375,) and about

egg ; though the instances of this form are of rare occurrence, the adytum being more frequently oviform than
the Temple; or serpentine,[43] because a serpent was the

one hundred feet further in the entrance into the outer court was
another stone of about twenty feet in height. Within the ditch was a
green walk of one hundred and five feet in breadth, which encompassed
the whole structure; and this was probably circumambulated by the
aspirant during the process of initiation. The building itself consisted
of two concentric circles, formed of upright and cross stones of gigantic size, the largest being twenty-five feet in height, and of a proportionate breadth and thickness. "The bulk of the constituent part is so
very great," says Stukeley, (Stonehenge, c. 1.) " that the mortaises and
tenons must have been prepared to an extreme nicety.; and like the
fabric of Solomon's Temple, every stone tallied, and neither axes nor
hammers were heard upon the whole structure." The outer circle was
one hundred feet in diameter, and consisted of sixty stones, alluding
to the sexagenary cycle of the Asiatics: one half being uprights and
the other imposts; the inner circle between eighty and ninety feet in
diameter, containing forty stones, in allusion probably to the forty days
prevalence of the diluvian waters. The adytum was oval, because an
egg was the constant symbol of the world ; the outer oval consisted of
ten stones, because ten was a perfect number, and amongst the Pythagoreans denoted Heaven, as being the perfection of all things, and the
inner oval contained nineteen stones, referring to the cycle of the Sun
and Moon, the two great arkite deities. The adytum contained an
altar.

[42] The remains of a small temple of this kind, consisting of sixty
stones, is still in existence at Addingham, in Cumberland, called Long
Meg and her daughters. The transverse diameter from east to west
is one hundred yards ; and the conjugate from north to south, eighty.
On the south side, at about the distance of twenty-three yards, stands
the stone called Long Meg, five yards high, and five yards in girt,
which was the idol or object of worship.

[43] The temple of Abury, one of the most stupendous erections which
ancient Britain could boast, and whose loss is a national calamity, was
constructed in the form of a circle, to which a vast Serpent was attached. It is considered to have been one of the earliest structures
erected in Britain, but now, alas ! totally desolated, and scarcely any
vestiges of its existence remain. Its name may probably have been
derived from the Cabiri, as Parkhurst, in loc. ingeniously supposes ;
because the Cabiric rites were undoubtedly celebrated within its precincts. Cabiri, or Abiri, signifies the Mighty Ones ; and the mysteries
were dedicated to those benevolent deities who invented and propagated the arts which elevated man from a savage to a civilized state of
being. This extraordinary monument of British ingenuity and per
severance, was erected on the summit of an eminence, in the centre of
an extensive plain, and consisted of a great circle, enclosed with a
stupendous vallum of earth, within which was a deep ditch. The area
of this part of the temple was twenty-eight acres. On the interior
bank was placed a circle of massive unhewn grey stones, generally
about twenty feet in height. Within this principal circle were two
smaller double concentric circles of stones, each seven feet high. In

symbol of the deity, who was no other than the diluvian
patriarch Noah, consecrated by the Druids under the
name of Hu; and the common emblem of a serpent
entwining himself over an egg, was intended to represent
Hu preserved in the Ark; or *winged*,[44] to figure the motion
of the divine spirit; or *cruciform*,[45] because a cross was the

the centre of one of these was a tall phallus, twenty-one feet in height,
and eight feet nine inches in diameter; and within the other was a cell
or adytum. A grand avenue, planted with large masses of stone, one
hundred in number on each side, at regular distances, proceeded from
the south-east part of this circle, which continued in a curvilineal form,
for more than a mile, and terminated in a chapel or cell; and from the
south-west of the temple proceeded another avenue in a contrary
direction, for about the same distance, tapering towards the end, and
terminating in the valley. About the centre of this latter avenue was
placed a cove or pastos, facing the south-east; the stones composing
which are still called by the country people, the Devil's Quoits. Each
avenue being on an inclined plane, a person advancing towards the
temple would have on all sides a most advantageous view of it. Thus
it formed the compound figure of a snake transmitted through a circle,
an unquestionable emblem of the deity, according to the creed of all
ancient nations. The circle represented the Demiurgus or Creator;
and the serpent referred to the divine emanation, to whose wisdom
the government of the universe was entrusted. (Maur. Ind. Ant., vol.
iv., p. 693.) Faber, however, is of opinion that the ring represented
the Ark, or Ceridwen; and the snake the great serpent-god Hu. (Pag.
Idol., vol. i., p. 193.) The avenue terminated with the head of the
snake, which was curiously situated on the apex of Hackpen hill, which
anciently derived its name from this circumstance; for, in the old
language, *hac* signifies a snake, (Hoare's Wiltshire,) and *pen*, the extremity, or head, (Owen's Dict., v. Pen.) whence hac-pen, the head or
the snake. The country people still hold this hill in high veneration;
and the little sanctuary which formed the serpent's head is still fresh
in their memory, having only very lately been destroyed. The whole
length of this magnificent structure was nearly three miles. Vid.
Stukeley's Abury, and letter to Mr. Gale; and Hoare's Anc. Wilts; to
which works I have been principally indebted for the above account
of this temple. Silbury hill, an artificial mound of earth, measuring
two thousand and twenty-seven feet in circumference at the base, one
hundred and twenty feet in diameter at the top; one hundred and
seventy feet in perpendicular height; three hundred and sixteen feet
in sloping height, and covering five acres of land, was erected in the
middle, between the head and tale of the snake, as an appendage to
the temple. Sir R. C. Hoare thinks it was a hill-altar.

[44] Stukeley mentions a winged temple which he found at Navestock,
in Essex; (Knave, from Canaph, or Kneph, the winged serpent deity
of Egypt;) and says he doubts not but there are many such temples
in the Britannic isles. Toland mentions a winged Druid-temple in one
of the Shetland islands.

[45] At Classerniss in the island of Lewis, Scotland, is a specimen of
this cruciform temple. It has a circle consisting of twelve stones; and

symbol of regeneration and life. They were variously
constructed as to the materials used in their composition.
In countries where stone was plentiful, they were composed of immense lumps of that substance, unhewn;
but where stone was scarce, rude banks of earth were
substituted, and the Temple was formed of a high vallum and ditch. But in the great national Temples
trouble and expence were not considered, and the two
forms were always united; the circle of rough stones,
unpolluted with a metal tool,[46] was encompassed by a high
embankment, and guarded generally by a deep ditch.
They were uncovered, because the Druids thought it
absurd to confine the Omnipotent Deity within the walls

three each on the east, west, and south sides placed in right lines;
while on the north is a double row of twice nineteen stones in two
perpendicular parallel lines, forming a superb avenue, with a single
elevated stone at the entrance. The whole number of stones was
sixty. In the centre of the temple stands, in an elevated situation,
the gigantic representative of the deity, to which the adoration of the
worshippers was peculiarly directed. (Borl. Ant. Corn., p. 193.)

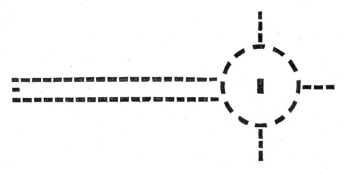

Another cruciform temple, of a different description, is found at New
Grange, in Ireland.

[46] There appears to have been a peculiar pollution attached to the
use of *metal tools* in the construction of the early temples. The
Almighty commanded Moses from the mount to raise a simple altar o.
earth; and if that should not prove sufficiently permanent, he was
directed to form it of *unhewn stone*, lest it should be polluted *by the
use of an iron tool*. (Ex. xx., 25.) And David, long afterwards, lamented the destruction of the intended temple, which he foresaw would
be effected by the *axes and hammers* of the surrounding idolaters.
(Psalm lxxiv., 6.) The temple itself, though an unequalled monument
of riches and architectural magnificence, was put together without
the assistance of ax, hammer, or any metal tool. (1 Kings vi., 7.)

of a religious edifice;[47] and were doubtless erected at the instance and under the direction of this priesthood to add dignity and authority to the rites of the national religion; and hence the most herculean labours were performed in their construction.[48]   Attached to the temple was generally placed a stone more elevated and of superior dimensions to the rest, which was worshipped as the representative of the deity.[49]

The general name of the sanctuary where the peculiar mysteries of Ceridwen were formally celebrated was *Caer Sidi*, the circle of revolution; so called from the well known form of the Druidical temples.[50]   It appears extremely probable that this sanctuary[51] consisted of a range

[47] This method of erecting temples consecrated to the celebration of divine rites, was consonant with primitive usage; for the most early patriarchal temples consisted of twelve stones placed in the open air, (Vid. Ex. xxiv., 4; Josh. iv., 9,) but the Druids added to the magnificence of their religious edifices, by an increased number of stones, arranged with an allusion to astronomical calculations.   They consisted chiefly of three, seven, twelve, nineteen, thirty, sixty, and one hundred and twenty stones, exclusive of the detached phalli which occupied places out of the circumference.   *Three* referred to the divine triad Hu—Ceridwin—Creirwy; *seven* to the seven heavens which they taught were placed in the upper regions of the air; *twelve* to the twelve signs of the Zodiac; *nineteen* to the Metonic cycle; *thirty* to the famous age or generation of the Druids; *sixty* to the sexagenary cycle of India, with which they were undoubtedly acquainted; and *one hundred and twenty* to the double sexagenary.

[48] It is asserted by Stukeley, that at the present time it would cost £20,000 to throw up such a mound as Silbury hill.

[49] The monument called Long Meg, is a fine specimen of this kind of idol.

[50] This phrase, according to Mr. Davies, implies "in the first place, the Ark in which the patriarch and his family were inclosed; secondly, the circle of the Zodiac, in which their luminous emblems, the sun, moon, and planets revolved; thirdly, the sanctuary of the British Ceres, which represented both the Ark and the zodiac." (Mytho. Druid., p. 516.)

[51] In the poem called Kadair Teyrn On, (Welch Arch., vol. i., p. 65,) we are told that there are four grand sanctuaries in the British dominions.   It would have been highly satisfactory if the bard had enumerated them.   The two principal ones were doubtless that of Stonehenge or Abury for the southern division of Britain; and probably the Temple at Shap, in Cumberland, which, as Stukeley affirms, (Itin., vol. ii., p. 15,) was constructed on the plan of a serpent transmitted through a circle, and full two miles in length, for the northern division.   In one of the Triads, however, (Meyrick. Cardig. Introd.,) the Bard says, "there are *three* principal Choirs in Britain," and names them as follows: The Knight Iltuds Bangor in Caer Worgorn

of buildings erected for the purpose, immediately adjoining their most sacred temples[52] in the centre of an impenetrable grove of oaks, consecrated with solemn rites to the service of the deity, and hallowed with the blood of human victims. In some parts of England the initiations were performed in the secret recesses of holy caverns formed by Nature with every convenience to give effect to their celebration; for a cavern was understood by the Epoptæ to represent the central cavity of the vast abyss, or the great receptacle of the diluvian waters;[53] or, in other words, Hades. The peculiar degree of sanctity attached to these awful inclosures, was calculated to produce a lasting impression on the aspirant, as well as to prevent the idle approach of the uninitiated. Considerable space was necessary for the machinery of initiation on its largest and most comprehensive scale. Apartments of all sizes, cells, vaults, baths, and long and artfully contrived passages, with all the apparatus of terror which was used on these important occasions could not have been contained within a small compass; although it is tolerably clear that initiation on a minor scale was performed in many parts of the island within the inclosure of caverns of moderate dimensions.

(Glamorganshire.) The Choir of Emrys (Ambres) in Caer Caradac, (Old Sarum, says Meyrick; I should rather think Stonehenge;) and Bangor Wydrin in the apple island, (Arallon or Glastonbury.)

[52] The three great labours of the Britons are represented in a famous triad to be, raising the stone of Cetti, or constructing the mystical Cromlech or adytum; Erecting the Emrys, or building the circular Temple with petræ ambrosiæ or consecrated stones; and Heaping the mount of Gyvrangon, or raising the mound or cairn in honour of the dead. In all these solemn duties gray stones were preferred. The adytum or ark of the mysteries was called a Cromlech, (Signs and Symbols, Lect. 6,) and was used as a sacred pastos or place of regeneration. It consisted of two or more upright stones as supporters of a broad flat stone which was laid across them, so as to form a small cell, within the area of which the aspirant was immured. The Carnedd was a heap of stones rudely piled together over the summit of a mountain or high hill for sepulchral or commemorative purposes. When used as a place of sepulture, the cairn was more commonly composed of earth; and in this case it was termed a tumulus or barrow: derived from the Celtic *tumba*, a tomb, and *byrig*, a mound of earth, or *byringenn*, sepultra.

[53] I once visited Poole's Hole, near Buxton, and found the noise of the waters to be absolutely stunning. It is, indeed, a cavern of horror.

7

It is well known that what was pure mythology in one age became romance in another;[54] and hence the fables current in this country about King Arthur and his knights connected with Merlin the enchanter;[55] their imaginary combats, and discomfiture of giants and powerful magicians, were all derived from occurrences that took place during the initiation of candidates into the highest mysteries of Druidism, which were of a complicated nature abounding with transformations, battles, and fearful ad ventures. Hence every remarkable structure in this island to which the name of Arthur is attached was doubtless connected with the initiations,[56] and the same may

[54] Vid. Fab. Pag. Idol., b. v., c. 8.

[55] " Merlin was the same as the Irish Tailgin St. Patrick; in other words, he was Noah, or the principal Telchin, whence he was denominated by the ancient Celts, Mer-Lin, or the marine god of the Lake." (Fab. Mys. Cab., vol. ii., p. 429.) " I am much inclined to conjecture," adds the author, " that the hardy knights of the Round Table were in fact, no other than the infernal, or Cabiric deities." (Ib., p. 437.)

[56] In the county of Westmoreland are two extraordinary monu ments connected with each other, the one called Maryborough, or more properly Mayburgh; the other, Arthur's Round Table. The former is a very striking specimen of the mixed architecture of the Druids, composed of stones and an embankment of earth, and lies about four hundred yards to the west of Arthur's Table. It consists of an eminence which rises gradually from the plain for about one hundred and forty paces, forming the lower section or base of a regular cone; the ascent is everywhere covered with wood, and the remains of timber trees of great size appear on every side. The summit of the hill is fenced round, save only an opening or entrance, twelve paces in width to the east; the fence is singular, being composed of an immense quantity of loose pebbles and flints which perhaps were gathered from the adjoining rivers. No kind of mortar appears to have been used in this work;· the stones lie uncemented, piled up to the ridge, near twenty paces wide at the base, and in height about twelve feet from the interior plain. Here and there time has scattered a few shrubs and trees over the pebbles, but in other places they are loose and naked on both sides. The space within consists of a fine plain of meadow ground exactly circular, one hundred and fifty paces in diameter; and inclining a little to the westward from the centre is *a large column of unhewn stone standing erect*, with its smaller end in the earth, eleven feet and upwards in height, and more than twenty-two feet in circumference at the middle. (Hutch. Comb., vol. i., p. 310.) The sacred character of this place has been handed down by tradition, even to the present time. In a correspondence which I had some time ago with the late Mr. Briggs of Kendal, he related the following anecdote respecting this Druidical circle : " Not many years since, an old man in neighborhood told me, there were

be said of all places to which a giant was a party.[57]   All ancient temples consecrated to religious worship, in whatever country, for the practice of all idolatrous nations was uniform in this particular, had places of initiation con-

four stones at the entrance, and he had heard old folks say that there had been four stones in the centre, but he could not recollect them. Those at the entrance he remembered very well, and they were destroyed by the landlord of the public house by the side of Arthur's Round Table, and his servant man.   But, added he, I think they did wrong to meddle with these ancient things, for one of the men soon after hanged himself, and the other lost his reason.   What must have been the veneration for this place," exclaims Mr. Briggs, "in the days of its greatest glory, when such a striking relic of superstitious respect is still fostered among the peasantry of the neighborhood!" Arthur's Round Table is a circular earthwork, one hundred and ten yards in diameter in the whole ; and has an elevated circular table in the centre of forty yards in diameter, which is surrounded by a ring twenty yards wide and the whole is encompassed by a fifteen yards ditch.   It is situated on a piece of elevated ground near Eamont bridge, and is wholly covered with a fine greensward.   It bears no marks of dilapidation.   It is composed wholly of earth, and there is not a stone about it, nor does it appear that there ever was.   It is now the theatre of an annual wrestling match, at which those gentlemen of the county, who have not previously obtained the honour, are formally installed knights of the Round Table ; of which order, Thomas Wyberg, Esq., is the present Grand Master.   It was in such places as this that the Britons used periodically to assemble for the purpose of witnessing the sports and games which were instituted to prove the strength and agility of their youth, and to amuse the people.   (Borl. Ant. Corn., p. 195.)

[57] In Cumberland, they have a legend respecting a monster of this nature, who resided in a cave on the banks of the river Eden.   He is represented to have been a terror to all the surrounding country.   His name was *Isir*.   He subsisted by spoiling the neighbouring fields of their cattle, and when hard pressed by hunger, did not hesitate to drag men into his cave and devour them.   When he washed his face, says the tradition, he placed his right foot on one side of the river, and his left on the other.   The Rev. G. Hall, of Rosegill, to whom I am indebted for this legend, adds, " this giant, like all other giants, died and went the way of all flesh.   When he died, tradition does not say ; but it *does* say that he was buried in Penrith churchyard ; and that the stones called the giant's gravestones, mark his grave and the length of his body."   This is evidently a legend of initiation transferred from mythology to romance.   The rites, as we have seen, were most commonly performed in caverns, and beside the pellucid waters of a running stream, where such conveniences could be placed in conjunction ; for candidates, during a certain part of the ceremony were immersed, and figuratively said to be metamorphosed into fishes.   The giant's name was strictly mythological.   The mysteries of Britain were sacred to Ceridwen, who was the same as Ceres or Isis, and she is represented by Taliesin as a *giantess*.   (Welch. Arch.

nected with them, and most frequently these places were
subterranean.   Few caverns in this country remain to
relate the wonders of Druidical initiation; but the stupendous grotto at Castleton, in Derbyshire,[58] called by
Stukeley, the Stygian Cave,[59] is sufficient to convince us
that these celebrations were of the most terrific nature;
were performed with the aid of complicated machinery,
and did not yield in interest and sublimity to those which
have been so highly eulogised in the more polished and
civilized nations of Egypt and Greece.   They were
usually constructed on the principles of secrecy and re-

vol. i., p. 166.)   The husband of Isis was Osiris: a word derived,
according to Vallancey, from two old Celtic words, signifying the
commander of a ship or ark; *Eiss-Aire*, or *Is-Ir*, the very name of
our Cumberland giant; who was no other than Osiris or Noah, and
was represented by every candidate during the initiations.   Gibson,
in Camden, (Col. 842,) says that this giant's cave or grotto was denominated *Isis Parlish*, or the cavern of Isis the perilous; and the
current legend, as we have seen, is, that the monster seized men and
cattle, and dragged them into his cave for a prey.   The cattle were
evidently brought there for sacrifice, and the men for initiation, during the process of which the aspirants were figuratively said *to be
devoured by the giantess Ceridwen or Isis*.   (Vid. infra. l. iii.)   Respecting the giant's grave I must refer to my former volume of Signs
and Symbols, Lect. VII.   A similar legend is recorded by Stukeley,
that a giant named Tarquin lived at Brougham Castle, in the same
neighbourhood, and that Sir Lancelet du Lake, then residing at Maryborough, attacked and slew him.

[58] Antiquities of Masonry, p. 107.

[59] Some very singular excavations have been discovered between
Luckington and Badminster, Wilts, called the Giants' Caves, which
are thus described in Childrey's Britannia Bacconica, and cited in the
Aubrey MSS.   "They are upon the top of a rising hill, in number
about nine; and some of them are or were formerly cemented with
lime.   Some of them are deeper, and some shallower, some broader and
larger than others.   They lie all together in a row   The manner of
them is two long stones set upon the sides, and broad stones set upon
the top to cover them.   The least of these caves is four feet broad,
and some of them are nine or ten feet long."   Sir R. C. Hoare pronounces them to be ancient sepulchres; but I conceive the learned
baronet to be mistaken in this point, for the author before cited says,
"the curiosity of some ingenious men, as it is reported, within these
forty years, tempted them to dig into it, and make search for some
ancient remains, but they found nothing but an old spur, and some few
other things not worth mentioning."   How could they be sepulchral
if no remains were interred within them?   The fact is, they were no
more sepulchral than were the pyramids of Egypt; and I have no
hesitation in saying that they were constructed for the selfsame purpose, viz. as places of initiation into the mysteries.

tirement from public observation. Long, dark, and in all practicable cases, intricate passages were the united essentials of the mysterious precinct; and it is evident that as religion could not be practised distinct from initiation, so places for the performance of these important rites were always constructed within or near the edifices consecrated to religious worship.

LECTURE VIII.

CEREMONIES OF INITIATION IN BRITAIN.

THE grand periods of initiation into these mysteries were quarterly, and determined by the course of the sun, and his arrival at the equinoctial and solstitial points.[1] These, at the remote period now under our consideration, corresponded with the 13th February; 1st May; 19th August; and 1st November.[2] But the time of annual celebration was May eve, and the ceremonial preparations commenced at midnight, on the 29th April, and when the initiations were over on May eve, fires were kindled[3] on all the cairns and cromlechs throughout the island, which burned all night to introduce the sports of May day. Round these fires choral dances[4] were performed, in honour of the Solar patriarch Hu, or Noah, who was at this season delivered from his confinement in the Ark.[5] The festival was phallic,[6] in honour of the Sun, the great

---

[1] Stukeley, Abury, p. 68.

[2] The monthly celebrations took place when the moon was six days old; and peculiar rites were appropriated to certain days, as appears from an ancient British poem, thus translated by Davies, "A song of dark import was composed by the distinguished Ogdoad, who assembled on the day of the Moon, and went in open procession. On the day of Mars, they allotted wrath to their adversaries. On the day of Mercury, they enjoyed full pomp. On the day of Jove, they were delivered from the detested usurpers. On the day of Venus, the day of the great influx, they swam in the blood of men. On the day of Saturn, ... On the day of the Sun, there truly assembled five ships, and five hundred of those who make supplication, &c."

[3] Toland, in his History of the Druids, (vol. i., p. 71,) says that two of these fires were kindled in every village of the nation; between which the men and beasts to be sacrificed were obliged to pass; one of them being kindled on the cairn, and the other on the ground.

[4] These were the fire dances mentioned by Porphyry, (l. i., p. 94,) and were probably used to propitiate that element which they believed was destined to destroy the world. (Ces. de bel. Gal., l. vi.)

[5] Signs and Symbols, Lect. v.

[6] Maur. Ind. Ant., vol. vi., p. 89. "It is remarkable that one of the most remarkable feasts of the Hindoos, called that of Auruna, the daystar, falls on the sixth day of the new moon, in May, and is dedicated to the goddess of generation, who is worshipped when the

source of generation, and consisted in the elevation of
long poles decorated with crowns of gold and garlands
of flowers, under which the youth of both sexes performed certain mysterious revolutions, for it was customary to adore the sun by circular dances.[7] These continued till the luminary had attained his meridian height;
and then retiring to the woods, the most disgraceful
orgies were perpetrated, and the festival ended with de-
bauchery and intoxication.[8]

The time of general meeting was figuratively said to
be when the Sun was at its due meridian;[9] in allusion to

morning star appears, or at dawn of day, for the propagation of
children and to remove barrenness." (Ibid., p. 93.)

[7] Vid. Asiat. Res., vol. ii., p. 333. The mythic circle had also a
reference to the historical period, commencing with the union of
heaven and earth, and ending with the return of Ulysses to Ithaca.
(Procl. in Phot. Bibl., p. 982.)

[8] This was doubtless the origin of the festivities which were practised in many parts of England, down to a very recent period, at the
same season of the year. The following description of these games
by Stubbs, (Anatomie of Abuses, 1595,) most unequivocally points
out their origin: "Against Maie-day, every parish, town, or village
assemble themselves, both men, women, and children; and either all
together, or dividing themselves into companies, they goe to the
woods and groves, some to the hills and mountains, some to one place,
and some to another, where they spend *all the night* in pleasant pas-
times, and in the morning they return bringing with them birch
boughes and branches of trees to deck their assemblies withal. But
their chiefest jewel they bring from thence is the maie-pole, which
they bring home with great veneration, as thus; they have *twentie or
fourtie yoake of oxen*, every oxe having a sweete nosegaie of flowrs
tied up to the tip of his hornes, and these oxen drawe home the May-
poale, which they covered all over with flowers and hearbes, bound
round with strings from the top to the bottome, and sometimes it was
painted with variable colours, having two or three hundred men, women, and children, following it with great devotion. And thus
equipped it was reared with handkerchiefes and flaggs streaming on
the top, they strawe the ground round about it, they bind green
boughs about it, they set up summer halles, bowers, and arbours,
hard by it, and then fall they to banquetting and feasting, to leaping,
and dancing, about it as the heathen people did at the dedication of
their idols. I have heard it credeblie reported, by men of great
gravity, credite, and reputation, that of fourtie, threescore, or a
hundred *maides* going to the wood, there have scarcelie the third
parte of them *returned home again as they went*."

[9] Their Gorseddaw were held in the open air, while the sun remained above the horizon. The bards assembled within a circle of
stones, and the presiding Druid stood before a large stone in the
centre. (Turn. Anglo Sax., vol. i., p. 197.)

that astronomical paradox founded on the globular form
of the earth, which, continually revolving on its axis,
makes the central Sun always at its meridian to some part
of its surface. The truth is, that the rites of the insular
sanctuary commenced at daybreak; and the rising of
their great deity, who was dignified with the appellation
of "the god of victory; the king who rises in light and
ascends the sky,"[10] was hailed with triumphant shouts
and loud hosannas. But the solemn initiations were
performed at midnight, to invest them with a higher
degree of dignity and importance. They contained
three independent steps or degrees, the first or lowest
being the Eubates, the second the Bards, and the third
the Druids.[11]

A careful preparation was used previously to the admission of candidates into the first degree; for it was considered that without mental and bodily purification, the •
arcana of a sacred establishment could not safely be
communicated. The heart must be prepared to conceal,
before the eyes are permitted to discover the truths
which often lie hid under significant emblems, the instruments, probably, of human industry; else the labour of
years may be unprofitably wasted in the thankless office
of committing seed to a barren soil, which will make no
return of fruit commensurate with the toil of cultivation.
They were purified by the Tolmen,[12] and then put to

[10] Gododin, Song xxii.

[11] This division did not include the preparatory ceremony of the
insular sanctuary, which partook rather of the nature of a qualification process than of a distinct degree. Thus Taliesin, in his poem
of The Spoils of the Deep, speaks of "that lore which was four
times reviewed in the quadrangular inclosure." (Dav. Druid, p. 518.)
And in his poem of The Battle of the Trees, the same bard describes
these four ceremonies of purification with great exactness. "I was
exorcised," says he, "by Math before I became immortal; I was
exorcised by Gwidion the great purifier of the Brython, of Eurowys,
of Euron and Medron, of the multitude of scientific teachers, children of Math. When the removal took place, I was exorcised by
the sovereign when he was half consumed. By the Sage of sages
was I exorcised in the primitive world, at which time I had a being."
(Dav. Druid, p. 541.)

[12] The Tolmen was a perforated stone which was used for the purpose of regeneration in the mysteries; and the hierophant or chief
Druid was hence denominated Tola. (Vid. Borl. Ant. Corn., p. 166.)
These consecrated petræ are common all over England and Wales;
and the act of passing through them was thought to convey extraor

their probation, which was very severe. Sometimes the candidate was doomed to a seclusion of twenty years,[13] which was spent amidst the secret recesses of an inaccessible forest,[14] in a close and devoted application to study and reflection, and the practice of gymnastic exercises. But this lengthened probation extended only to such as were regularly educated and initiated into the mysteries, for the express purpose of occupying the most elevated situations in the civil or ecclesiastical departments of the state. These were instructed in all the sciences of which the Druids made profession. They were excited to emulate the heroic deeds of their progenitors, whose bravery was inculcated in verse, that it might never be banished from the recollection.[15]

The aspirant for mere initiation, was clad in a robe striped alternately with *white*, *skyblue*, and *green*,[16] which were the sacred colours of Druidism, and emblematical of *light*, *truth*, and *hope*; and confined in a cromlech without food three days prior to his admission into each of the two first degrees;[17] that is, he was placed in the pastos with the usual ceremonies on the evening of the first day,[18] remained an entire day enclosed, or *dead* in the language of the mysteries, and was liberated for initiation, or in other words, restored to life on the third.[19]

dinary purity. In some parts of Britain they were denominated Main Ambres; and the ingenious Dr. Stukeley conjectures that the primitive name of Stonehenge was "the Ambres," whence was derived the name of Ambresbury, a village in the immediate vicinity of that celebrated monument of antiquity.

[13] Cesar. l. vi. [14] Gollut. Ax. 1.
[15] Borl. Ant. Corn., p. 82. [16] Owen's W. Dict., v. Glain.
[17] Signs and Symbols, Lect. vi.

[18] "It was customary with the Hebrews," says the Abbé Fleury (Manners of the Ancient Israelites, p. 4, c. 3,) "to express a whole day by the terms, *the evening and the morning*; or by these, *the night and the day*; which the Greeks express by their *nuchthemeron*; and which as well signifies any particular part of the day or night, as the whole of it. And this is the reason why a thing that has lasted *two nights and one whole day*, and a part only of the preceding and following days, is said by the Hebrews to have lasted *three days and three nights.*"

[19] This was symbolical of the patriarch Adam, who died on one day, the world before the Flood being so esteemed; remained in the tomb another day, i. e., during the continuance of the post-diluvian world; and will rise again to judgment on the third or eternal day; and being purified from his corruptions, will remain for ever happy

7*

The Welsh triads contain a hint of this solitary confinement in the cromlech when speaking of the initiation of Arthur, who is there said to have been imprisoned "three nights in the inclosure of Oeth and Anoeth, and three nights with the lady of Pendragon, and three nights in the prison of Kud, under the flat stone of Echemeint; and one youth released him from the three prisons, namely, Goreu, the son of Cystenin, his nephew."[20]   The last of these prisons was evidently the cromlech, in which it is certain the candidate endured a confinement of much more extended duration,[21] before he was admitted to the last and most distinguished privilege of Druidism.

When the sanctuary was prepared for the solemn business of initiation, the Druids and their attendants, ceremonially arranged, properly clothed, crowned with ivy and protected by amulets; a hymn to the sun was

in a place of light. It was further symbolical of Noah, who entered into the Ark in one year; remained inclosed a year, and was emancipated from his confinement, or *reborn*, in the third year. Much confusion arose in the mythology of the ancient world from this doctrine. The aspirant, like Noah, is supposed to have lived in the old world, and was hence esteemed a venerable *old man;* but he was new-born from the mysteries, as Noah was from the Ark, and hence he was considered but *an infant.* Noah built the Ark, and it was consequently represented as *his daughter;* but he was united with the Ark, and they together floated over the all-pervading wave; hence she was taken for *his wife;* and ultimately he was born from the Ark, which, from this circumstance, sustained the character of *his mother.* Again, when he is said to die, the Ark is *his coffin;* when a child, it is *his cradle;* and when he is supposed to sleep in deep repose during the prevalence of the waters, it is *his bed.* (Vid. Fab. Pag. Idol., vol. ii., p. 281.) The confusion this would necessarily create could not be reconciled without having recourse to a multiplication of deities, and therefore in Greece, as *the father* of the female principle or Ark, Noah was termed Saturn; as *her husband* he was termed Jupiter, and as *her son,* Bacchus; and when the *solar* and the *arkite* superstitions were connected, he became Apollo, and soon branched off into a number of collateral deities which peopled their imaginary heaven, and tended to mystify their system of religion, and place it entirely out of the reach of ordinary comprehension; and the unravelment of this intricate machinery formed one grand secret of the Greater Mysteries, in which the hierophant reduced all the complicated pantheon of idolatry to one single god. (Cudworth, Intel. Syst., l. i., c. 4.) This subject is also handled at length in Faber's Pagan Idolatry, (b. i., c. 1, s. 10–12.)

[20] Welsh Archæol. Triad. 50. Dav. Druid. p. 404
[21] Welsh Archæol., vol. i., p. 19.

chanted,[22] and *three blessed drops*[23] of the Spirit were
earnestly implored. The candidate was then introduced,
and placed under the care of the officer who was stationed to receive him "in the land of rest." Soon,
however, the active duties of initiation were commenced.
The aspirant, who was denominated a blind man,[24] was
appointed to kindle a fire under the cauldron. As the
cauldron was a mystical word to express the whole circle
of science taught in the mysteries, so the act of kindling
a fire under it must have had an evident reference to
those preliminary ceremonies which were practised before the disclosure of any part of the august secrets of
the Order. A pageant was then formed, and the several
candidates were arranged in ranks consisting of *threes,
fives,* and *sevens,* according to their respective qualifications,
and conducted nine times round the sanctuary in circles
from east to west by the south;[25] proceeding at first
"with solemn step and slow," amidst an awful and death-
like silence, to inspire a sacred feeling adapted to the reception of Divine truths; at length the pace increased,
until they were impelled into a rapid and furious motion

[22] Maur. Hist. Hind., vol. ii., p. 170.

[23] Signs and Symbols, Lect. viii.

[24] The ceremonies of initiation which I am about to describe and
illustrate, have been transmitted to us by Taliesin, in a poem of extraordinary merit, called Hanes Taliesin; which contains a mythological account of the candidate's progress through the different
stages, to his ultimate state of perfection. A translation of this
poem may be found in Dav. Druid, p. 189, 213, 229.

[25] Diodorus informs us that the temple of Stonehenge was the peculiar abode of Apollo; and that the god amused himself with a
dance once in nineteen years, amongst his established train. On
this observation, Davies remarks, that "as it was the known practice for certain priests, in the celebration of the mysteries, personally to represent the sun and moon, I conjecture that the Druids, in
their great festival of the cycle, dressed up a pageant of their own
order, to personate this luminous divinity." The same may be said
of the dance called Betarmus, which was used during the initiations
in honour of the solar orb, and his attendant planets; and of the
Egyptian Pyrrhic dance, afterwards used by the Greeks, which was
performed at the summer solstice, accompanied by the singing of
dithyrambic odes; and the same idolatrous dances were performed
by the Israelites, which they had learned in Egypt. In the Raas
Jattra, or the dance of the circle in India, the performers proceeded
sometimes from left to right, as amongst the Romans; and sometimes
from right to left, as with the Greeks and Britons. And the Greeks
used a similar movement while their choruses were performing.

by the tumultuous clang of musical instruments, and the screams of harsh and dissonant voices, reciting in verse the praise of those heroes who had been brave in war,. courteous in peace, and devoted friends and patrons of religion.[26] This sacred ceremony completed, an oath of secrecy was administered, and hence the waters of the cauldron were said to deprive the candidates of utterance.[27] The oath was ratified by drinking out of the sacred vessel; and thus sealed, its violation could only be expiated by death.[28]

In the prosecution of the consecutive ceremonies, the following characters were successively sustained by the aspirant. Taliesin applies them to himself in his poem of Angar Cyvyndawd.[29] I have been a blue salmon; I have been a dog;[30] I have been a roebuck on the mountain; I have been a stock of a tree: I have been a spade; I have been an axe in the hand; I have been a pin in a forceps for a year and a half; I have been a cock, variegated with white, upon hens in Eidin; I have been a stallion upon a mare; I have been a buck of yellow hue in the act of feeding; I· have been a grain of the arkites which vegetated on a hill, and then the reaper placed me in a smoky recess,[31] that I might be compelled freely to yield my corn, when subjected to tribulation;[32] I was received by a hen[33] with red fangs and a divided crest;[34]

---

[26] The dance was somewhat similar to the wild ceremonial dances of the Corybantes; and is mentioned by Taliesin, in his poem of Kadair Teyrn On; (Welsh Archæol., vol. i., p. 65,) and more particularly described in another poem, where the bard says, "The assembled·train were dancing after the manner, and singing in cadence, with garlands (of ivy) on their brows; loud was the clattering of shields round the ancient cauldron in frantic mirth," &c. (Dav. Druid., p. 576.) Toland, in his History of the Druids, may also be usefully consulted on this ceremony; and Borlase in his Antiquities of Cornwall. [27] Turn. Vindicat., p. 283.

[28] Taliesin, Preiddeu Annwn. Welsh Archæol., vol. i., p. 45.

[29] Welsh Archæol., vol. i., p. 36.

[30] We have already witnessed the profuse use of this animal in the mysteries: and we shall find as we proceed, that similar canine phantoms were exhibited in the mysteries of Britain.

[31] The dark cavern of initiation.

[32] Or in other words, that the austerity of initiation might humanize and improve the heart, and elicit the fruits of morality and virtue.

[33] The arkite goddess, Ceridwen, was represented in the initiation as a hen with red fangs.

[34] Emblematical of the lunette, or six days moon.

I remained nine months an infant in her womb;[35] I have been Aedd,[36] returning to my former state; I have been an offering before the sovereign;[37] I have died; I have revived;[38] and conspicuous with my ivy branch;[39] I have been a leader, and by my bounty I became poor.[40] Again was I instructed by the cherisher with red fangs.[41] Of what she gave me[42] scarcely can I utter the great praise that is due."[43] And in his poem of Cad Goddeu, the same poet gives a further account of his numerous adventures during the ceremony of initiation. "I have been a spotted adder on the mount; I·have been a viper in the lake;[44] I have been stars among the superior chiefs; I have been the weigher of the falling drops, drest in my priest's cloke and furnished with my bowl."[45] These extraordinary transformations were undoubtedly effected by means of masks, shaped like the heads of those animals[46] which the aspirant was feigned to represent, and garments composed of their skins.[47]

[35] Alluding to the pastos or cromlech.

[36] The helio-arkite god, or his priest.

[37] When presented to the archdruid after initiation.

[38] Another allusion to the cromlech, in which the aspirant suffered a mythological death and revivification.

[39] It has been already observed that the aspirant was crowned with ivy.

[40] A mystical poverty was the characteristic of a candidate during the process of initiation.

[41] Ceridwen.

[42] Instruction in all mysteries and sciences, human and divine.

[43] Dav. Druid, p. 573.

[44] Serpents, as we have already seen, were much used in all the ancient mysteries.

[45] Dav. Druid, p. 544.

[46] Figures of men with the heads of animals are very common on the monuments of Egypt. (Vid. the plates to Belzoni's Researches.) Dr. Pococke says (Descrip. of the East, vol. i., p. 95,) "in some of the temples I have observed that the human body has always on it the head of some bird or beast."

[47] From a tradition of this practice arose that prevailing opinion, that "the spectres of Britain were hellish, more numerous than those of Egypt, of which some are yet remaining," says Gildas, "*strangely featured and ugly*, and still to be seen both within and without the forsaken walls, looking stern and grim, after their usual manner." (Gibson's Camd., xxxv.) The practice was continued as a *mummery* or holiday sport down to a comparatively recent period. "There was a sport," says Strutt, (Sports, p. 188,) "common among the ancients, which usually took place in the Kalends of January, and probably formed a part of the Saturnalia, or feasts of Saturn. It consisted in

The second part of the ceremony commenced with
striking *the blind man* a violent blow on the head with an
oar, and a pitchy darkness immediately ensued,[48] which was
soon changed into a blaze of light which illuminated the
whole area of the shrine, for now the fire was kindled.
This was intended to shadow forth the genial effects of
that great transition from darkness to light which the
arkite patriarch experienced on emerging from the gloom
of the Ark to the brightness of a pure and renovated
world, enlightened by the rays of a meridian sun. The
light was, however, suddenly withdrawn, and the aspirant
again involved in chaotic darkness. His heart thrilled
with horror. The most dismal howlings, shrieks, and
lamentations, saluted his astonished ears ; for now the
death of their great progenitor, typified by his confinement in the Ark, was commemorated with every external
mark of sorrow.[49] This was succeeded by the howling
and barking of dogs,[50] the blowing of horns,[51] and the

mummings and disguisements; for the actors took upon themselves
the resemblance of wild beasts, or domestic cattle, and wandered about
from one place to another; and he, I presume, stood highest in the
estimation of his fellow, who best supported the character of the
brute he imitated. This whimsical amusement was exceedingly popular, and continued to be practised long after the establishment of
Christianity." It was, indeed, very common in the reign of Henry
VIII. and was doubtless the remains of the system of metamorphosis
which was used during the Druidical initiations ; the memory of which
was retained long after the institution itself was buried in oblivion;
for the mummers were always decorated with ivy leaves, the characteristics of the priesthood, and the insignia of the mysteries. The
Christmas morris dances of the present day are perhaps the last
remains of this idolatrous superstition.

[48] The oar is an unequivocal emblem of the Deluge ; and the darkness represented the state of obscurity in which Hu was involved
while confined within the gloomy recesses of the Ark.

[49] This was the origin of the coronach or funeral dirge, used by the
Celts to a very recent period ; and even now imitated by the wild peasants of our sister country, at the funeral of a deceased friend or relation.

[50] The tale of Pwyll in the Cambrian Register (vol. i., p. 177,)
records this circumstance : " Pywll entering fully upon the chase, and
listening to the cry of the pack, *began to hear distinctly the cry of
another pack* which was of a different tone from that of his own dogs,
and was coming in an opposite direction." The whole of this tale is
worth considering, as it contains many plain intimations relative to the
ceremonies of initiation.

[51] Tale of Pywll, as above. Taliesin. Kadair Teyrn On.

voices of men uttering discordant cries. His timidity increasing, he would naturally attempt to fly, without knowing where to look for safety. Escape was, however, impossible, for wherever he turned, *white* dogs, with shining *red* ears,[52] appeared to bay at his heels. Thus he was said to be transformed into a hare;[53] evidently in allusion to the timidity which was the natural consequence of all the horrors to which he was necessarily exposed.[54] The gigantic goddess, Ceridwen, in the form of a proud mare,[55] emerging from behind the veil, now seized the astonished candidate, and by main force bore him away to the mythological sea of Dylan, into whose purifying stream he was immediately plunged by the attendant priest, and hence he was said to be changed into a fish;[56]

[52] Tale of Pywll. The Druids were habited during the performance of these ceremonies in *white* vestments, and crowned with *red* diadems. Dogs were generally considered to be effective agents under supernatural circumstances. Morgan, in his history of Algiers, gives a curious instance of this. He says, that "the Turks report, as a certain truth, that the corpse of Heyradin Barbarosa was found, four or five times, out of the ground, lying by his sepulchre, after he had been there inhumed; nor could they possibly make him lie quiet in his grave, till a Greek wizard counselled them *to bury a black dog* together with the body. This done, he lay still, and gave them no farther trouble."

[53] Hanes Taliesin. The tale of Pywll, however, likens the aspirant to a stag.

[54] I am inclined to think that the career of the aspirant was frequently contested by real or imaginary opponents to prove his personal courage. These contests were probably of a nature somewhat similar to the subsequent practice of the Crusaders during the process of admission into the superior orders of knighthood. The following passage in the poem of Gododin, (Song xxii., Dav. Druid., p. 365,) generally, and perhaps truly, referred to the slaughter of the Britons at the fatal banquet given by Hengist to Vortigern, at Stonehenge, forcibly points out the probable danger which surrounded the candidate at this period of the initiation. "Whilst the assembled train were accumulating like a darkening swarm around him, without the semblance of a retreat, his exerted wisdom planned a defence against the pallid outcasts with their sharp pointed weapons."

[55] Or rather fiend mare. She is here represented as a monstrous animal, compounded of a mare and a hen. (Dav. on British Coins.)

[56] Dylan, according to Mr. Davies, (Druid, p. 100.) was the patriarch Noah; and his *sea*, the Deluge; and he cites the following passage from Taliesin's Cad Goddeu in support of his opinion.

> " Truly I was in the ship
> With Dylan, son of the sea,
> Embraced in the centre
> Between the royal knees,

and to remain a whole year in the deep, in the character of Arawn, the arkite.[57] The pursuit of his terrible persecutors did not end here. The same appalling noises still assailed his ears; and his pursuer, transformed into an otter, threatens him with destruction. Emerging at length from the stream, the darkness was removed, and he found himself surrounded with the most brilliant coruscations of light.[58] This change produced in the attendants a corresponding emotion of joy and pleasure, which was expressed by shouts and loud pæans, to testify their supreme felicity at the resuscitation of their god, or in other words, his egress from the purifying wave. The aspirant was here presented to the Archdruid, seated on his throne of state, who expatiated on the design of the mysteries; imparted some portion of the cabalistical knowledge of Druidism; and earnestly recommended the practice of fortitude to the exhausted aspirant; for the exercise of this virtue constituted, in the opinion of the Druids, one leading trait of perfection.[59]

After his lustration and subsequent enlightening, the novice was said to become a bird who penetrates the regions of the air towards the lofty arch of heaven, to figure out the high and supernal privileges he had just attained; the favour of heaven and the protection of the gods. He was now instructed in the morality of the order; incited by precept to act bravely in war; taught that souls are immortal, and must live in a future state;[60] solemnly enjoined to the duties of divine worship, to

> When, like the rushing of hostile spears,
> The floods came forth
> From heaven to the great deep.

As Dylan was Noah, so Stonehenge was denominated the mundane ark, which was feigned to have been conveyed across the Irish channel by Hu, another name for Dylan, who, as the legend is recorded by Christian writers, is represented as the prince of darkness, the devil. (Drayton. Poly-Olbion, Song 4.)

[57] "It was proposed that Pywll should assume the form of Arawn, and preside in the deep in *his* character and person for one complete year." (Tale of Pywll.)

[58] "At the completion of the year, Pywll returns from the palace of the deep, into his own dominions, and providing a solemn sacrifice, beheld the sign of the *Rainbow* glittering in all its brilliancy of colouring under the character of a lady mounted upon a horse of a pale, bright colour, great and very high." (Tale of Pywll.)

[59] Diog. Laert. Prooem.   [60] Mela., l. iii., c. 2.

practise morality; and to avoid sloth, contention, and folly; and ultimately was invested with some sacred badges of Druidism. The crystal,[62] an unequivocal test of initiation,[63] was delivered to him, as an undoubted preservative from all future dangers; and if not intended for the highest offices of the priesthood, he was brought before the sacred fire, three hymns were chanted to the honour of Hu and Ceridwen, accompanied by the bardic harps; the mead was solemnly administered by the attendant officer, and the initiated aspirant was dismissed with solemn ceremonies.

But, after having surmounted the two former degrees, he was still deemed *exoteric*, and few attained the character of *esoteric*, or thrice born ; for this degree was administered to none but persons of rank and consequence; and if a noble candidate aspired to a higher degree of perfection than had been already communicated, he underwent other and more arduous ceremonies of purification. He was compared to a grain of pure wheat, emblematical of his perfect fitness for the highest mysteries of Druidism; and committed to the secluded solitude of the cromlech for the space of nine months, during which time he applied himself to the study of theology, natural philosophy, and divination, cosmography, astronomy, geography, rhetoric, logic, arithmetic, and music. This tedious period was devoted to study and reflection, that the candidate might be prepared to understand, more perfectly, the sacred truths in which

[61] Diog. Laert. Prooem.

[62] This Amulet was variously shaped. Sometimes like a round bead of glass; (Owen's Dic., v. Glain.) at others, like a crescent, or glass boat; (Kadeir Taliesin. Welsh Archæol., vol. i., p. 37,) now it was denominated a glass circle, (Preiddeu Annwn., Dav. Druid. Append., No. iii.) and now a glass house. (Ibid.) In each case it was a powerful talisman of protection; and its colour was merely the mark of distinction between the different orders. The Druids' crystal was white ; the bards' skyblue, the eubates' green, and the aspirants' was distinguished by a mixture of all these colours. The secret of manufacturing them rested solely with the Druids.

[63] " A crystal ring Abdaldar wore ;
The powerful gem condensed
Primeval dews that upon Caucasus
Felt the first winter's frost.
. . . . .it may have charms
To blind or poison."
Southey's Thalaba, vol. i., p. 84, .108

he was now about to be fully instructed. It was the death and burial of the mysteries; and on its expiration he was said to be newly born from the womb of Ceridwen, and was pronounced a regenerate person, cleansed from his former impurities by the mystical contents of her cauldron. When his term of probation expired, his qualifications were ascertained by propounding many abstruse queries in the branches of science to which his attention has been directed.[64]

This confinement and subsequent emancipation was represented by a continuation of the former kind of symbols. The candidate, while under the supposed form of a grain of pure wheat, was encountered by his pursuer, Ceridwen the fury,[65] in the shape of a high-crested hen,[66] who selected him from the heap amongst which he lay, and swallowed him. He is said to have remained nine months in her womb, to depict the period of his seclusion from the world in the Pastos, the door of which was reputed to be under the guardianship of the terrible divinity Buanawr,[67] armed with a drawn sword, whose vindicative rage, excited by the pusillanimity, or unworthiness of the aspirant, would make earth, hell, and heaven itself tremble.[68] When the full

[64] The nature of this intellectual investigation may be estimated from the following specimen selected out of Davies's Druids. (p. 50). "At what time and to what extent will land be productive? What is the extent and diameter of the earth? Who is the regulator between heaven and earth? What brings forth the glain from the working of stones? Where do the cuckoos, which visit us in the summer, retire during the winter? Who carried the measuring line of the Lord of causes—what scale was used when the heavens were reared aloft; and who supported the curtain from the earth to the skies? Knowest thou what thou art in the hour of sleep; a mere body, a mere soul, or a secret retreat of light? What supports the fabric of the habitable earth? Who is the Illuminator of the soul; who has seen—who knows him?" &c.

[65] Geridwen wrach. Welsh Archæol., vol. i., p. 19.

[66] Vid. Davies. Remarks on British Coins.

[67] Dav. Druid. Append., No. vii.

[68] The duty of this relentless Janitor was, to prevent unlawful intrusion, and to see that the candidate went through his probation with becoming fortitude and perseverance. On the flat stone which covered this miserable place of penance, denominated by Taliesin, *the gate of hell*, (Priddeu Annwn. W. Archæol., vol. i., p. 45,) a sheathed sword was placed, to denote equally a love of justice and peace, (Owen's Dict. v. Cromlec.) and a certain retribution if the sanctuary were profaned by cowardice or irresolution.

period of gestation in the womb of Ceridwen was complete, the aspirant was prepared for the consummation of his knowledge; and, after a very dangerous process had been successfully braved, he received the highest and most ineffable degree of light and purity which mortal man was esteemed able either to confer or receive. This was emblematically performed by placing *the new-born infant* in a coracle,[69] or small boat, covered with a skin, and committing it to the mercy of the winds and waves. The candidate was actually set adrift in the open sea on the evening of the 29th of April,[70] and was obliged to depend on his own address and presence of mind to reach the opposite shore in safety. This dangerous nocturnal expedition was the closing act of initiation, and sometimes proved the closing scene of life. If he possessed a strong arm and a well fortified heart, he might succeed in gaining the safe landing-place on *Gwyddno's wear*, which was the typical mountain where the Ark rested when the waters of the Deluge had subsided; but, if either of these failed during the enterprise, the prospect before him was little less than certain death. Hence, on beholding across a stormy sea, at the approach of night, the dashing waves breaking on the wear at an immense and almost hopeless distance, the timid probationer has frequently been induced to distrust his own courage, and abandon the undertaking altogether. A refusal which brought on a formal and contemptuous rejection from the hierophant, and the candidate was pronounced unworthy of a participation in the honours and distinctions to which he aspired; and to which, from this moment, he was for ever ineligible. "Thy coming without external purity;" thus was he addressed in a prescribed formulary, "is a pledge that I

[69] This description of boat is still used by the fishermen of Wales. "These coracles," says Wyndham, in his Tour through Wales, "are generally five feet and a half long, and four feet broad; their bottom is a little rounded, and their shape is exactly oval. They are ribbed with light laths, or split twigs, in the manner of basket work, and are covered with a raw hide and strong canvass, pitched in such a manner as to prevent leaking. A seat crossed just above the centre towards the broad end. The men paddle them with one hand, and fish with the other; and when their work is finished, bring their boats home on their backs."

[70] Fab. Pag. Idol., vol. iii., p. 177.

will not receive thee. Take out the gloomy one. From my territory have I alienated the useful steed;—my revenge upon the shoal of earthworms is, their hopeless longing for the pleasant allotment. Out of the receptacle which is thy aversion did I obtain the Rainbow."[71] But the fearless aspirant who surmounted all these dangers was triumphantly received from the water on May eve[72] by the Arch-druid, the representative of Gwiddno, and his companions, and unhesitatingly announced his own inspiration by proclaiming himself capable to foretell future events. Thus the three precious drops of efficacious water from the cauldron of Ceridwen; or, in other words, the three mysterious degrees, were no sooner attained, than the candidate received the undisputed power of vaticination in its highest form.[73] The fermented contents of the cauldron were reputed poisonous, after the three efficacious drops had been disengaged from the boiling vessel, and appropriated to the fortunate aspirant, which referred to the doctrine of regeneration; for the refuse of the concoction was supposed to be deeply impregnated with all the impurities of which the renovated novice was now disburdened. But the three drops in which the accumulated virtues of the cauldron were concentrated, had the reputation of conveying, not only unlimited wisdom and knowledge, but also the inestimable gift of immortality.

The completion of the Three Degrees was termed being *thrice born;*[74] the adept thenceforward was denomi-

---

[71] Welsh Archæol., vol. i., p. 165.   Dav. Druid., p. 251.

[72] The following custom may have originated from an indistinct tradition of this ceremony.   "Near Clifton is a famous spring where the people go annually every May-day to drink, *by a custom beyond all remembrance;* they hold it an earnest of good luck in the ensuing year to be there and *drink of the water before sunrise.*" (Stukeley. Itin. Cur., vol. ii., p. 45.)

[73] How questionable soever these powers might be, they conferred an *actual* superiority on the initiated, which he seldom failed to exert to his own personal advantage.   Let us raise our hands in devout gratitude to Him who brought life and immortality to light, for delivering us from the power of such a gross and dreadful superstition as that under which the first occupiers of our soil were enthralled!

[74] In a poem of Taliesin, to which I have often referred, he pronounces himself *thrice born* after the concluding scene of his initiation.   First he was born of his natural parent; then from the

nated Dedwydd, (*Εποπτης*) and could say to the multitude of the profane, Stand by, come not near me, I am
holier than ye!⁷⁵ and the benefits resulting from this
privilege were so various and important, as amply to
compensate for the danger necessarily incurred in the
process. These benefits rendered the possessor eligible
for any ecclesiastical, civil, or military dignity, and consisted of every species of instruction which had a tendency to store the mind with wisdom, fortitude, and
virtue. The whole circle of human science was open to
his investigation;⁷⁶ the knowledge of divine things was
communicated without reserve; he was now enabled to
perform the mysterious rites of worship, and had his
understanding enriched with an elaborate system of
morality.

womb of Ceridwen, the mythological Ark, where he was a representative of the Arkite patriarch; and lastly from the coracle, or
Ark itself. To this effect also the Brahmins say, "The first birth
is from a natural mother; the second from the ligature of the zone;
the third from the due performance of the sacrifice (of initiation); such
are the births of him who is usually called thrice born, according to
the text of the Veda." (Ordin. of Menu. Sir W. Jones' Works, vol.
iii., p. 106.) The Greeks also styled their Epopts, *τριγονος,* thrice
born; and the last birth, like that of Taliesin, was from an Ark. A
passage in the Geeta, (p. 67,) assigns perfection to the Yogee who
had accomplished *many births.*

⁷⁵ Isaiah lxv., 5.

⁷⁶ This superior knowledge was that particular species of worldly
wisdom on which the Prophet pronounces this severe invective.
Every man is brutish by his knowledge. (Jerem. li., 17.)

LECTURE IX.

THE initiations were finally completed at day-break; and at the rising of the sun, an awful period with those who practised the Sabian idolatry, as a decisive proof of his cabalistic attainments, the adept was required to exhibit his skill in the art of divination. These mystical performances were of various kinds. On high occasions the entrails of sacrifices afforded them every information they could desire on all subjects which came under their consideration. They predicted future events from the flight of birds;[1] by white horses;[2] by the agitation of water, or hydromancy, and by lots.[3] The latter process, being the most celebrated, may merit a brief description. *One hundred and forty-seven* shoots were cut from the apple tree, with many superstitious ceremonies; they were exactly of the same length, but with a varied diversity of branchings and ramifications, each being a secret symbol representing a word, a letter, or an idea. These were the elementary principles by which the result was effected. Being cast into a white napkin, after certain incantations the divine will was ascertained on any specified subject by taking an indifferent number of these tallies indiscriminately from the napkin, and skilfully developing the mysterious ideas which they appeared to convey. Of all the secrets of Druidism, this appears to have been the most highly esteemed. It

[1] Taliesin. Mic Dinbych. Welsh Archæol., vol. i., p. 67.
[2] Borl. Ant. Corn., p. 134.
[3] Taliesin. Kadair Teyrn On. Welsh Archæol., vol. i. p. 65. Sir R. C. Hoare discovered in a tumulus near Stonehenge, amidst some ashes and burned bones, four small bone trinkets, which he supposes were used for casting lots. They are oblong, about three quarters of an inch one way, by half an inch the other, and about one-eighth of an inch in thickness. One side is flat and the other convex, and they are each adorned with a separate and distinguishing device. This great antiquary ranks them amongst the most eminent curiosities which he had been fortunate enough to discover in all his laborious and comprehensive researches; and considers them as forming a step towards the use of letters.

was celebrated by the bards in all the language of grave and lofty panegyric; and even the possession of an orchard containing one hundred and forty-seven apple trees of equal size, age, and beauty, with wide spreading branches, and pure white blossoms, succeeded by delicious fruit, was a prize more splendid and desirable than any temporal dignity or spiritual rank.[4]

It is to be remarked that one hundred and forty-seven was a magical number, produced by multiplying the square of *seven* by the sacred number *three;* for, like the rest of the world, the Druids paid the most sacred regard to *odd numbers.* In them, some unusual charm was supposed to exist which would propitiate the favour of the deity, and secure to the pious worshipper the blessing of divine protection. The number *three* was held in peculiar veneration by this order of men; and hence the arrangement of classes both in civil and religious polity partook of a ternary form.[5] Nothing could be transacted without a reference to this number. On solemn occasions, the processions were formed *three times* round the sacred inclosure of Caer Sidi;[6] their invocations were *thrice* repeated, and even their poetry was composed in *triads.*[7] The *ternary* deiseal,[8] or procession from east to

---

[4] Myrdyin's Avallenau, in Dav. Druid., p. 465.
[5] Thus Gaul was divided into three provinces, the Belgæ, the Acquitani, and the Celtæ; the inhabitants were of three classes, the Druids, the Equites, and the Plebs; and the hierarchy consisted of three gradations, the Druids, the Bards, and the Eubates. Wales, England, and Scotland, were denominated Cymru, Lloeger and Alban; and Robert of Gloucester gives these names to the three sons of his fabulous king Brutus.

> But this noble prince sones had thre,
> By hys wyf Innogen, noble men and fre,
> Locryn and Kamber and Albanak al so, &c.

[6] Pennant's Tour in Scotl., P. ii., p. 15.
[7] The triads of the bards, like the proverbs of every country in the world, were a series of truisms wrapt up in pithy sentences adapted to oral transmission; and it appears highly probable that many of the abstruse secrets of religion; the sacred lore of Druidism; the institutional maxims of the bards, were communicated in this form, as well calculated for being treasured up in the memory; for we have it on record that these secrets were contained in 20,000 verses, which required twenty years' study to understand perfectly. (P. Mela, l. 3, c. 2. Ces., l. 6, c. 2.) The public triads, however, which were scattered amongst the people, did not exceed three hundred, according to tradition (W. Arch., vol. 2, p. 75), of which little more than a third part have descended to our times (Dav. Dru., p. 30).
[8] Toland. Druids, p. 108.

west by the south,[9] accompanied all their rites whether
civil or religious,[10] and nothing was accounted sanctified
without the performance of this preliminary ceremony.[11]
They entertained a similar veneration for the number
seven;[12] taught that the upper regions of the air contained
seven heavens; and gave to man *seven* external senses,
appetite and aversion being added to hearing, seeing,
feeling, tasting, and smelling.   The combinations oi
seven and three were hence, in all their forms, esteemed
sacred.   Thus their great period of *thirty* years was produced by the sum of seven and three multiplied by
three; and we have already seen that the magical number one hundred and forty-seven was so much esteemed
because it proceeded from the square of 7×3.   Several
Druid monuments are still in existence, consisting of
nineteen upright stones $(7+3+3^2)$, in allusion to the
cycle of the sun and moon, commonly called the Metonic
cycle, which was familiar to the Druids of Britain.[13]

[9] This custom might probably have been adopted from the Pythagorean philosophy, which represented Light by the circular motion
from east to west, and Darkness by the contrary course.   Thus
Timœus the Locrian says, in a disquisition on the science of astronomy, "The sun maketh day in performing his course from east to west,
and night by motion from west to east."
[10] Jamieson. Scot. Dict. in vo. Widdersinnis.
[11] It may be added that this number was invested with peculiar
properties, by every nation under heaven, some referring its origin to
the *three* great circles in the heavens, two of which the sun touches
in his annual course, and the third he passes over; and others to
some ancient, though mutilated tradition of either the Trinity, or the
arkite triad.
[12] Vide ut supra, Lect. 7, in notâ.
[13] Diod. Sic., l. xii., c. 6.   A striking monument of Druidism, both
with respect to form and situation, still exists near Keswick, which
contains an adytum in complete preservation, and has been constructed
with a due regard to the sacred numbers.   It is called Carles or
Castle Rigg, and is about *thirty* paces $(7+3 \times 3)$ from east to west,
and twenty-one (3×7) from north to south.   The adytum is situated
at the *eastern* extremity, and consists of a quadrangular inclosure
seven paces by *three*.   At about *three* paces without the inclosure on
the west, stood a single upright stone which is now broken, so that
the primitive elevation cannot be ascertained.   It was a representative of the deity.   From this august temple a view was presented to
the eye of the superstitious Briton, calculated to awaken all his energies, and rouse the latent sparks of devotion.   The holy mountain of
Skiddaw, with its single elevated peak soaring up to heaven; Carrick
Heigh with its two peaks; and Saddleback, or more properly, Blenc-
Arthur, with its perfect character of three distinct peaks, were all

The possession of the orchard containing one hundred and forty-seven apple trees above noticed was, however, figurative. The orchard represented the place of initiation; the apple trees were the Druids; the white blossoms, their garments; the fruit, their doctrine, while the strong and vigorous branches represented their power and authority, which, in many cases, exceeded that of the monarch. They were the sole interpreters of religion, and consequently superintended all sacrifices, for no private person was allowed to offer a sacrifice without their sanction. They possessed the power of excommunication, which was the most horrible punishment that could be inflicted; and, from the effects of this curse, the highest magistrate was not exempt. They resided in sumptuous palaces, and sat on thrones of gold.[14] The great council of the realm was not competent to declare war or conclude peace without their concurrence. They determined all disputes by a final and unalterable decision;[15] and even had the power of inflicting the punishment of death.

visible from this consecrated spot; lending alike their aid to light up the fire of religion in his soul; and to expand his mind with veneration for the powerful author of such stupendous imagery.

[14] Dion. Chrys., cited by Borlase. Ant. Corn., p. 79.

[15] The Logan, or rocking stone, was a fearful engine of Druidical judgment, and erected for the purpose of imposing a degree of reverence for the persons of the Druids, which was unattainable by ordinary means. This kind of artificial curiosity is of great antiquity. Faber (Mys. Cab., vol. i., p. 111,) says, that it was in allusion to the scriptural Bethel (Gen. xxviii., 19), that Sanchoniatho mentions "that Uranus contrived stones, called Betulia, *which possessed the power of motion as if they were instinct with life.* These were, in all probability, sacred Rocking Stones; numbers of which, erected by the Druids, are to be found in various parts of our own island." The people were impressed with an idea that no power but the all-controlling fiat of the divinity could move these stones upon their basis, and hence they were referred to as oracles to determine the innocence or guilt of an accused person. A stupendous specimen of the Logan is found at Brimham Craggs in Yorkshire, which is thus described by Mr. Rock in the Archæology (vol. viii.): "It rests upon a kind of pedestal, and is supposed to be about one hundred tons in weight on each side. On examining the stone, it appears to have been shaped to a small knob at the bottom to give it motion, though my guide, who was about seventy years old, born on the moors, and well acquainted with these rocks, assured me that the stone had never been known to rock; however, upon my making trial round it, when I came to the middle of one side, I found it moved with great ease. The astonishing increase of the motion with the little force I gave it

The lowest degree of the mysteries conveyed the power of vaticination in its minor divisions. Borlase says,[16] "The Eubates or vates were of the third or lowest class; their name, as some think, being derived from *Thada*, which, amongst the Irish, commonly signifies *magic*, and their business was to foretell future events; to be ready on all common occasions to satisfy the inquiries of the anxious and credulous." The Druids practised augury for the public service of the state;[17] while the Eubates were merely fortune-tellers, and dealers in charms and philtres, to recover lost treasure, or to excite the soft passion of love; and they were the authors of an abundance of ridiculous superstitions and absurd ceremonies to promote good fortune or avert calamity, many of which remain to this day.[18]

Symbolical instruction is recommended by the constant usage of antiquity; and retained its influence throughout all ages, as a system of mysterious communication. Even the Deity himself, in his revelation to man, condescended to adopt the use of material images for the purpose of enforcing sublime truths, as is evident

---

made me very apprehensive the equilibrium might be destroyed; but, on examining it, I found it was so nicely balanced that there was no danger of it falling. The construction of this equipoised stone must have been by artists well skilled in the powers of mechanics." Dr. Borlase has described these stones with much minuteness (Ant. Corn., b. iii., c. 4).

[16] Ant. Corn., p. 67.

[17] "We have many instances," says Stukeley (Itin. Cur., vol. ii., p. 14), "of Druid men and women endued with the spirit of prophecy. I shall mention but one out of Josephus (Ant. Jud., xviii.). The Jewish Agrippa fell into the displeasure of Tiberius, who put him in bonds. As he stood leaning against a tree before the palace, an owl perched upon that tree: a German Druid, one of the Emperor's guards, spoke to him to be of good cheer, for he should be released from those bonds, and arrive at great dignity and power; but bid him remember that when he saw the bird again, he should live but five days. All this came to pass. He was made king by Caligula;—St. Paul preached before him; and Josephus speaks of his death agreeably to the prediction."

[18] The system of vaticination was ultimately prostituted by the Druids themselves to unworthy purposes, in which fraud and pecuniary emolument appear to be the most striking features. Dr. Borlase and Meyrick have enumerated, at great length, these glaring impositions on a superstitious and abused people, and their respective works may be referred to by those who feel any curiosity on the subject (Ant. Corn., b. ii., c. 21. Meyrick. Hist. Cardig. Introd.)

throughout the prophetical and inspired writings.[19] The mysterious knowledge of the Druids, in like manner, was imbedded in signs and symbols. Taliesin, describing his initiation, says, " The secrets were imparted to me by the old giantess, *without the use of audible language.*"[20] And again, in the poem called his Chair, he says, " I am a *silent* proficient."[21] The symbols which could contain the learning and morality of the Druids, must necessarily have been both numerous and significant. From a multiplicity of these emblems, I have selected the following, as being decidedly characteristic of the people and of the institution.

The *anguinum ovum* was a very important symbol, and contained some highly mysterious allusions. As an Egg is the fountain of life, this serpent's egg referred, properly, to the Ark while it floated on the expanse of waters, and held within its inclosure every living creature. It was attended by *a serpent* entwined round the centre of the amulet, to signify the superintending care which an *eternal* Being affords to his worshippers.[22] It had the reputed

[19] See, particularly, the books of Jeremiah and Ezekiel; the Parables of Our Saviour, and the Apocalypse. In the Theocratic Philosophy of Freemasonry, Lect. vii., the subject is copiously explained. [20] Welsh Archæol., vol. i., p. 166.

[21] Ibid., p. 37. The Druids were great lovers of *silence*, and enforced the observance of it with much rigour at their public assemblies. If a loquacious member incautiously violated the solemn stillness of their meetings, he was publicly admonished three several times. A repetition of the offence was punished by placing a conspicuous mark upon his robe, and declaring that *the sword was naked against him;* (Priddeu Annwn, Welsh Arch., vol. i., p. 45,) and if this failed to correct the impropriety of his conduct, expulsion ensued; and, in exaggerated cases, a still more severe and signal punishment.

[22] The anguinum, or Druids' egg, was said to be produced by a knot of serpents, and, being propelled into the air, was caught in the vestment of the priest, and carried off with great rapidity, to avoid the fury of its parents. This egg, if genuine, was said always to float, so did the Ark. The method of its formation was, however, fabulous, or, to use the words of Mr. Davies, (Myth. Dru., p. 210,) " was but so much dust thrown into the eyes of the profane multitude." The Druids were the serpents, and the eggs were crystals curiously contrived to conceal within their substance the mysterious tokens of the highest orders, which were not even revealed to the person in whose custody they were placed, but on full and substantial proof of his wisdom and prudence, and in union with the solemn investiture of their ineffable degrees of perfection, to which no person was eligible as a candidate who could not produce one of these magical crystals, as a token of due preparation and previous acceptance.

virtue of procuring favour to the possessor,[23] and was
believed capable of conveying a decided advantage in
any legal suit or process.[24] The *serpent* and *egg*[25] was a
symbol of the Ark and its tenant Hu, and no other proof
is wanting of the importance which the Druids attached
to this emblem, than the fact, that the temple of Abury,
one of the most stupendous erections which ancient
Britain could boast, was constructed in the precise form
of a circle, an acknowledged symbol of the arkite egg, to
which a vast serpent was attached.[26]

The *Rainbow* was the Druidical emblem of protection;
it was believed, figuratively, to surround the aspirant
when delivered from his confinement in the pastos or
Ark. Thus the Bard says, " My belt has been a *Rainbow.*"[27] The *Boat* bore a reference to the Ark, or its
representative Ceridwen. The glain was a *boat of glass*,
and was probably presented during the ceremonies of the
insular sanctuary, to the successful probationer, as a
testimony of his competence to be admitted to the
superior degrees.[28] The *Wheel* was a famous Druidical

[23] Toland. Hist. Druids, vol. i., p. 60.
[24] So extensively was this belief propagated, that the Emperor
Claudius Cesar actually put a gentleman of Rome to death for pleading
a cause with the anguinum in his bosom. (Plin. Nat. Hist., l. xxix.,
c. 3.)
[25] A splendid variety of this amulet was found by Sir R. C. Hoare,
in a large tumulus in the vicinity of Stonehenge, which Stukeley distinguished by the name of Bush Barrow. It consists of a curious
perforated stone of the kind called tabularia, moulded into the form
of an egg, and highly polished, and containing, in the veins of the
fossil, an intricate mass of small serpents entwined together in every
possible combination. From the situation in which this extraordinary
amulet was found, I should pronounce it to be the burial place of the
Supreme Archdruid of the British dominions; and, more particularly,
as the same tumulus contained, also, a rich breastplate of gold, in the
form of a lozenge, and highly decorated with carved work and devices.
[26] In war, the British armies were attended by a magical banner,
which had been ritually consecrated by the Druids, and emblazoned
with a symbolical device. In the centre was a serpent, surmounted
by the meridian sun, and supported by the great father and mother of
the human species, personified in Hu and Ceridwen.
[27] Marwnad Uthyr Pendragon. Davies, p. 559.
[28] The glain and anguinum were evidently artificial, and composed
of some vitrified substance, the secret of which was known only to the
Druids. They were considered equally potential in the communication
of benefits. This boat of glass was a sign or diploma of initiation,
which was capable of introducing the possessor to the sacred solemni-
ties without examination or proof

symbo,, and has been thought to refer to the astronomical cycles. It was, in fact, a representation of the mundane circle, as were also the round temples of Britain. It had a further reference to the rainbow.[29] The *White trefoil* was a symbol of *union*, not only from the circumstance of its including the mystical triad; but also because the Druids saw or pretended to see, in every leaf, a faint representation of the lunette, or six days moon, which was an object of their veneration, from its resemblance to a boat or ark.[30] It was the powerful pledge or symbol which demanded and conveyed mutual aid in the moment of peril; a never-failing token of everlasting brotherhood, esteem, goodwill, and assistance, even unto death. The *Chain* was symbolical of the *penance* imposed on every candidate for initiation by his confinement in the pastos. The phrase, he submitted to the chain, implied that he had endured the rigours of preparation and initiation with patience and fortitude. The *Spica, or ear of corn*, was an emblem of *plenty* and prosperity; and a *Wheat straw* was an invaluable symbol, and the conservater of many potent virtues.[31]

The *Oak* was a symbol of an expanded mind; the *Reed*, of deceitfulness; and the *Aspen leaf*, of instability.[32] The *oak tree* was the visible representative of Don or Daron, and was considered as peculiarly sanctified by the gods, if not their immediate residence. The fairest tree[33] in the grove[34] was, therefore, solemnly consecrated to this

[29] Thus, Arianrod (Iris) is termed by the bards, the goddess of the silver wheel, who throws her gracious beams of protection round the candidate when his initiation is completed. (Davies on Ancient British Coins.)

[30] The commencement of their local divisions of time, months, years, and ages, were regulated by the moon when six days old. (Plin. Nat. Hist., l. xxv., c. 44.)

[31] A wheat straw, formed into a dart, was supposed, by some inherent magical sympathies, to be capable of destroying wild beasts and noxious animals;—by the same fragile article, compacts were formed; and, by breaking the straw, an agreement was dissolved. (Vid. Dav. Celt. Res., p. 178.)

[32] Dav. Celt. Res., p. 247.

[33] This represented the central tree in the garden of Eden, (Gen. ii., 9,) and was a transcript of a similar superstition all over the world. Isaiah gives a curious illustration of this practice, as used by the idolaters for purification. (Isaiah lxvi., 17.)

[34] Plin. Nat. Hist. l. xii., c. 1.

god with many superstitious ceremonies.[35] Sometimes it was divested of its collateral branches, and one of the largest was so fixed as to preserve the form of a gigantic cross.[36] The *Misletoe* of the oak was a symbol of protection in all dangers and difficulties, whether mental or corporeal. Its medicinal properties were so highly estimated, that it acquired the comprehensive name of *All Heal*, and was considered a never-failing remedy for all diseases.[37] It was reputed to counteract the effects of poison, to prevent sterility; and, in a word, it was esteemed a grand preservative against all evils, moral and physical.[38] The *Selago*, *Samolus*, and other medicinal plants, were gathered with similar ceremonies, and invested with peculiar virtues. The *Beehive* was used as an emblem of industry; but the hive referred to the Ark, and the initiated, or thrice born, were termed bees.[39] Another symbol of the Ark was the *Beaver*; and a *Cube* was the emblem of truth.[40]

The Druids had also a comprehensive system of symbolical language.[41] Thus it was said of the uninitiated:

[35] Probably from an old tradition of the *trees of knowledge and life* in the garden of Eden, (Gen. iii., 5, 22,) for it is certain that the ideas of *science* and *immortality* were combined in this sacred tree.

[36] Borl. Ant. Corn., p. 108.

[37] Its efficacy depended, however, in a great measure, on the superstitions used at the ceremony of detaching it from the tree. The archdruid, himself, was alone deemed worthy to pluck the misletoe; and, lest it should sustain pollution in the act of gathering, and thus expose the whole nation to divine vengeance, he very carefully purified himself with consecrated water. Two white bulls, secured for the first time by the horns, (Maur. Ind. Ant., vol. vi., p. 85,) were provided as an offering of propitiation, and when the moon was six days old, the archdruid, clad in his white vestment and red tiara, ascended the tree with naked feet, severed the plant with a golden hook, held in his left hand, which had never before been used, and received it in the *sagus* or sacred vest, amidst the shouts and acclamations of the people. The bulls were then sacrificed, and prayers offered to the gods, that they would sanctify their own gift.

[38] Plin. Nat. Hist., l. xvi., c. 44. Acorns were offered in sacrifice to their deities. (Welsh Archæol.. vol. i., p. 66.)

[39] In Egypt, the bee was an emblem of a prince ruling his subjects in prosperity and peace.

[40] Borl. Ant. Corn., p. 82. "The Bards had a secret," says Meyrick. "like the Freemasons, *by which they knew one another;* and, indeed, it has been supposed by some, that Masonry is Bardism in disguise.' (Hist. Card., Introd.)

[41] Thus the sacred phrase the language of the Chair, which origin

" They know not on what day the stroke will be given; nor what hour the agitated person would be born; or who prevented his going into the dales of Devwy. They know not the brindled ox, with the thick headband, having seen seven score knobs in his collar."[42] Here we have an evident, though concise, description of certain ceremonies characteristic of the Three Degrees through which th candidate has been successively passed. The stroke and the new birth have been already explained. The ox with the thick headband had an undoubted reference to a peculiar ceremony, which was practised during the initiations.[43] It was said to be attended by three Cranes,[44] one of which perched on his head, another on the middle of his back, and the third at the extremity, near the tail. These birds emblematically represented the Sun[45] at his rising, meridian, and setting, personified in the three principal officers in the mysteries. A crane symbolized the vigilant priesthood, and was sacred to the sun;[46] and hence the strict propriety of the emblem. The *headband* pointed out the state of subjection to which the animal

ally denoted the sacred method of communicating the most sublime mysteries of the Order, without the actual pronunciation of words, was at length clothed with the highest degree of importance by being identified with the chief dignity of Druidism; for the archdruid, at the time of his installation, was invested with absolute sovereignty, and received the significant appellation of Cadeiriaith, the literal meaning of which is, the language of the chair.

[42] Taliesin. Priddeu Annwn, translated by Dav. Dru., Append. iii.

[43] This animal, which was otherwise termed Beer Lled, or the flaming Bull, was a symbol of the patriarch Hu, who subjected him to the yoke, and instructed the Britons in the art of agriculture, from whence he derived the name of Centaur, ($\kappa\varepsilon\nu$ $\tau\alpha\nu\varrho\sigma\varsigma$) or the tamer of the bull. It referred also to the Sun, of which Hu was the representative. "Baal, the sun," says Mr. Faber, "was not unfrequently represented under the form of the Noetic symbol, the Bull; while the goddess Baaltis or Baalah, bore the figure of a heifer. Baal and Baaltis are the same mythological characters as Osiris and Isis (or Hu and Ceridwen,) whose symbols were, in a similar manner, a bull and a heifer; and who were Noah and the Ark, adored in conjunction with the Sun and Moon". (Fab. Mys. Cab., vol. i., p. 189.)

[44] Borl. Ant. Corn., p. 106.

[45] Here we have in Britain, as in Persia, the emblem of the Bull and Sun.

[46] The Egyptian crane received its name Ibis (אש Fire, אב Father,) because it was consecrated to the god of Light; perhaps from the colour of the bird, which rendered it sacred.

had been reduced, alluding to the long and weary confinement of the candidate in the pastos, where, in the
language of the bard, he was " subjected to the yoke for
his affliction ;" and the seven score knobs,[47] was a combination of the sacred number s*seven* and *three* ; $((7+3+3^2)$
$\times7+7)$ and doubtless had some mysterious astronomical
allusion.

The divine unity was a doctrine admitted by the
Druids.[48] They taught that time was only an intercepted
fragment of eternity ; and there are strong grounds for
believing that they held the Pythagorean hypothesis of
an endless succession of worlds; for it is well known
that they believed the earth to have sustained one general
destruction by water; and expected that it would undergo another by fire.[49] They admitted the doctrines of
the immortality of the soul,[50] a future state,[51] and a day
of judgment which will be conducted on the principle of
man's responsibility. In a word, the primitive religion
of the Druids was purely patriarchal ;[52] and they retained some knowledge of the redemption of mankind through
the death of a mediator.[53] Their place of eternal punishment was a quagmire of never-ending frost, and abounding with noxious insects and venomous reptiles. But,
though the most early Druids practised, with some varia-
tions, the rites of true worship, yet, in process of time,
other deities were introduced into the system ; and at
length, they paid divine honours to deceased mortals, who
were considered the representatives of the sun, the moon,
and all the host of Heaven.[54] A tradition of the Deluge[55]

[47] In Maurice's Plates of the Indian Avaters, the sacred Cow is uniformly depicted with a collar composed of a similar wreath of knobs.
[48] We learn from Selden that their invocations were made to the
ONE all-preserving power ; and they argued that, as this power was not
matter, it must necessarily be the deity ; and the sacred symbol used
to express his Name was O.I.W. (Signs and Symbols, Lect. 2.)
[49] Conditum mundum credebant, says Cesar, et aliquando igni peri-
turum.   [50] Borl. Ant. Corn., p. 98.
[51] Cesar de bel. Gal., l. vi., c. 13.
[52] Stukeley, Itin. Cur., vol. ii., p. 14.   [53] Cesar, ut supra.
[54] Vide my Hist. of Beverley, p. 19, in notâ 14.
[55] The legend preserved amongst the British Druids is inserted in
Signs and Symbols, (Lect. 5,) and History of Beverley, (p. 11,) where
it is evident that the vessel without sails was the Ark of Noah ; (Gen.
vi., 14,) the bursting of the lake referred to the description of the
great central abyss; (Ibid. vii., 11,) the service performed by the Ychen

was perpetuated in these rites; perverted, indeed, and localized, like that of most other nations; and the circumstances attending this tradition appear to have pervaded their most solemn rites and ceremonies. The doctrine of transmigration formed a leading feature in the Druidical system,[56] and was extended to the belief tha the departed soul of a virtuous individual possessed the secret power of infusing itself at pleasure into any substance, whether animate or inanimate.[57]

The Druids cultivated, and taught to their disciples, many of the liberal sciences,[58] and particularly astronomy, in which they attained a considerable proficiency, displayed in the construction of their religious edifices.[59]

Banawg. or the oxen of Hu Gadarn, was emblematical of the sun drying up the waters from the face of the earth; (Ibid. viii., 13,) for Hu was the helio-arkite deity; and the assurance of preservation, commemorative of Noah's rainbow, (Ibid. ix. 13,) was undoubtedly symbolized in the Chair of Ceridwen.

[56] Cesar, de bel. Gal. l. vi., c. 14.

[57] Hence a deceased friend could give force to a warrior's sword; could occupy his shield, or avert a flying javelin, armed with destruction. This is amply illustrated in the poem of Cynddelw, addressed to Owen Cyveiliawy, Prince of Powis. (Dav. Dru., p. 15.) "In the form of a vibrating shield before the rising tumult, borne aloft on the shoulder of the leader—in the form of a lion before the chief with the mighty wings—in the form of a terrible spear with a glittering blade—in the form of a bright sword spreading fame in the conflict, and overwhelming the levelled rank—in the form of a dragon (banner) before the sovereign of Britain,—and in the form of a daring wolf, has Owen appeared."

[58] Alcuin, an Anglo-Saxon writer, says, that in these early times a liberal education comprised grammar, rhetoric, arithmetic, geometry, music, and astrology. (Alc. Gram. apud Canis., tom. ii., par. i., p. 508.) Aldhelm extended it to the seven liberal sciences of Freemasonry. (Ald. de laud. vir., p. 331.)

It must be confessed, however, that at the period of the Roman invasion under Cesar, the people were still extremely rude in their diet and mode of life. (Strabo, l. 4, Diod. Sic., l. 4.) Some went entirely naked; Xiphil., l. 21.) others were clothed in the skins of beasts; (Cesar, l. 5, c. 14,) and the state in which they were found, induced the Romans to style them barbarians. (Herodian., l. 3, Pomp. Mela., l. 3. c. 6.)

[59] The time of celebrating public worship sprang from an application of this science. Thus their ordinary times of devotion were regulated by the phases of the moon; and the more solemn quarterly assemblages took place when the sun arrived at the equinoctial and solstitial points; (Stukeley, Abury, p. 68,) which at the era of their establishment, about 4000 years ago, corresponded with our 1st May, which was their grand annual festival, the 19th August, 1st November, and

They considered day as the offspring of night, because
night or chaos was in existence before day was created ;[60]
and hence their computations were made by nights in
preference to days.[61]   They divided the heavens into constellations, and were conversant with the laws and
motions of the planets, from which they made celestial
observations to determine the result of any important
transaction, and to foretell the prominent events which
were fated to distinguish the lives or fortunes of individuals ; thus converting a noble science to the puerile
purposes of judicial astrology.

Their botanical knowledge was extensive, and applied
chiefly to the art of healing; hence Pliny terms the
Druids physicians.   They investigated, with great precision, the structure of the human body, and were the
most complete anatomists at that time existing in the
world.[62]   They understood foreign languages, according
to Cesar and Tacitus, and used the Greek character in
their writings ;[63] they cultivated the liberal sciences; and
their system of morality may claim and ensure our appro-
bation, if the Welsh triads are of any authority.   In the
Mythology of the British Druids,[64] Mr. Davies has given
a copious collection of the moral precepts which were

13th February.   The four seasons of the year were denominated
Gwanwyn (Spring), Hâv (Summer), Hydrev (Autumn), and Ganav
(Winter.)
    [60] Seld. in Gibs. Camd., col. xv.
    The Hebrews had the same peculiarity.   The evening and the
morning were the first day.   (Gen. i., 5.)   This mode of computing
time is still retained among us, for seven days are usually expressed
by the word sen'night; fourteen days by fortnight, &c.   The Druids
used lunar observations, and regulated their festivals by the aspect of
the moon.   Their ages were of thirty years' duration, each year containing twelve lunations, or 354 days.
    [62] It is presumed that they acquired much information on the sub-
ject of medicine from Pythagoras, who learned it in Chaldea, (Apuleius)
and practiced his own precepts by using the most temperate system
of diet, his food being chiefly composed of bread, herbs, and honey.
(Porph. de Abstin.)   The same practice was recommended by the
Druids, and hence the longevity of this order of men is satisfactorily
accounted for.   Pythagoras wrote a treatise on medicinal herbs, and
another on the sea onion, (Plin. Nat. Hist.,) which, it is said, he communicated to the Druids; and his instruction, added to their own
sedulous investigations into the causes of diseases, soon conferred on
them a high and merited celebrity in the science of medicine.
    [63] Cesar, de bel. Gal., l. vi.   [64] Page 76-79.

derived from the Druidical institution; and these precepts often produced a corresponding purity of thought, for it is confidently asserted that the bards had such a sacred regard for *the truth*[65], that it constituted the motto of their Order;[66] and it is even said that they would have had less reluctance in sacrificing their lives, than in renouncing a strict adherence to the truth in every situation and transaction of life.

[65] Hence the records they have left behind them, whether in the form of triads or historical poems, may be depended on as containing an allusion to pure historical facts or moral precepts. And though sometimes highly figurative, yet they may be referred to with some degree of confidence, as the depositories of moral, religious or political events which distinguished the times of which they profess to treat.

[66] Gerop. Becan.

LECTURE X.

HISTORY OF INITIATION INTO THE GOTHIC MYSTERIES.

THE Gothic Mysteries[1] were introduced by Sigge, a Scythian prince; who, it is said, abandoned his native country when it became oppressed by a population too dense for the comforts and necessities of a pastoral life; and. with a chosen band of followers, wandered in search of another settlement.[2] Travelling to the north-west of Europe, he assumed the name of Odin, the supreme deity

---

[1] The Gothic Mysteries were practised by all the northern nations of Europe. Mr. Turner (Angl. Sax., vol. iv., p. 18) says, "we are not authorized to ascribe to the Saxon deities the apparatus and mythology which the northern Scalds of subsequent ages have transmitted to us from Denmark, Norway, and Iceland;" meaning, undoubtedly, the mythology of the Eddas. I am inclined to think, however, that the Norwegians, Danes, and Saxons all practised the Gothic superstition, as it was remodelled by Sigge, who assumed the name of Odin a few years before the birth of Christ. This celebrated individual, after having established himself in Scandinavia, placed his sons in the territory around him as viceroys, and their respective divisions, after his death, became independent kingdoms. Suarlami had assigned to him a part of Russia; Baldeg had Western Saxony, and Segdeg East Saxony (Mal. North. Ant., vol. i., p. 62); and they would, doubtless, introduce his system of Religion amongst their new subjects, because they had experienced its advantages in enslaving the minds of an ignorant and superstitious people, and placing them implicitly under the control of their superiors. At this period the religion of Europe may be divided into four grand divisions—the Roman, the Celtic, the Sclavonian, and the Gothic; and, as the Saxons were a Gothic people, they would, undoubtedly, practise the Gothic superstitions. "The ancient Germans," says Bishop Percy. "Scandinavians, &c., being of Gothic race, professed that system of polytheism afterwards delivered in the Edda; and the Franks and Saxons who afterwards settled in Gaul and Britain, being of Gothic race, introduced the polytheism of their own nation, which was in general the same with what prevailed among all the other Gothic or Teutonic people, viz., the Germans, Scandinavians," &c. (Mal. North. Ant., Intr., vi., Note.)

[2] The Scythian and Hyperborean doctrines and mythology may be traced in every part of these eastern regions; nor can we doubt that Wod or Odin, whose religion, as the northern historians admit, was introduced into Scandinavia by a foreign race, was the same with Buddh, whose rites were probably imported into India nearly at the same time, though received much later by the Chinese, who softened his name into Fo. (Asiat. Res., vol. i., p. 425.)

of the Scandinavians,[3] and in his progress founded many empires, and performed such prodigies of valour, as are wholly incredible, except to the believers in Scandinavian tradition. In every country which he subdued, he introduced the eastern mysteries, modelled into a form subservient to his own secret purposes.[4] He placed over the celebrations twelve hierophants, whom he styled Drottes, and invested them with uncontrollable authority; they were alike priests, and counsellors of state, and judges, from whose decision there was no appeal.[5] Their power was extended to its utmost limits, by being allowed a discretionary privilege of determining on the choice of human victims for sacrifice. Even the monarch was not exempt from this choice. Hence arose the necessity of cultivating the esteem of these sovereign pontiffs; for if an officer of the highest dignity in the state became obnoxious to the Drottes, as the dreaded arbiters of life and death, from whose decision there was no appeal, his life was held by a very uncertain tenure; for at the very next celebration it was almost sure to be offered up in sacrifice to the gods.

This privilege was an abundant and never-failing source of wealth as well as influence; for the superstitious people, in the hope of averting a calamity so exceedingly dreadful, were profuse in their offerings and oblations; and in times of general calamity, when the blood of human victims[6] was necessary to appease their sanguinary

[3] Mal. North. Ant., vol. i., c. 4.

[4] The fact is, that the system of the warlike Sacas was of a military cast, and hence differed materially from the corresponding system practised by the hierophants of India, Greece, and Britain, derived, as they were, from the same source, on the plains of Chaldea. In a word, the two great Sects into which primitive idolatry had been divided, to serve the ambitious policy of their professors, were practised by the Britons and the Saxons, two immediate neighbours, who were ultimately blended into one and the same people.

[5] Mal. North. Ant., vol. i., p. 65. From this order proceeded the establishment of British juries, consisting of the same number of men, invested with similar powers.

[6] These sacrifices were all conducted on a principle of veneration for the sacred numbers three and nine; for every thrice three months, thrice three victims, many of them human, on each of the thrice three days of the festival's continuance, were offered in sacrifice to the tri-une god. (Mal. North. Ant., vol. i., p. 133.) "The number *nine* has long been held in great veneration among the Tartars, whence, probably, the Scandinavians derived their origin. All presents made

deities, tne oblations of the Drottes were of increased value, in proportion with the expected danger of the trembling suppliant. Hence, as this order of men, like the Israelitish priesthood, was restricted to one family, they became possessed of unbounded wealth, and erected splendid palaces for their residence. These immunities and distinctions increasing their power in every age, they ultimately became so proud, overbearing, and tyrannical, as to be objects of terror to all other classes of the community, which, in the end, accelerated their destruction. It was, indeed, credulity on the one hand, as well as artifice and imposture on the other, which originally placed the people thus at the entire disposal of the priest; but they at length grew weary of the increased oppressions under which they groaned; and, with minds thus prepared for any change which might promise to deliver them from the tyranny of priestly domination, the inhabitants of Scandinavia embraced the offer of Christianity with enthusiasm; and, inspired with a fanatical spirit of vengeance for accumulated and long-continued suffering, they retaliated with dreadful severity on their persecutors, and destroyed every vestige of the ancient religion. The palaces and temples, the statues of their gods, and all the paraphernalia of heathen superstition, perished in one common ruin;[7] and nothing remains to show the character of this religion, but a few Cromlechs; some stupendous monuments of rough stone which human fury was unable to destroy; certain ranges of caverns hewn out of the solid rock for the purpose of initiation, and some natural grottos which were, undoubtedly, applied to the same purpose.

The great festivals, annually commemorated by this

to their princes consist, in general, of *nine* of each article. At all their feasts this number and its combinations are always attended to in their dishes of meat, and in their skins of wine, and other liquors. At one entertainment, mentioned by the Tartar king Abulgazi Khan, there were nine thousand sheep, nine hundred horses, ninety-nine vessels of brandy, &c. Even the roving Tartars rob the caravans by this rule; and will rather take *nine* of anything than a greater number. Abulgazi Khan, in the preface to his history, says, "I have divided it into *nine* parts, to conform myself to the custom of other writers who all have this number in particular esteem." (Rich. Dissert. p. 270.)

[7] Mal. North. Ant., vol. i., p. 129.

people, were three; the most magnificent of which commenced at the winter solstice, and was celebrated in honour of Thor, the prince of the power of the air.[8]   It was commemorative of the creation; for, being the longest night in the year,[9] they assigned to it the formation of the world from primeval darkness, and called it MOTHER-NIGHT.[10]   This festival was denominated Yule Juul, or Yeol,[11] and was a season of universal festivity.[1] At the nocturnal meetings of this sacred celebration, the initiations were performed on a superb scale; for it was believed that the succeeding season would be fruitful or unpropitious, in proportion with the sumptuous[13] or

[8] Verstegan says, that " in the ayre hee gouerned the wyndes and the clowdes; and, being displeased, did cause lightning, thunder, and tempests, with excessive rain, and all il weather.   But, being wel pleased by the adoration, sacrifice, and seruice of his supplyants, hee then bestowed upon them most fayre and seasonable weather; and caused corne abundantly to growe; as also all sortes of fruites, &c., and kept away from them the plague, and all other evill and infectious diseases." (Rest. Dec. Intell., p. 75.)

[9] The feast was, in fact, sacred to Darkness, that great and awful principle which was a stumbling-block to the whole heathen world.

[10] Mal. North. Ant., vol. i., p. 358.

[11] Vid. Jamieson. Scott. Dict., v. Yule.

[12] When Christianity was first promulgated in the northern nations, the missionaries found the inhabitants unwilling to relinquish this annual rejoicing; the festival was, therefore, applied to the nativity of Christ; and hence the Yule Feast was denominated Christmas.   On the eve of the first day of the festival or *Mother-Night*, fires *of wood* blazed throughout the whole extent of northern Europe; hence the origin of our *Yule-clog*.   The peace-offerings dedicated to Thor at this season were cakes of flour sweetened with honey; hence the *Yule-cake*.   Subjects at this festival presented their annual gifts or benevolences to their sovereign (Johnston, Antiq. Celto-Scand., p. 230); hence *Christmas-boxes, New-year-gifts, &c.*   The candles of the Sun were said to illuminate the northern dwellings on the night before Yule; and hence arose the custom of burning large candles at this solemnity; for it boded ill luck to the family for the succeeding year if a second candle were lighted; whence our *Yule-candles*. (Vid. Jamieson, Scot. Dict., v. Yule, vi.)   I am informed by a Danish Brother, that cakes are still made in Denmark, of a particular form, at this season, composed of the finest flour, eggs, currants, and other ingredients; and are called *Juule-Kåger*.

[13] " The ancient inhabitants of the North were never at a loss for the means of celebrating their Yule.   Johnson (Antiq. Celto-Normann. has a note referring to this subject, which exhibits their character in its true light.   The Scandinavian expeditions, he says, were anciently conducted in the following manner: A chieftain sailed with a few ships for Britain, and collected all the scattered adventurers he could find in his way.   They landed on the coast, and formed a temporary

parsimonious manner in which this festival was conducted. The next celebration was dedicated to Frea,[14]
the goddess of pleasure ;[15] and commenced on the first
quarter of the second moon in the new year; and the
third was celebrated in honour of Odin, the god of battles. It commenced at the beginning of Spring, and was
celebrated with great magnificence in the hope of a successful warfare in the ensuing campaign.[16] These were
the three principal times of celebration ; but the initiations were performed at innumerable other smaller festi-

fortress. To this strong hold they drove all the cattle, and, having
salted them, the freebooters returned home, where they spent their
Jol [Yule] or brumal feast with much glee. Such an expedition was
called *Strandhoggua*, or a strand slaughter." (Jamieson, Scot. Dict.,
v. Yule, iii.)

[14] This goddess was the same as the Grecian Mylitta or Venus, and
probably derived her name from *Phree*, to be fruitful.

[15] Frea was esteemed equally the wife and daughter of Odin. (Mal.
North. Ant., vol. ii., p. 30.)

[16] It was esteemed disgraceful in any individual to quit these festivals
sober. (Mal. North. Ant., vol. i., p. 137.) Hence excessive drinking
introduced the attendant custom of vows and pledges. Each person
present, before he put the cup to his mouth, made some vow to the
tutelary deity of the festival, for the purpose of securing his protection.
When this had been performed by the whole company, the ceremony
of pledging each other commenced. The president, or chief person,
taking the Cup, called publicly on the next in rank to pledge him, and,
after drinking, placed the cup in his hand. The next inferior personage
was drank to in the same manner, and so the toast proceeded round
the board. Hence the origin of drinking Healths. This social custom
was introduced into Britain by Hengist, at a banquet prepared by him
in honour of Vortigern. "At this feast, Rowena, instructed by her
uncle, presented to the aged prince a cup of spiced wine, and, with
smiles, welcomed him with the words *Waes heal hlaford Cyning* ;
i. e., Be of health, my lord king; to which, through his interpreter, he
answered, *Drinc heal*, or, I drink your health." (Brady, Clav. Cal.,
vol. ii, p. 320.) Or, as it is more poetically expressed by Milman
(Samor, Lord of the Bright city),

> ————— She, by wond'ring gaze
> Unmov'd, and stifled murmurs of applause,
> Nor yet unconscious, slowly won her way
> To where the King, amid the festal pomp,
> Sate loftiest. As she rais'd a fair clasp'd cup,
> Something of sweet confusion overspread
> Her features ; something tremulous broke in
> On her half-failing accents, as she said,
> " Health to the King !" the sparkling wine laugh'd up
> As eager 't were to touch so fair a lip.

It was a custom of this people to indulge themselves in drinking a
liquor made from *honey* for thirty days after the marriage of their
principal men ; whence arose our phrase of *the Honey-moon*.

vals; which, in fact, could be held as frequently as
individuals chose to subject themselves to the expense.

The palace of Thor, which is thus described in the
Edda,[17] was nothing more than a cavern[18] of initiation

---

[17] Fab. 11, apud. Mal. North. Ant., vol. ii., p. 65.

[18] The northern nations abound with natural caverns which were
admirably adapted to the purposes of initiation; and were, doubtless,
applied by this people to the celebration of their mysterious rites.
One of these caves was personally inspected by Bishop Pontoppidon,
and, as it bears a striking resemblance to our own cavern at Castleton,
in the Peak of Derbyshire, in which the Druidical mysteries were
unquestionably celebrated, I shall make no apology for describing it in
that author's own words. "Hearing at the parsonage of Oerskoug,
that. in the district of the annexed chapelry of Strande, not far from
thence a stream had been found, which issued through a rock from
the side of a mountain called Limur, and over it a cavern which,
probably, followed the stream, but of the length of which I could
procure no account; I resolved to examine it myself, as on my visitation
to Nordal I was to pass near it. I furnished myself with a tinder-box,
candle, a lantern, and a long line to serve me instead of Ariadne's
clue. My boat put me ashore at the foot of the aforesaid mountain of
Limur. But, being extremely steep, we were obliged to climb with
our hands as well as feet, and sometimes we were hard put to it to
clear our way through the hazel and alder-bushes. On the side of
this laborious ascent, we met with a rivulet streaming out, which
directed us to the cavern. It is, indeed, something wonderful, being
a kind of natural conduit, formed purely by the force of the water
through the solid rock, which was a compound mass, mostly consisting
of grey pebbles, but about the conduit, of a clear, grey marble, with
blueish veins; had this natural structure been raised by human skill,
it would have been a work of no small expense; for a few paces after
getting through the thicket, which almost hides the aperture of the
cavern, one is surprised with a vaulted passage of pure marble, without
the least flaw or breach, but with several angles and protuberances,
all so polished, as if it had been a paste moulded into smooth, globular
forms. About a hundred paces forward, the passage continues in a
straight direction, then winds off to the right with ascents and
descents, and in some places growing narrower, and in others widen-
ing to double its former breadth, which, according to my admeasure-
ment, was about four or five ells, and the height about three; thus
two persons could go abreast, except that they were now and then
obliged to stoop, and even creep, and then they felt a damp vapour
like that of a burial vault. This prevented my penetrating so far as
I had intended. Another thing remarkable, was the terrible roaring
of the waters under us, the course of which was what most excited
my wonder, as over it lies a pavement of smooth stone, inclining a
little like a vault on each side, but flat in the middle, and not above
three fingers thick, with some small crevices through which the
water may be seen." (Pontop. Hist. Norw., p. 48.) Here we find
every characteristic which attended the process of initiation. The
roaring of the waters; the narrow subterranean passages, which

into the mysteries. "The most illustrious among the
gods is Thor. His kingdom is called Thrudwanger. He
possesses there a palace in which are five hundred and
forty halls. It is the largest house that is known;
according as we find mentioned in the poem of Grimnis.
There are five hundred and forty halls in the winding
palace of the god Thor; and I believe there is no where
a greater fabric than this of the eldest of sons."

This magnificent structure is termed, *a winding palace*.
The caverns of initiation were usually constructed with
a variety of intricate windings and turnings excavated
with great care and ingenuity, the mazes of which were
difficult to thread, except by those who were intimately
acquainted with every private mark, placed as a clue to
direct their progress.[19] Hence in the eastern nations
they were frequently termed labyrinths.

It contained *five hundred and forty halls*. The usual
residence of this rude people consisted chiefly of wretched
huts, or burrows in the earth, where they existed in
almost a state of torpidity when unengaged in warlike
expeditions. Hence every habitation which excluded
the open air, if it contained only a single apartment, was
dignified with the name of a Hall;[20] if it included several
rooms it was termed a Palace.[21] If an intricate cavern
terminated in a spacious vault, as the Mithratic grottos,
or places of initiation, always did, it was esteemed, in
this inhospitable climate, a residence, or palace, fit for

---

formed the descent into the bowels of the mountain; the water of
purification; the pastos, replete with a damp vapour like that of a
funeral vault, the emblem of which it undoubtedly was. It is not
likely that this people would overlook a cavern which Nature had
provided; decorated with superb pillars of polished marble, and furnished with an apparatus capable of performing almost all the machinery of initiation.

[19] Worm. Monum. Dan., l. i., p. 6.   Many of these stupendous works
of art still remain in Norway and Sweden.

[20] Bede, l. ii., c. 13.

[21] Oliver's Hist. Beveri., p. 38.   This might also refer to the solar
system.   From the path of the planets moving in their orbits at
various distances from the sun, it is called a *winding palace;* and the
540 Halls referred, most probably, to the precession of the equinoxes.
The eastern nations, from whom the Scandinavians derived their
origin, thought that the fixed stars advanced at the rate of 54 minutes
in the first sexagenary cycle, which gives exactly 540 minutes for the
entire change in the great luni-solar period of 600 years.

the reception of the celestial gods. Hence arose the veneration of the initiated for these grottos. The enthusiastic recollections which the ceremonies of initiation never failed to inspire, joined with the splendid appearance exhibited in the sacellum on these occasions, which is described in the Edda[22] as glittering with burnished gold, could scarcely fail to leave an indelible impression on the mind of the astonished candidate, who, before this time, had, perhaps, never entered an apartment which displayed any appearance of comfort or convenience.

This palace was the residence of Thor, the Sun. This luminary was a conspicuous object of adoration in all the ancient mysteries, particularly those of Persia, the great model on which the Scandinavian system was founded; the one being consecrated to *Thor-As*, and the other to *Mi-Thr-As;* the same god, possessed of the same attributes and almost the same name; and alike esteemed by their respective votaries, as the first begotten Son, and a Mediator, as well as visibly represented by the Sun.[23]

It was situate in the kingdom of Thrudwanger; the literal meaning of which, according to M. Mallet, is *a place of refuge from terror.* Now the great Hall of this palace, or, in language less metaphorical, the sacellum of the grotto of initiation, literally answered this description; for the candidates were not introduced into it until the rites were all finished; and, consequently, at the portal of this sacellum, their fears would naturally subside. And when introduced into the sacred presence, called, by way of eminence, Gladheim, or the abode of joy,[24] they saw the twelve Drottes, seated on as many thrones, habited like the twelve celestial gods, in robes of exquisite richness, shining with gold, and jewels, and precious stones;[25] they might naturally fancy themselves in

---

[22] Fab. 1. Mal. North. Ant., vol. ii., p. 2.

[23] I doubt not, though the Eddas are wholly silent on the subject, but in the principal Hall of this palace or place of initiation, divided, probably, into twelve compartments, in reference to the twelve Signs of the Zodiac, the god was designated by a Plate of burnished gold placed conspicuously in the centre of the roof, and strongly illuminated by flaming torches.

[24] Edda. Fab. 7.   [25] Ibid., Fab. 1.

the regions of the blessed; of which this was, indeed, the avowed representation. And, as the succeeding ceremonies were all pleasurable, it is not surprising that they should adopt an hyperbolical phraseology, and esteem this magnificent place as a palace of the gods in the ever-blessed kingdom of Thrudwanger.

It would be useless to repeat minutely the forms of initiation, after the many specimens you have already heard; suffice it to say, that the candidate, being duly prepared[26] by fasting and mortification, and the usual preliminary ceremonies and sacrifices, dances, and circular processions being accomplished,[27] he was introduced, with naked feet,[28] into the sacred cavern, and conducted by a winding descent to the tomb of Volva the prophetess, amidst the shades of darkness and the terrific howling of dogs. Passing onward, however, with resolute intrepidity, he soon beheld, in a thin flame of light, the canine guardian of the holy sepulchre, whose fangs appeared to be smeared with the blood of some hardy adventurer,

[26] Pontoppidan, in his History of Norway (p. 248), thus describes the robust exercises practised by the inhabitants of the northern nations. "King Olaf Tryggeson was stronger and more nimble than any man in his dominions. He could climb up the rock Smalserhorn, and fix his shield upon the top of it; he could walk round the outside of a boat, upon the oars, while the men were rowing; he could play with three darts, alternately throwing them in the air, and always kept two of them up, while he held the third in one of his hands; he was ambidexter, and could cast two darts at once; he excelled all the men of his time in shooting with the bow; and in swimming he had no equal. Sigmund Brestesen used to practise these exercises with the king, viz., swimming, shooting, climbing the rocks, and all other manly exercises which heroes and warriors practised in those times, and none could come so near the king in all these, as Sigmund."

[27] I am not sure whether the disease called St. Vitus's dance (chorea S. Viti) may not have had some connection with this ceremony. There were three Vituses amongst our Saxon ancestors, who were worshipped as deities. Rugi-Vitus, who was represented with seven faces; Pon-Vitus, with five heads; and Swanto-(sancto) Vitus, with four heads. This latter worthy was worshipped by a *circular dance;* and every year, ninety and nine persons were offered to him in sacrifice. He had a white horse, which was placed in charge of the priests, *and dedicated to the sun.* This horse is supposed by Schedius to be the original of the silver horse in the shield of the Hengist; and probably also of the Hanoverian horse which still occupies a quarter of the escutcheon of pretence in the royal arms of Great Britian. Sammes in his Britannia, has given engravings of the above deities.

[28] Strabo, l. vii.

whose life had recently paid the forfeit of his rash attempt to explore the forbidden recesses of the consecrated vault.[29] The hollow caverns re-echoed with his howlings. Regardless of the posture of defiance assumed by this hideous monster, the candidate was urged forward by his conductor, and, passing this unreal shape, entered the portal, and in the east found a spacious apartment, in the centre of which was the Pastos or Tomb where the oracle was immured.[30] In the distance, a vision of the regions of death (hela) was presented to his eyes, and he beheld a splendid throne which appeared designed for some person of distinction; but it was empty.[31]

Here the mysterious rites of invocation commenced; magical characters were inscribed in squares, triangles, and circles; and charmed rhymes of irresistible potency were repeated. The incantations being complete, the reluctant prophetess signified her intention of uttering an oracular response.[32] The candidate was instructed to question her respecting the fate which awaited Balder, a benevolent deity who was under the protection of the celestial gods; and, though deemed invulnerable, was, nevertheless, supposed to be in imminent danger from the unsuspected effort of subtlety and malice. To this demand the prophetess answered, that Balder should suffer by the intervention of Loke, the adversary of the gods,[33] who, by a sprig of misletoe in the hands of a

---

[29] "*The dog* who guards the gates of death, meets him. His breast and his jaws are stained with blood; he opens his voracious mouth to bite, and barks a long time at the father of magic." (Ancient Runic Poem in Mal. North. Ant., vol. ii., p. 220.)

[30] "Odin pursues his way; his horse causes the infernal caverns to resound and tremble; at length he reaches the deep abode of death, and stopped near the eastern gate where stands the tomb of the prophetess." (Ancient Poem, as above.)

[31] Runic Poem.

[32] "He sings to her verses adapted to call up the dead. He looks towards the north; he engraves the Runic characters on her tomb; he utters mysterious words; he demands an answer; until the prophetess is constrained to arise, and thus utter the words of the dead. 'Who is this unknown that dares disturb my repose, and drag me from my grave, wherein I have lien dead so long, all covered with snow, and moistened with the rains,'" &c. (Ancient Poem, as above.)

[33] This people believed in the existence of an evil principle, who was named Loke, and was esteemed the great adversary of gods and men. This pernicious deity was the prince of fraud and perfidy; a perfect master of all the arts of dissimulation, and addicted solely to the prac-

blind man, shall inflict wounds producing instant death.
The candidate, pressing onwards, soon heard the cries
and bewailings for the death of Balder,[34] who was bitterly
lamented by the deities who had been the innocent cause
of his destruction. He was then confined within the
Pastos,[35] a cell composed of three sharp-edged stones,

tice of evil. He married the daughter of the giantess *Anger-Bode*
(Messenger of Evil), by whom he had three children of portentous
character, who were doomed to destroy the whole host of deities,
when the ship Naglefara should be completed from the nails of dead
men. The first-born was a gigantic wolf, called Fenris, who was
destined to devour the supreme god Odin, and swallow the Sun.
This monster was bound by the gods to a rock in indissoluble chains
until the much-dreaded *twilight of the gods* shall arrive, and all nature
be consumed in a general conflagration. The next offspring of these
two evil beings was an enormous serpent, called Midgard, who was
the destined destroyer of the god Thor. He was precipitated by Odin
to the bottom of the sea, where he attained so vast a bulk, that he
was able to coil himself round the globe, and repose with his tail in
his mouth. The third dreadful issue of Loke and Anger-Bode, was
Hela, or Death, who was cast into hell by the gods, there to await
the appointed time of destruction, and to receive into her dismal
abode all such as died of sickness or of old age.

[34] It appears that Balder, who was esteemed invulnerable, had placed
himself in sport as a mark in the general assembly, at which the gods
respectively exercised their skill and dexterity, in casting darts and
missiles; for Odin and Friga had previously exacted an oath of safety,
in favour of this god, from everything in nature, except the misletoe,
which was omitted on account of its weak and contemptible qualities.
(Edda. Fab. 28.) Loke, always bent on mischief, discovered the
exception; and, privately procuring a sprig of this herb, placed it in
the hands of Hoder, who was bereft of sight, and persuaded him to
cast it at the devoted victim, who fell, pierced through with mortal
wounds. His body was then placed in a ship or boat, and set afloat
on the waters. while all the gods mourned for his decease. The fable
of Balder and Loke, with the lamentations of the gods for the death of
Balder, bears such an obvious relation to those of Osiris and Typhon,
Bacchus and the Titans, Cama, Iswara, &c., &c., that I entertain no
doubt but it constituted the legend of initiation; as it is, indeed, the
exact counterpart of all other systems of mysterious celebration. It
is true, the legend of Odin and Freya, including the wanderings of the
latter, as related in the Edda of Snorro, bears some resemblance to the
wanderings of Ceres, and Isis, and Rhea; but I think the preceding
fable unquestionably contains the identical incidents which were perpetuated in the Gothic mysteries.

[35] The Pastos was a representation of the Ark of Noah. "And God
said unto Noah.... make thee an ark of Gopher wood.... *the door of*
the ark shalt thou set in the side thereof.... In the self same day
entered Noah.... into the ark.... *and the Lord shut him in*." (Gen.
vi., 13, 14. 16; vii., 13, 16.) The account in the text, in connection
with the Rainbow, evidently relates to the Deluge.

and guarded by Heimdal, the light-eared door-keeper of the gods, armed with a naked sword;[36] and when the term of his penance was completed, he was instructed to search for the body of Balder,[37] and to use his utmost endeavours to raise him from death to life. Being, therefore, prepared for this dangerous expedition, he was solemnly recommended to the protection of the gods. He then descended through *nine* subterranean passages, dark, damp, and dismal, attended by the usual guide. Under a full persuasion that his mysterious conductor possessed the power of raising the dead and commanding the elements, every sight presented before his eyes, every sound which assailed his ears, in his progress through the regenerating medium, was invested with the awe and terror attached to a supernatural occurrence. If the glare of burning torches gleamed through a fissure of the rock and imparted a temporary illumination to the dark cavern through which he passed, it presented to his inventive imagination the god descending in a sheet of flame. If a sound resembling distant and continued thunder was heard to reverberate through the hollow passages, it was referred to the dreadful " twilight of the gods,"[38] when all nature shall be involved in universal

---

[36] This place of penance was termed the Celestial Fort, said to be situated at the foot of the bridge Bifrost (Edda. Fab. 7), or the Rainbow, which reached from earth to heaven, and which celestials only could ascend. The sentinel was possessed of a trumpet of so loud a blast, that the sound might be heard through all the worlds. (Edda. Fab. 15.)   [37] Edda. Fab. 29.

[38] The twilight of the gods is thus described in the Edda (Fab. 32). "In the first place, will come the grand, 'the desolating' winter; during which the snow will fall from the four corners of the world; the frost will be very severe; the tempest violent and dangerous; and the sun will withdraw his beams. Three such winters shall pass away, without being softened by one summer. Three others shall follow, during which war and discord will spread through the whole globe. Brothers, out of hatred, shall kill each other; no one shall spare either his parent, or his child, or his relations. See how it is described in the Voluspa: 'Brothers becoming murderers, shall stain themselves with brothers' blood; kindred shall forget the ties of consanguinity; life shall become a burden; adultery shall reign throughout the world. A barbarous age! an age of swords! an age of tempests! an age of wolves! The bucklers shall be broken in pieces; and these calamities shall succeed each other till the world shall fall to ruin.' Then will happen such things as may well be called prodigies. The wolf Fenris will devour the sun: a severe loss will it be found to mankind. Another monster will carry off the moon, and render her

ruin. Arriving, at length, on the banks of a sluggish
stream, he was directed to plunge into the waters of
purification and explore the caverns situate on the opposite bank. Soon his progress was intercepted by the

totally useless; the stars shall fly away and vanish from the heavens;
the earth and the mountains shall be seen violently agitated; the
trees torn up from the earth by the roots; the tottering hills to tum-
ble headlong from their foundations; all the chains and irons of the
prisoners to be broken and dashed in pieces. Then is the wolf Fenris
let loose; the sea rushes impetuously over the earth, because the great
Serpent, changed into a spectre, gains the shore. The Naglefara is set
afloat; this vessel is constructed of the nails of dead men; for which
reason great care should be taken not to die with unpared nails; for
he who dies so supplies materials towards the building of that vessel,
which gods and men will wish were finished as late as possible. The
Giant Rymer is the pilot of this vessel, which the sea breaking over
its banks, wafts along with it. The wolf Fenris, advancing, opens his
enormous mouth; his lower jaw reaches to the earth, and his upper
jaw to the heavens, and would reach still farther, were space itself
found to admit of it. The burning fire flashes out from his eyes and
nostrils. The great Serpent vomits forth floods of poison, which
overwhelm the air and the waters. This terrible monster places
himself by the side of the wolf. In this confusion the heavens shall
cleave asunder; and by this breach the Genii of Fire enter on horseback. Surtur is at their head; before and behind him sparkles a
bright, glowing fire. His sword outshines the sun itself. The army
of these Genii, passing on horseback over the bridge of heaven, break
it in pieces: thence they direct their course to a plain, where they
are joined by the wolf Fenris and the great Serpent. Thither also
repair Loke and the Giant Rymer, and with them all the Giants of
the Frost, who follow Loke even to death. The Genii of Fire march
first in battle array, forming a most brilliant squadron on this plain,
which is an hundred degrees square on every side. During these
prodigies, Heimdal, the door-keeper of the gods, rises up; he violently
sounds his clanging trumpet to awaken the gods, who instantly assemble. Then Odin repairs to the fountain of Mimis, to consult what he
ought to do, he and his army. The great Ash Tree Ydrasil is shaken;
nor is anything in heaven or earth exempt from fear and danger. The
gods are clad in armour; Odin puts on his golden helmet, and his
resplendent cuirass; he grasps his sword, and marches directly against
the wolf Fenris. He hath Thor at his side; but this god cannot
assist him, for he himself fights with the Great Serpent. Frey
encounters Surtur, and terrible blows are exchanged on both sides,
till Frey is beat down; he owes his defeat to his having formerly
given his sword to his attendant Skyrner. That day also is let loose
the dog, named Garmer, who hath hitherto been chained at the
entrance of a cavern. He is a monster dreadful even to the gods; he
attacks Tyr, and they kill each other. Thor beats down the Great
Serpent to the earth, but at the same time recoiling back *nine* steps,
he falls dead upon the spot, suffocated with floods of venom, which
the serpent vomits forth upon him. Odin is devoured by the wolf
Fenris. At the same instant, Vidar advances, and, pressing down the

sacred door of expurgation; on passing which, he entered
into the illuminated sacellum, and found Balder enthroned
in a situation of the highest distinction.

At his entrance into this enchanting place, the aspirant
was saluted with an anthem of congratulation; and the
utmost cheerfulness was displayed in the rejoicings which
now took place for the resuscitation of the benevolent
god. The Scalds,[59] to the flute and harp, chanted hymns
descriptive of the generation of gods, the Creation of the
world, the Deluge, and the restoration of man. They
celebrated in strains of highest panegyric the warlike
acts of heroes; the praise of wise and valiant chiefs; the
fatal overthrow of hosts and hostile armies. They sang
the irresistible valour of Odin, and dwelt on the immortal
renown which his high achievements had secured, with
a view of exciting in the candidate a spirit of emulation
to great and warlike deeds. A solemn oath[40] was then
administered *on a naked sword*, which was used for this
purpose, because it was considered as a symbol of the
supreme god.[41] The aspirant entered into voluntary

monster's lower jaw with his foot, seizes the other with his hand, and
thus tears and rends him till he dies. Loke and Heimdal fight, and
mutually kill each other. After that, Surtur darts fire and flame over
all the earth; the whole world is presently consumed." The description of this event, in the Voluspa, concludes with the following very
remarkable passage:—" The sun is darkened; the earth is immerged
in the sea; the shining stars fall from heaven; a fiery vapour ascends;
a vehement heat prevails, even in heaven itself." (Goranson, Hist.
26, apud Mallet.)

[39] "The historical monuments of the north are full of the honours
paid to the Scalds both by princes and people; nor can the annals of
poetry produce any age or country which reflects more glory or lustre
upon it. They were men especially honoured and caressed at the
courts of those princes who distinguished themselves by their great
actions, or passion for glory. Harold Harfager, for instance, placed
them at his feasts above all other officers of his court. Many princes
intrusted them, both in peace and war, with commissions of the utmost
importance. They never set out on any considerable expedition without some of them in their train. Hacon, Earl of Norway, had five
celebrated poets along with him in that famous battle when the warriors of Jomsburg were defeated; and history records that they sung
each an ode to animate the soldiers before they engaged. Olave, King
of Norway, placing three of them one day around him in battle, cried
out with spirit, ' You shall not relate what you have only heard, but
what you are eye-witnesses of yourselves.' " (Mal. North. Ant., vol.
ι., pp. 386, 389.)

[40] Mal. North. Ant., vol. i., p. 217.

[41] Justin (Hist., l. xliii., c. 3) says, that the ancient Scythians wor-

obligations to pay due submission to the chief officers of the state, whether civil or religious ; to practise devotion to the gods ; and to defend and protect his initiated companions, at the hazard of his life, from all secret and open attacks of their enemies; and, if slain, to avenge their death. The oath was sealed by drinking mead out of a human skull.[42]

shipped swords and spears—a practice common with all who practised the Buddhic superstition.

[42] The word *skull* was commonly used for a drinking vessel, which, probably, " received this name from the barbarous custom which prevailed among several ancient nations, of drinking out of the skulls of their enemies. Warnefrid, in his work, de gestis Longobard, says, Albin slew Cunimund, and having carried away his head, converted it into a drinking vessel; which kind of cup is with us called *schala*, but in the Latin language it has the name of *patera*." (Jamieson, Scot. Dict., v. Skul.

LECTURE XI.

THE splendour and importance of the mysteries gave them such a vast and overwhelming influence, even with the principal nobility of every ancient nation, that the high-born youth displayed the utmost anxiety to endure the fatigue and danger of initiation, that they might be assimilated with that distinguished society, into which no other formula could introduce them. For this purpose every peril was braved, and every risk cheerfully encountered; and loss of life in the process was preferred to the dishonour of remaining voluntarily amongst the uninitiated and profane. Nothing but this unconquerable principle could have induced men to press forward through such a series of opposing difficulties as we have just enumerated.

The candidate was now invested with a sword, a shield, and a lance, and declared equal to the toil of combat, hunting, and providing for his own subsistence, from which latter duty his parents were henceforth wholly relieved, although he had now only attained his fifteenth year. His shield was *white*, and termed "the shield of expectation." A specified period was assigned for his probation in arms, and if he failed to distinguish himself in battle before the expiration of this term, the phrase *Niding* was applied to him, and he was shunned by all his former associates.[1] This, however, did not often happen; and when he had performed any distinguished achievement, he was permitted to have a design painted on his shield, as a testimony of his prowess. This privilege, however, led, in process of time, to innovations in the device and fashion of the shield which endangered

[1] The word *Niding*, amongst the Scandinavians, was esteemed so contemptuous that it would provoke even a coward to single combat. It was equal to giving the lie in our own country; and has now merged into the phrase—You are a good-for-*nothing* fellow. (Vid. Mallet, vol. i., p. 218.)

the distinction between lord and vassal; and, at length,
a code of directions became necessary to regulate the
practice; and the distinction of a painted shield was
limited to the families of princes and heroes.[2]

The sacred sign of the Cross was then impressed upon
nim; and, as a concluding ceremony, a Ring was delivered to him as a symbol of the divine protection, which
he was enjoined to preserve as an invaluable amulet, the
gift of Balder the good.[3] This ring, he was told, was
not only capable of affording him protection in times of
imminent danger and adversity,[4] but it was also to be considered as an inexhaustible fund, whence riches, honours,
and all other benefits would undoubtedly flow.

The whole system of creation and providence, as far as
it was understood by this people, was now unfolded to
the aspirant's view; he was taught mysterious doctrines
wrapped up in hieroglyphical symbols; the art of magic,
and the important secret of preparing amulets and incantations. And, as a final charge, he was solemnly enjoined
to make himself perfect in athletic exercises;[5] and was
assured that the sole method of being translated to the

[2] This may, probably, have been the origin of patrimonial badges and
armorial bearings with the northern nations of Europe, although it is
well known that the Gauls and Germans had armorial distinctions
long before. Diodorus says (l. v.). the Gauls used long shields,
distinguished by particular marks; and Tacitus (de mor. Germ., s.
6) tells us, that the Germans distinguished their shields by different
colours.

"Diodorus Siculus adduces a corresponding custom in Egypt; and
among the Greeks we observe that the shield of Agamemnon bore a
lion's head; that of Alcibiades, a serpent; that of Cadmus, a dragon;
and that of Ulysses, a dolphin." (Wait's Antiq., vol. i., p. 149.)
More anciently, the distinguishing symbols were placed upon the
helmet. Thus, the crest of Osiris was a hawk; of Horus, a lion; &c.

[3] It is said in the Runic mythology, that when Hermod descended
into hell to search for Balder, he found the murdered deity occupying
a distinguished situation in the palace of Death; and failing, through
the artifices of Loke, to procure his return to Valhall, the supernal
palace of the gods, he bore a ring to Odin. as a token of remembrance,
from his deceased friend, which possessed the miraculous power of
producing, every ninth night, eight rings of equal weight and utility.

[4] Plin. Nat. Hist., l. xxxiii., c. 1.

[5] These were, "to fight valiantly; to sit firmly on horseback; to
inure himself to swimming and skating; to dart the lance, and to
become skilful at the oar." (Ode of Harold the Valiant, in Mal.
North. Ant., vol. ii., p. 237.)

hall of Odin, was to die in battle, covered with wounds, valiantly fighting against the enemies of his country.[6]

The most prominent symbols in these celebrations were, the Cross and Ring already mentioned;[7] the Ash tree, the Point within a Circle, the Rainbow,[8] and a Cube the emblem of Odin.[9]

---

[6] When Odin perceived that his end drew nigh, "he would not wait till the consequences of a lingering disease should put a period to that life which he had so often bravely hazarded in the field; but, assembling the friends and companions of his fortune, he gave himself nine wounds in the form of a circle with the point of a lance, and many other cuts in his skin with his sword. As he was dying, he declared he was going back into Scythia to take his seat among the other gods at an eternal banquet, where he would receive with great honours all who should expose themselves intrepidly in battle, and die bravely with their swords in their hands. As soon as he had breathed his last, they carried his body to Sigtuna (the ancient capital of Sweden), where, conformably to a custom introduced by himself into the north, his body was burned with much pomp and magnificence." (Mal. North. Ant., vol. i., p. 6.) Hence in battle the Scandinavians were inspired with the most furious bravery and contempt of death, under the impression that all who died bravely in the field would certainly be received by Odin into his paradise, designated by the endearing appellation of Valhalla, and be rewarded with an honourable seat in his presence; there to enjoy a continual feast of warriors, served up by the Valkyriæ, who were virgins of the most exquisite beauty; serenaded with martial music, and drinking hydromel or mead out of the skulls of vanquished enemies, until the destruction and final renovation of the earth and heavens. The Edda (Fab. 20) thus describes these envied joys, which incited the barbarians of Northern Europe to court death in every violent shape; and inspired an undefined horror at the prospect of a death proceeding from disease or old age. "The heroes who are received into the palace of Odin, have every day the pleasure of arming themselves, of passing in review, or ranging themselves in order of battle, and of cutting one another in pieces; but as soon as the hour of repast approaches, they return on horseback, all safe and sound, back to the Hall of Odin, and fall to eating and drinking. . . . . . . Their beverage is beer and mead; their cups are the skulls of enemies they have slain. A crowd of virgins wait upon the heroes at table, and fill their cups as fast as they empty them." (Mal. North. Ant., vol. i., p. 120.) Hence Ragnor Lodbrok, in his death song, consoles himself with this reflection, "I shall soon drink beer from hollow cups made of skulls." (St. 25 Worm. Liter. Dan., p. 203. Jamieson, Scot. Dict., v. Skul. Mal. North. Ant., vol. ii., p. 232.)

[7] Vid. ut supra, p. 265.

[8] Signs and Symbols, Lect. 8, 9. "The Ash tree *Udrasil*," says the Edda, (Fab. 20,) "is the greatest of trees; *Skidbladner*, of vessels; *Odin*, of gods; *Sleipner*, of horses; *Bifrost*, of bridges; *Brage*, of scalds or poets; *Habroc*, of hawks; and *Garmer*, of hounds."

[9] Fab. Mys. Cab., vol. i., p. 308.

We now come to the system of Magic[10] inculcated by
the Scandinavians. The Scalds and Diviners established
a great reputation, and consequent influence over the
people, by the boasted power of composing charms, or
amulets, which possessed the quality of conferring favour
and protection on friends, and of hurling destruction on
their enemies.[11]   This superstition was derived from
Odin, who acquired the reputation of being a skilful
magician, and was styled, by way of eminence, the father
of magic, from his introduction of the mysteries with
all their terrific machinery amongst this ignorant and
superstitious people.   This potent individual boasted a
very high degree of mystical knowledge, which he imparted to but few, even of his most intimate companions;
for it was a maxim with him, that "whatever is known
only to one's self, is always of the greatest value."[12] He
proclaimed himself capable of rendering the arms of his
enemies powerless; to burst, by the repetition of a single
rhyme, the strongest chains of captivity; to inspire his
foes with the utmost veneration for his person; to strike
his adversary dead with a curse; to pass through the
world with the rapidity of thought; to assume at pleasure, the forms of wild and ferocious beasts; to calm
tempests, disconcert magicians, and even to raise the
dead.[13]

[10] "Magic in general," says Wait, in his Oriental Antiquities, (p.
135,) "may be conceived to have arisen from the mysteries of Persia
or Chaldea, and from the various illusions to which the Epopts were
submitted."
[11] A belief in the efficacy of these incantations, produced much real
and imaginary evil amongst the inhabitants of Scandinavia. "Helga,
a Scandinavian sorceress, when wishing to give efficacy to some Runic
character for doing injury to others, observed this mode. Taking a
knife in her hand, she cut the letters in the wood, and besmeared
them with her blood. Then singing her incantations, *oc gech aufug
rangsaelis um treit*, she went backwards and contrary to the course
of the sun around the tree. Then she procured that it should be cast
into the sea, praying that it might be driven by the waves to the
island Drangsa, and there be the cause of all evils to Gretter." (Hist.
Gretter, apud Berthol. Caus. Contempt. Mortes, p. 661.   Jamieson,
Scot. Dic., v. Widdersinnis.)
[12] Ancient Runic Poem.
[13] These are the enchantments which the Scriptures pronounce as
ever attendant on the practice of a false worship. Thus the sorcerers
of Egypt, when contending against Moses, are said to use enchantments, (Exod. vii., 11) which were prohibited to the Israelites. (Levit.

These pretensions, sanctioned by the timidity which superstition never fails to produce in an untaught mind, would naturally invest this politic prince with an authority which his successors would be desirous to retain. Hence they pronounced that the supernatural powers which Odin was believed to possess,[14] were vested in the three orders of men, the Drottes, the Scalds, and the Diviners, to whose custody the mysteries had been entrusted. In succeeding ages these boasted powers were publicly converted to the purpose of emolument; and charms, amulets, and philtres were openly exposed for sale. And as they were reputed to be effectual antidotes against the effects of poison, to cure diseases, to inspire affection,[15] and to enable the possessor to work miracles; every individual was anxious to be furnished with a charm which promised to counteract the secret machinations of his enemies, in a country where private disputes usually terminated in bloodshed; and hence the composers of such invaluable jewels rose in the public estimation, and became finally invested with uncontrollable authority. These amulets consisted chiefly of Runic characters or letters,[16] inscribed on a tablet made of the

xix., 26.) And the punishment of them is announced by Isaiah: "Behold they shall be as stubble, the fire shall burn them, and they shall not deliver themselves from the power of the flame." (Isai xlvii.. 14.)

[14] " Hence oracles, auguries, divinations, and a thousand practices of that kind quickly sprang up in crowds from this erroneous principle. Accordingly, in all our ancient fables and chronicles, we see the northern nations extremely attached to this vain science. They had oracles, like the people of Italy and Greece, and these oracles were not less revered, nor less famous than theirs. Their diviners were honoured with the name of prophets, and revered as if they had been such. Some of them were said to have familiar spirits who never left them, and whom they consulted under the form of little idols. Others dragged the ghosts of the departed from their tombs, and forced the dead to tell them what would happen." (Mal. North. Ant., vol. 1, p. 143, 146.)

[15] Turn. Ang. Sax., vol. iv., p. 186.

[16] Letters were first introduced into Scandinavia by Odin, and from the ignorance of the people respecting their nature and effects, he taught them to believe that by their use he was empowered to work miracles. Hence he was called *Run-Hofdi*, and *Runom-Fauthr*, King of Spells and Father of Letters. Thus originated the custom of vaticination and fortune-telling; which is not yet fully exploded, and scarcely will be while superstition maintains its empire over the human

wood or bark of the birch tree, in magical form; either
in a circle described from east to west by the south; in
a triangle; in a direct line from the top to the bottom;
or by a retrograde movement from the bottom to the
top; from left to right, or from right to left,[17] according
to the circumstances of each peculiar case; every form
being adapted to its own particular service. They were
frequently carved on walking sticks,[18] sword scabbards
implements of husbandry, and other articles of common
use. Those which were intended to bring woe and destruction on their enemies were termed *Noxious;*[19] those
which were used to avert calamity, to prevent ship-
wreck, to obtain the affections of a beloved female, to
counteract the treachery of an enemy, &c., were called
Favourable; and those which were invested with the

mind. Traces of this practice are still visible in most of the countries
of Europe; and even our own land, though enlightened by the perfection of science, exhibits in every province, many evidences of the prevalence of superstition, in the implicit reliance placed by our rustic
population in amulets, charms, and incantations.

[17] Mal. North. Ant., vol. i., p. 146.

[18] Verstegan tells us, that the people "used to engrave upon certain
square sticks about a foot in length, or shorter or longer as they
pleased, the courses of the moones of the whole yeare, whereby they
could alwayes certainly tel when the new moones, ful moones, and
changes should happen, as also their festival dayes; and such a carved
stick they called an *Al-mon-aght*, that is to say, *Al-moon-heed*, to wit,
the regard or observation of all the moones; and here hence is deryved
the name of Almanack." (Rest. Dec. Int., p. 58.)

[19] In our own country this practice was very prevalent a century or
two ago. "King James, in his Dæmonology, (b. ii., c. 5,) tells us that
the devil teacheth how to make *pictures of wax or clay*, that by roast-
ing thereof, the persons that they bear the name of may be continually
melted, or dried away by continual sickness. Blagrave, in his astrolo-
gical practice of Physic, (p. 89) observes, that the way which the
witches usually take for to afflict man or beast in this kind is, as I
conceive, done by image or model, made in the likeness of that man or
beast they intend to work mischief upon; and by the subtility of the
devil, made at such hours and times when it shall work most power-
fully upon them by thorn, pin, or needle, pricked into that limb or
member of the body afflicted."

> "Witches which some murther do intend
> Doe make a picture and doe shoote at it;
> And in that part where they the picture hit,
> The parties self doth languish to his end."
> Constable's Diaria. Decad. II., Son. 2, 1594.

(Vid. Brand's Popul. Ant., vol. ii., p. 376.)

property of curing diseases, were termed *Medicinal*.[20] The most trifling error in the composition[21] of these wonder-working amulets, was said to be fatal to the artist himself, or to endanger the life of his dearest friend; and hence none dared to attempt the formation of a charm but he who, by initiation, had become perfectly instructed in the various ceremonies, which were indispensably attached to every particular service.

The doctrines inculcated in these mysteries embraced disquisitions on the nature of the gods, the creation of the world, the Deluge, and the present and future condition of man. The early inhabitants of Scandinavia believed in a god, who was "the author of every thing that existeth; the eternal, the ancient, the living and awful being, the searcher into concealed things, the being that never changeth."[22] The name given to this

[20] "All these various kinds differed only in the ceremonies observed in writing them, in the material on which they were written, in the place where they were exposed, in the manner in which the lines were drawn, whether in the form of a circle, of a serpent, or a triangle, &c. In the strict observance of these childish particulars consisted that obscure and ridiculous art, which required, to so many weak and wicked persons, the respectable name of priests and prophetesses, merely for filling rude minds with jealousy, fear and hatred." (Mal. North. Ant., vol. i., p. 316.)

[21] The superstition of the "Hand of Glory" is still firmly believed in some parts of Germany. Its composition was as follows: "Take the hand of a person hanged and exposed on the highway; wrap it up in a piece of a shroud or winding sheet, in which let it be well squeezed to get out any small quantity of blood that may have remained in it; then put it into an earthen vessel with zimat, saltpetre, salt, and long pepper, the whole well powdered; leave it fifteen days in that vessel; afterwards take it out, and expose it to the noontide sun in the dog days, till it is thoroughly dry, and if the sun is not sufficient, put it into an oven, heated with fern and vervain. Then compose a kind of candle with the fat of the hanged man, virgin wax and sesame of Lapland. The Hand of Glory is used as a candlestick to hold this candle when lighted. Its properties are, that wheresoever any one goes with this dreadful instrument, the person to whom it is presented will be deprived of all power of motion. Hence it was used by housebreakers to enter houses at night without fear of opposition. But there was a counter charm which would deprive the Hand of Glory of its effects. The threshold of the door of the house and other places where the thieves might enter, was to be anointed with an unguent composed of the gall of a black cat, the fat of a white hen, and the blood of a screech owl, which mixture must necessarily be prepared in the dog days." (Grose. Provincial Glossary, and Popular Superstitions.)

[22] Edda. Fab. 12.

9*

most high god, was Odin,[23] who was also believed to
send plagues into the world when provoked by the
wickedness of its inhabitants; and his anger could only
be appeased by human sacrifices, prayer and repentance.[24] Idols and visible representations of the deity
were originally forbidden, and he was directed to be
worshipped in the lonely solitude of sequestered forests,
where he was said to dwell, invisible and in perfect
silence.[25] But after the irruption of Sigge and his followers, other objects of adoration were introduced;[26] to
each of which was assigned a particular dominion; and,
hence, every object of the creation soon became placed
under the care of its presiding divinity. The trees, the
houses, fire, water, sun, stars, and even thunder and
lightning, wind and rain, had each its protecting deity;

[23] " Odin is believed to have been the name of the one true God
among the first colonies who came from the East and peopled Germany and Scandinavia, and among their posterity for several ages.
But, at length, a mighty conqueror, the leader of a new army of adventurers from the East, overran the north of Europe, erected a great
empire, assumed the name of ODIN, and claimed the honours which
had been formerly paid to that deity. From thenceforward this deified mortal became the chief object of the idolatrous worship of the
Saxons and Danes in this island, as well as of many other nations.
Having been a mighty and successful warrior, he was believed to be
the god of war, who gave victory, and revived courage in the conflict.
Having civilized, in some measure, the countries which he conquered,
and introduced arts formerly unknown, he was also worshipped as
the god of arts and artists. In a word, to this Odin, his deluded
worshippers impiously ascribed all the attributes which belong only
to the true God: to him they built magnificent temples, offered many
sacrifices, and consecrated the fourth day of the week, which is still
called by his name in England, and in all the other countries where
he was formerly worshipped." (Henry's Hist. of Eng., vol. ii.)
[24] Mallet, vol. i., c. 7.
[25] Tacit. de mor. Germ., l. ix., c. 35. There is a peculiar degree of
solemnity in a primitive grove. A writer on the scenery of America,
thus expresses himself respecting one of the vast woods of that continent: " When the air is calm, scarcely a sound of anything is to be
heard; for the few birds that flit athwart the gloom are dumb. It is
impossible for any one to enter such solitudes without dread; nor
can the traveller contemplate his condition without anxiety and fear.
The comparison of a gothic cathedral to the grove, is old and trite;
but the associations which the vast forest aisles and embowered
arches awaken, make the sense of a present divinity far more power-
fully felt, than in the greatest cathedrals with all their gorgeous talismans of devotion."
[26] Verst. Rest., p. 69.

who were thus, united or individually, enabled to visit the good with benefits, and to punish the wicked with destruction. These inferior deities considered at first only as Mediators, were, at length, invested with supreme authority; and as courage, strength, and superior valour were the chief traits of excellence in this rude people; the first cause soon became compounded with the god of war, and was hence esteemed a sanguinary being; terrible to his enemies; clad in vengeance as in a garment; and delighting in desolation and carnage, slaughter and blood.[27]

The splendid temple on the river Sala, the present site of Upsal, which is said to be of great antiquity, dating its existence from the time of Ninus,[28] was decorated with a profusion of costly ornaments, plates and chains of burnished gold,[29] and contained a representation of the Scandinavian triad Odin—Thor—Frea.[30] These deities were placed beside each other in a line. On the right stood Odin, a gigantic figure bearing his emblematical characteristic, the Sword. In the centre stood Thor, his first born son, and the reputed mediator between God and man, of an equal stature, and bearing

[27] Mallet. North. Ant., vol. i., p. 86.
[28] Olaus Magnus, c. vi., p. 104.
[29] The astonishing riches exhibited in some of these heathen temples exceeds our comprehension. "In the great temple of Belus built by Semiramis, we find three prodigious statues of beaten gold, representing Jupiter the father of all, Juno the queen of heaven, and Rhea the universal mother. The statue of Jupiter appeared erect, and in a walking attitude; it was forty feet in height, and weighed a thousand Babylonian talents. The statue of Rhea also weighed the same number of talents, but was sculptured sitting on a throne of massy gold, with two lions standing before her, as guardians of the statue, accompanied with two huge serpents in silver, that weighed each thirty talents. The statue of Juno was in an erect posture, and weighed eight hundred talents; her right hand grasped a serpent by the head, and her left a golden sceptre incrusted with gems. Before these three colossal figures stood an altar of beaten gold, forty feet in length, fifteen in breadth, and of the weight of five hundred talents. On this altar stood two vast flagons weighing each thirty talents; two censers for incense, probably kept continually burning, each weighing five hundred talents; and finally three vessels for the consecrated wine, of which the largest, that assigned to Jupiter, weighed three hundred talents, and those to Juno and Rhea six hundred talents." (Diod. Sic., l. ii., p. 98, apud Maur. Ind. Ant., vol. vii., p. 459.)
[30] Mallet, vol. i., p. 96.

the symbolical crown, sceptre, and mace,[31] showing his unlimited dominion over the earth and elements; and to depict his astronomical character, twelve stars were arranged in a circle round his head.[32] And on the left was placed Frea,[33] represented as an hermaphrodite,[34] and adorned with a variety of symbolical decorations pointing out her dominion over marriage, conception, and parturition.[35]

The legends of the creation and the Deluge were rather fanciful, but not more so than those of some other idolatrous nations. Chaos was described as a vast abyss, which being gradually filled up by the formation of successive strata of congealed vapours, the giant Ymer or Aurgelmer[36] was formed of icy exhalations melted by a genial south wind. The copious perspiration which issued from this monster, produced a corrupt race of giants called the Hrimthussi; who, at length, rising in rebellion against their progenitor, he was slain by the sons of Bore;[37] Odin, Vile, and Ve, who proceeded from

[31] Maur. Ind. Ant., vol. v., p. 782.

[32] Verst. Rest. Dec. Intel., p. 74.

[33] Friga, the Scandinavian Venus, was sometimes confounded with the moon, because they were equally thought to possess an influence over the increase of the human species; and hence the time of the full moon was considered a most favourable period for marriages.

[34] Cudw. Intel. Syst., l. i., c. 4.

[35] Maur. Ind. Ant., vol. v., p. 781. These emblems bore a reference commensurate with the eastern phallus and linga, but did not lead to the same scandalous excesses. So chaste were this otherwise barbarous people, that their continence and absolute deference to the weaker sex, gained the applause of all polished nations. Even Tacitus could say, that amongst this people the females were safe from personal insult; and the sanctity of the matrimonial bond was so devotedly venerated, as to merit the most unqualified applause. (Tacit. Germ., c. 18.) And Salvian says, that these barbarians were worthy of admiration on account of their continence; and that they were literally the reformers of the Roman manners! (Salv. de gub. dei., l. vii.)

[36] The giant Ymer was the same with Typhon or the ocean; and the drying up of the waters of the Deluge is expressed under the figure of the destruction of the monster. Mr. Faber thinks it "not improbable that the gothic name Ymer or Umer is the same as the Persic name Cai-Umersh; an appellation which is applied to Adam.". (Pag. Idol., vol. i., p. 217, in notâ 2.)

[37] Or Bo, who, himself, or probably some successor of Sigge who assumed his name, was represented as a valorous chieftain, and his name was held in such dread for many centuries after his death as to

the cow Andumbla,[38] a creature formed from the particles of dissolved ice. The torrents of blood issuing from his wounds, caused an inundation which overflowed the whole earth, and destroyed all the giants of the frost (i. e., the human race), except Bore or Bergelmer[39] and his family, who succeeded in keeping a boat afloat on the surface. The sons of Bore now formed the earth out of the body of Ymer which they dragged from the abyss of Ginnungagap for this especial purpose. The land was formed from his flesh, the water from his blood, the mountains were composed of his bones, the rocks of his teeth, and the arch of heaven of his scull, supported at four equi-distant points by as many dwarfs, whose names were East, West, North, and South, and teeming with clouds formed from his dispersed brains. They afterwards created a man and woman of two logs of wood, the former of *ash*, the latter of *elm*, and called them Askus and Embla.[40]

It was taught in these mysterious institutions, that when the multiplied iniquities of men should overwhelm the earth with deeds of violence; when the parent should arm his hand against his children, and the child against his parent; when murder, treason, and ingratitude should

be used by soldiers on the approach of an enemy, as a war-cry to inspire their opponents with a panic fear. The Irish continued the practice of this custom till the reign of our Henry VII., when it was prohibited by authority. It is still used by the English rustic as an epithet of terror. Bore was the same mythological personage as the hellenic Boreas, the north wind; and meant, undoubtedly, the patriarch Noah, as his three sons Odin, Vile, and Ve, may be identical with Shem, Ham, and Japheth.

[38] This cow was the ark, from which the triple offspring of the patriarch proceeded.

[39] Thus was a tradition of the Deluge, as well as of the antediluvian patriarchs preserved in Scandinavia. From *Aurgelmer* (Adam), say they, proceeded *Thrudgelmer* (Lamech), from whom *Bergelmer* (Noah) sprang, *while the earth was deluged by the ocean.* This is preserved in the Edda of Saemund.

> "When wintry storms o'erspread the sky,
> Ere yet from ocean rose the earth,
> Great Bergelmer had his birth.
> Thrudgelmer was his father's name,
> He from great Aurgelmer came."
> Song of Vafthrudnis. Cottle's Version.

[40] Edda. Fab. 1, 2, 3, 4, 5. Hence the Ash was sacred to Odin, the Birch to Thor, and the Elm to Frea.

stain the earth with blood; when a series of unmixed wickedness and vice should supersede piety and virtue:[41] then the present system shall fall into annihilation, and all the gods as well as men shall perish in the general ruin; while the mysterious ship Naglefara floats amidst torrents of mixed fire and water, and defies the desolating tempest under the direction of its mighty pilot. After which a new world shall arise like a phœnix from the ashes of its parent, splendid as the meridian sun, adorned with stately palaces all glittering with gold and precious stones, where the brave and virtuous shall enjoy everlasting happiness and delight; while in the inhospitable regions of the *north*, a place of punishment shall also be formed, abounding with serpents and other noisome reptiles, where the pusillanimous and wicked shall be for ever entombed amidst pestiferous vapours; some plunged in rivers of liquid poison distilled from the mouths of serpents; others perpetually bitten and devoured by ravenous wolves; and all condemned to suffer various torments, unpitied and hopeless, amidst the accumulated horrors of everlasting filth and nastiness.

Such were the secret doctrines taught to the aspirant by our Saxon ancestors in the wilds of Scandinavia. And they afford an evident proof of the eastern derivation of their mysteries, although disguised by names and

---

[41] The morality inculcated in these Mysteries has been preserved by Saemund surnamed the Learned, in a Poem called the Havamaal, or the Sublime Discourse of Odin. From this code I subjoin a few extracts to shew the nature of their moral instruction. "Many are thought to be knit in the ties of sincere kindness: but when it comes to the proof, how much are they deceived. Slander is the common vice of the age. Even the host backbites his guest."—"Whilst we live let us live well; for be a man ever so rich, when he lights his fire, Death may, perhaps, enter his door, before it be burnt out."—"There is no malady or sickness more severe, than not to be content with one's lot."—"The heart alone knows what passes within the heart: and that which betrays the soul, is the soul itself."—"*Seek not to seduce another's wife* with the alluring charms of Runic incantations." —"Where is there to be found a virtuous man without some failing? or one so wicked as to have no good quality?"—"The fire drives away diseases; the oak expels the stranguary; straw dissolve enchantments." Hence, probably, is derived the custom of laying two straws crosswise in the path where a witch is expected to come. "Runic characters destroy the effect of imprecations; the earth swallows up inundations; and death extinguishes hatred and quar-rels." (Mal. North. Ant., vol. ii., p. 206, &c.)

circumstances which display the ingenuity of the hierophants; and their anxiety to frame a system which
should aid, by the correspondence of its doctrines, to
cement the military frame-work of society, and confirm
the veneration of the people by an appeal to the prevailing taste for patriotism, and a respect for the institutions of their country.

LECTURE XII.

AMERICA was evidently peopled from the old continent, because there were only eight persons saved at the Deluge; and the principal part of their posterity, during the whole of the first century after that event, occupied the very centre of Asia. Some say that America was peopled by the Carthaginians[1] who possessed the Cape Verd Islands, which are only three weeks sail from that continent. Their ships, having women and children on board, might miss the intended Islands, before the invention of the compass; and if so, they would inevitably be driven by the Trade Winds to the coast of America. Others, judging from the similarity of some religious rites, have conjectured that it was peopled by the Ten Tribes at the dispersion of Israel.[2] Some think it received its population from China or Japan; others that it was colonized by some wandering tribes of Japheth, who penetrated into the trackless regions of North America by the straits of Anian.[3] Some have been bold enough to assert that America was not inundated at the Deluge, and that, consequently, the aborigines were antediluvians, and the most ancient people on earth. Others suppose that there were few individuals preserved on this vast continent at the Deluge, that it might be without difficulty repeopled. And we are told, " that America was peopled after the Deluge, at the same time, as it were, (communibus aliis) with other parts of the earth equidistant from the spot whereon the Ark is acknowledged to have grounded. For *the grand division of the Eastern and Western hemispheres through the natural effect of causes operating from the Deluge, did not take place till about half a century after that event;* and thus a subject that has uniformly puzzled the most learned historians and philosophers, and given ground for the most elaborate disserta-

---

[1] Rel. Cerem. of various Nations, p. 278.   [2] Ibid.
[3] Bochart. Phaleg., l. iii., c. 1.

tions, namely, the manner by which America was peopled, appears to be made simple and easy, as are all those questions that are submitted to the ordeal of truth, the infallible attestations of Holy Writ.[4] M. Humboldt[5] seems to insinuate that the " tribes of the Tartar race passed over to the north-west coast of America, and thence to the south and east towards the banks of Gila, and those o. the Missouri." Robertson[6] also supposes the Americans to have derived their original from the Asiatics; and supports his conjecture by some ancient traditions amongst the Mexicans, which ascribe their primitive population to a horde from a remote country to the north-west; whose gradual progress from the northern coast, where they landed, to the interior provinces, is distinctly traced. And, in the infancy of Christianity, Mexico is said to have been in a more advanced state of civilization than Denmark, Sweden, and Russia.[7]

[4] New theory of the two hemispheres, Pamphl., vol. v. Mr. Thompson deduces his theory from Genesis x., 25. " Peleg—in his days *was the earth divided*".

[5] Research. in Amer., vol. i., p. 147. [6] Hist. Amer., b. iv.

[7] Humboldt. Research. in Amer., vol. i., p. 83. A most interesting evidence of the early existence of the arts in these regions, has recently been discovered by the captain of an American vessel, named Kay, on the coast of Peru, in the environs of Garvay, Province of Fruscillo, in an ancient buried city of considerable extent. Following the course of some excavations which he made, he found the walls of the edifices still standing, and many of them in a complete state of preservation. He infers, from the number and extent of them, that the population of the city could not have been less than 3000 souls. Great numbers of skeletons and mummies in a perfect state of preservation were found among the private and sacred edifices, and a great number of domestic utensils, articles of furniture, coins, and curious antiquities. The earthquake, by which it would appear the city was engulfed, appears to have surprised the inhabitants like those of Pompeii, in the midst of their daily avocations, and many of them were singularly preserved, by the exclusion of atmospheric air, in the precise action or employment of the moment when overwhelmed. One man, standing up as if in the act of escaping, was dressed in a light robe, in the folds of which coins were found, which have been sent to the scientific institutions of Lima for investigation. A female was also found sitting in a chair, before a loom, which contained an unfinished piece of cotton stuff, which she was in the act of weaving. The cotton-stuff (which is of a gaudy pattern, but very neatly fabricated) is about eight inches in diameter, and appears to have been only half completed. A great number of antiquities and curiosities found in this American Herculaneum grave have been sent to the museum of Lima.

From what people soever the Americans descended, or in whatever manner that vast continent was originally furnished with human beings ; it is certain that the first inhabitants brought with them a system of mysteries which they applied to the purposes of religious worship ;[8] and though this system, in process of time, was almost entirely lost amongst the scattered tribes which led an erratic life in its deepest wilds, yet many of the truths on which it was founded, were preserved in a deteriorated form, by the two great nations which had planted themselves on each side of the Isthmus of Panama.

The entire system adopted by the Mexicans, though highly symbolical, bore a character of dark and gloomy austerity. "The priests were wont to select for their religious incantations, rocky caverns, lofty mountains, and the deep gloom of eternal forests."[9]   They worshipped many deities,[10] the chief of which were Teotl, the invisible and supreme being ;[11] Virococha, the creator,[12] Vitzliputzli or Huitzilopochtli, as the name is spelt by Humboldt, the god of mercy ;[13] Tescalipuca, the god of vengeance ; Quetzalcoatl, the Mexican Mercury,[14] or god

---

[8] Sir W. Jones says truly, that the religion of Mexico and Peru was substantially the same as that practised by the various nations of the eastern hemisphere. (Asiat. Res., vol. i., p. 268.)   And why should it not ?   It was evidently derived from the same source ; the Scythic superstition as practised by the architects on the plain of Shinar.

[9] Fab. Pag. Idol., vol. iii., p. 200.   See also Maur. Ind. Ant., vol. ii., p. 39. Purch. Pilgr., b. viii., c. 12, and Humb. Res. Amer., vol. ii., p. 244.

[10] Some say they had two thousand gods. (Univ. Displ., vol. i., p. 176.)

[11] Humb. Res. Amer., vol. i., p. 83.   [12] Acosta. Hist. Ind., p. 380.

[13] Even this deity, with all the benign attributes which some ascribe to him, is represented as delighting in the blood of human victims. It is said in an old tradition, that "he came into the world with a dart in his right hand, and a buckler in his left, and his head covered with a helmet crowned with green feathers.   His first feat at his birth was to kill his brothers and sisters ;" and hence originated the sanguinary rites that were offered to him.   (Humb. Res. Amer., vol. i., p. 220.)

[14] "Quetzalcoatl, whose name signifies *Serpent clothed with green feathers*, from *coatl*, serpent and *quetzalli*, green feathers, is the most mysterious being of the whole Mexican mythology.   He was a white and bearded man, high priest of Tula, legislator, chief of a religious sect, which, like the Sonyasis and Buddhists of Hindostan, inflicted on themselves the most cruel penances.   In a Mexican drawing in the Vatican library, I have seen a figure representing Quetzalcoatl appeasing by his penances the wrath of the gods, when 13,060 years after

of the air; Mictlancihautl, the goddess of hell; Tlaloc-
teutli, who corresponded with Neptune, and Ixcuina, with
Venus.[15]   To Vitzliputzli was ascribed the renovation of
the world; and his name was deemed ineffable, and referred to the principal luminary, the Sun.   He was said
to be the offspring of a virgin, who was impregnated by
a Plume of Feathers which descended from heaven into
her bosom invested with all the colours of the Rainbow.[16]
Hence a Rainbow with a serpent attached to each end of
it was a Mexican symbol,[17] and referred to the two
parents of the human race who were miraculously preserved from the effects of the Deluge by the intervention
of Serpents.   Vitzliputzli was represented in his temple
by the figure of a man, whose countenance was disfigured
by certain black lines drawn across his forehead and nose.
He was seated on a globe,[18] which was a symbol of his
universal power, over a lofty altar, which was borne in
procession during the celebration of the mysteries, supported on four long poles, each end of which was ornamented with a serpent's head.[19]   His right hand grasped
a snake, and his left a buckler with arrows; all charged
with emblematical devices, each of which conveyed some
mysterious signification, and inculcated some useful
lesson upon the initiated.[20]

   The office of Tescalipuca was to punish the sins of men
by the infliction of plague; famine and pestilence, disease
and death.   He was represented as a black man with a

the creation of the world, (I follow the vague chronology of Rios,)
a great famine prevailed in the province of Culan. The saint had
chosen his place of retirement near Tlaxapuchicalo on the volcano
Catcitapetl, (Speaking mountain,) where he walked barefoot on agave
leaves armed with prickles. He finally disappeared at the mouth of
the river Goasacoalco, after having declared to the Cholulans that
he would return in a short time to govern them again and renew their
happiness." (Humb. Res., vol. i., p. 92.)

[15] Codex Borgianus MSS., fo. 73, apud Humb. Res., vol. i., p. 228.

[16] Clavigero. Mexico.

[17] Purch. Pilg., b. ix., c. 12.

[18] Mr. Faber thinks that the globe on which this god was said to be
seated, was in reality no other than the calix of the lotos, and the deity
himself was the triplicated great father, or Noah. (Fab. Pag Idol.,
vol. ii., p. 316.)

[19] The temples of Mexico were replete with representations of this
reptile; particularly of the amphisbæna, or mysterious serpent with
two heads. (Humb. Res., vol. i., p. 131.)

[20] Purch. Pilg., b. viii. c. 11.

hideous countenance, enthroned upon an altar, and decorated with rich jewels and valuable trinkets. His anger could only be appeased by human sacrifices.[21] The symbol of this terrible divinity was *a blue feather*, which was generally appended, in some conspicuous situation, about his person. "From his hair, tied up with a golden fillet, there hung an ear, which was another symbol, by which the afflicted soul and repenting sinner was taught, that he might confide in the divine mercy, who would listen to his prayers. He held four darts in his right hand, signifying the punishment for sin, and the vengeance of Heaven, which manifests itself to man by plagues, war, poverty, and famine. His left hand held a golden mirror, extremely smooth, and so bright as to receive the objects clearly and distinctly. With the same hand he held, behind this mirror, a fan made of feathers, of all kinds and colours, signifying that nothing was hid from

---

[21] A terrible picture of this insatiate monster has been drawn by Marmontel, (Incas, vol. i., p. 77,) which makes the reader shudder. Montezuma, in his distress, applies to the sovereign Pontiff for advice, who thus addresses him: "Sir," said he, "I would not have you be surprised at the weakness of our gods, or at the ruin which seems to await your empire. We have called up the mighty God of Evil, the fearful Telcalepulca. He appeared to us over the pinnacle of the Temple, amidst the darkness of the night. Clouds rent by lightning were his seat. His head reached up to Heaven; his arms, which stretched from north to south, seemed to incircle the whole earth: from his mouth the poison of pestilence seemed ready to burst forth: in his hollow eyes sparkled the devouring fire of madness and of famine: he held in one hand the three darts of war, and in his other rattled the fetters of captivity. His voice, like the sounds of storms and tempests, smote our ears: Ye mock me: my altars thirst in vain: my victims are not fattened: a few half starved wretches are all the offerings ye bestow on me. Where is now the time when twenty thousand captives in one day lay slaughtered in my temple? Its rock returned no other sound but groans and bitter wailings, which rejoiced my heart; altars swam in blood; rich offerings lay scattered on my floor. Hath Montezuma forgotten that I am Telcalepulca, and that all Heaven's plagues are the ministers of my wrath? As for the other gods, let him send them away empty, if he will; their indulgence exposes them to contempt: by suffering it they encourage and deserve it: but let him know that it is folly in the extreme to neglect a jealous god, the God of Evil." Terrified at this portentous intelligence, Montezuma gave instant orders that the captives should be surveyed, and a thousand of them picked out to immolate to their incensed god, that they should be fattened up with all possible expedition; and that as soon as every thing was ready, they should be offered up in solemn sacrifice.

that vindictive god. Round the idol were a great number of emblematical figures."[22]

The System of the Mexicans was barbarous and bloody in the extreme. Their Temples were covered with representations of monstrous serpents,[23] tigers and all sorts

---

[22] Rel. Cerem. of Various Nations, p. 316.

[23] The temples of religion in most nations were decorated with serpents to indicate their sacred character. (Pers., Sat. i., 113, and see Signs and Symb., Lect. 3.) From the general use of this hieroglyphic in systems of idolatry, we may trace its introduction into the legends of romance. For this idea I am indebted to Mr. Faber, and shall transcribe from his elaborate work, on the Origin of Pagan Idolatry, a passage in support of the proposition. "In British fiction, we have a Lady of the Lake, who is said to have been the sister of King Arthur, and who is celebrated by the name of Morgana, or Viviana. Boiardo represents her as gliding beneath the waters of an enchanted lake, while she caresses a vast serpent, into which form she had metamorphosed one of her lovers. And other romance writers describe her as the perfidious paramour of Merlin, who was wont to denominate her the White Serpent. Her character has been taken from that of the White Goddess, who presided over the Sacred Lake, and who, as the navicular serpent, was the diluvian vehicle of the great universal Father." (Fab. Pag. Idol., vol. iii., p. 321.) And again, in the Arabian Tales, contests between the good and evil demons are very frequently introduced, and sometimes they are represented in the form of serpents, agreeably to the universal belief of all the east. In one of these tales, the malignant serpent, or an evil genius in that form, is represented as endeavouring to destroy the beneficent genius, depicted also as a winged snake. The passage is as follows, and is an extraordinary incident which occurred to Zobeide, after her sisters had cruelly thrown her overboard, and she had miraculously succeeded in gaining the land. "I laid myself down," said she to the caliph of Bagdad, "in a shade, and soon after I saw a winged serpent, very large and long. coming towards me, wriggling to the right and to the left, and hanging out his tongue, which made me think he had got some hurt. I arose and saw a larger serpent following him, holding him by the tail, and endeavouring to devour him. I had compassion on him, and, instead of flying away, I had the boldness and courage to take up a stone that by chance lay by me, and threw it with all my strength at *the great serpent, whom I hit on the head and killed him.* The other, finding himself at liberty, took to his wings and flew away. I looked a long while after him in the air, as an extraordinary thing: but he flew out of sight, and I lay down again in another place in the shade, and fell asleep. When I awaked, judge how I was surprised to see by me a black woman, of a lively and agreeable complexion. I sat up and asked her who she was. I am, said she, *the serpent whom you delivered not long since from my mortal enemy,*" &c., &c.—Mr. Faber, whose opinions are entitled to considerable respect, thus endeavours to account for that universal degeneracy of principle which induced mankind to offer the rites of divine worship to this disgusting symbol. "Serpents," he says, "were accounted the greatest of gods, and the

of uncouth and horrible figures, compounded of men and animals. "They had dark houses full of idols, great and small, and wrought of sundry metals. These were all bathed and washed with human blood an inch thick on the walls of the houses, and a foot thick on the floors."[24] Their sacred chapel at Mexico was decorated with the skulls of those unhappy wretches who had been slain in sacrifice and their priests were clad in garments made of their skins.[25]

The celebration of their mysterious rites was preceded by long and painful fastings and mortification. The candidate was subjected to all the terrors, sufferings, and penances which attended the purifications of the eastern world. He was scourged with knotted cords; his flesh was cut with knives,[26] or cauterized with red hot cinders; and many other severities was he compelled to undergo, that his fortitude might be fully proved before he was admitted to those distinctions which conferred the high privilege of personally sacrificing his fellow men. The probation was pressed with such unrelenting cruelty, that many perished under it. And should the wretched candidate, even under the most excruciating infliction,

---

leading principles of the universe; and as such they were invariably introduced both into the Temples, and into the due celebration of the Mysteries The real ground of their being accounted the greatest of the gods was this : they were employed, according to their sexes, to symbolize the great father and the great mother. And in this manner we find them venerated in every quarter of the globe." (Fab. Pag. Idol., b. ii., c. 7.

[24] Gage. Surv. of the West Indies, p. 12.

[25] Human victims were sacrificed in Tlacaxipehualitztli the first month of the Mexican year, for the purpose of procuring their skins for the priests. (Humb. Res., vol. i., p. 290.) The origin of this revolting custom may be found in the following legend, which is recorded in a folio, entitled, " The Ceremonies and Religious Customs of various Nations," (p. 316). " Tozi, that is to say, our Grand Mother, was of mortal extraction. Vitzliputzli procured her divine honours by enjoining the Mexicans to demand her of her father, who was King of Culhucacan, for their queen; this being done, they also commanded him to put her to death, afterwards to flay her, and to cover a young man with her skin. It was in this manner she was stripped of her humanity, to be translated among the gods."

[26] Quetzalcoatl "introduced the custom of piercing the lips and ears, and lacerating the rest of the body with the prickles of the agave leaf, or the thorns of the cactus, and of putting reeds into the wounds, in order that the blood might be seen to trickle more copiously." (Humb. Res., vol. i., p. 92.)

utter so much as a sigh, a groan, or an impatient exclamation, he was dismissed with contempt, and from that moment considered unworthy the honour of admission into the society of his equals. One striking shade of difference is observable between the preparations of the Mexicans, and those of other idolatrous nations. The purifications of the latter were performed with water, the other by blood.[27] The candidate's habit was also black,[28] instead of the white garments of other nations, in accordance with that ferocity of disposition which the habitual practice of sacrificing men must necessarily produce. Before initiation he was anointed with an ointment ritually prepared,[29] which was said "to dispel fear, and invigorate courage. It was made of the juice of the most venomous creatures at the altar of the idol, the ashes of which were pounded in a mortar, and mixed with tobacco, to which they added live scorpions, and some other venomous insects. They heightened this composition with a herb which has the property of disturbing the brain, as also with soot and rosin. This is what they call the repast or sustenance of the gods "[30]

The Temple of Vitzliputzli, in Mexico, was of such an extraordinary magnitude, that a city consisting of five hundred houses[31] might have been erected within the compass of its walls.[32] Its form was that of a truncated

---

[27] Rel. Cerem. of Various Nations, p. 318.

[28] Faber says, "their orgies appear to have been of a peculiarly gloomy and terrific nature, sufficient to strike with horror, even the most undaunted hearts." (Fab. Pag. Idol., vol. iii., p. 188.)

[29] Fab. Pag. Idol., v. iii., p. 188.   [30] Univ. Displayed., v. i., p. 190.

[31] Rel. Cerem. of Various Nations, p. 316.

[32] " The group of pyramids of Teotihuacan is in the valley of Mexico, 8 leagues N. E. from the capital, in the plain that bears the name of Micoatl, *the Path of the Dead.* There are two large Pyramids, dedicated to the sun (Tonatiuh) and to the moon (Mextli), and these are surrounded by several hundreds of smaller pyramids, which form streets in exact lines from north to south, and from east to west. Of these two great teocallis, one is 55 metres, (180,450416 feet,) and the other 44 metres, (144,3603 feet,) in perpendicular height. The basis of the first is 208 metres, (682,4306 feet in length. The small pyramids are scarcely 10 metres, (32,80916 feet) high; and served, according to the tradition of the natives, as burial places for the chiefs of the tribes. On the top of the great teocallis were two colossal statues of the sun and moon; they were of stone, and covered with plates of gold, of which they were stripped by the soldiers of Cortes.' (Humb. Res., vol. i., p. 84.)

pyramid,[33] on the flat top of which were one or two chapels, which contained the colossal idols of the divinity;[34] and it served for an observatory as well as for sacrifice.[35] Here it was that the Mexican mysteries were celebrated on a grand scale;[36] and here it was that all the crimes of a bloody and revolting superstition were concentrated, and all the horrible phantasies of a dark and barbarous worship were exhibited in full perfection. The young aspirant, notwithstanding he had been anointed with a stupifying unguent, was overwhelmed with horror at beholding his fellow creatures wantonly immolated under the pretence of explaining an otherwise incommunicable mystery.[37]

He now descended into the dark and cheerless caverns of initiation[38] which had been excavated beneath the

[33] Purch. Pilg., b. viii., c. 12.   [34] Humb. Res., vol. i., p. 82.
[35] Ibid., p. 100, 103.
[36] "It is impossible," says M. Humboldt, (Res., vol. i., p. 82,) "to read the descriptions which Herodotus and Diodorus have left us of the Temple of Jupiter Belus, without being struck with the resemblance of that Babylonian monument to the teocallis of Anahuac."
[37] These abominable sacrifices were performed as follows: "The sovereign priest carried a large and sharp knife in his hand, made of a flint; another priest carried a collar of wood, wrought in the form of a snake; the other four priests who assisted, arranged themselves in order adjoining the pyramidal stone; being directly against the door of the chapel of their idol. This stone was so pointed, that the man who was to be sacrificed, being laid thereon upon his back, did bend in such sort as occasioned the stomach to separate upon the slightest incision of the knife. When the sacrificers were thus in order, they brought forth such as had been taken in war, and caused them to mount up those large stairs in rank to the place where the ministers were prepared. As they respectfully approached those ministers, the latter seized them, two of them laying hold of the two feet, and two more of the two hands of the unhappy victim, and in this manner cast him upon his back upon the pointed stone, while the fifth fastened round his neck the serpentine collar of wood. The high priest then opened his stomach with the knife, with wonderful dexterity and nimbleness, tearing out his heart with his hand, which he elevated smoking towards the sun, to whom he did offer it, and presently turning towards the idol, did cast the heart towards it, besmearing his face with the blood. In this manner were all the victims sacrificed, and the bodies afterwards precipitated down the stairs, reeking with their gore. There were forty or fifty victims at the least thus sacrificed." (Acosta's Hist. of the Ind., p. 383.)
[38] "In Persia, numerous galleries built with stone, and communicating with each other by shafts, fill up the interior of the artificial hills." (Humb. Res., vol. i., p. 102.) Many of these excavations have been discovered in different parts of this continent. Two fine caves,

foundations of this stupendous temple,[39] and passed through the horrible mysteries of the Mexican religion, which emblematically represented the wanderings of their god. These caverns were denominated, *the path of the dead.* Here he saw such sights as made his blood run cold. The phantoms of slain victims passed before his eyes; this moment seen, the next lost in the darkness. Now he heard the groans of the dying, the shrieks of despair, and the howlings of hopeless grief, rendered still more dismaying by the ominous sound of the sacred horn,[40] while he passed, with tottering footsteps, the dungeons where religious victims were confined. Every step he took, some horrible object flitting across the gloom met his eyes; some sound, appalling to his senses,[41] struck upon his ear; and he proceeded with measured pace, fearful lest the knife of the sacrificing priest should be next applied to him ; or that an incautious step might precipitate him into some deep and hidden pitfall, where

resembling the extraordinary caverns in the peak of Derbyshire, have recently been found about twelve miles from Albany. (Gent's. Mag., Jan., 1822.)

[39] "I have been assured," says M. Humboldt, (Res., vol. i., p. 90,) "by some Indians of Cholula, that the inside of the pyramids is hollow ; and that during the abode of Cortes in this city, their ancestors had concealed in the body of the pyramid a considerable number of warriors, who were to fall suddenly on the Spaniards ; but the materials of which the teocalli is built, and the silence of the historians of those times, give but little probability to this latter assertion. It is certain, however, that in the interior of the pyramids there are considerable cavities, which were used as sepulchres," &c.

[40] Univ. Displayed, vol. i., p. 194.

[41] "A traveller of credit gives us an account, in the Philosophical Transactions, of a remarkable cave, some leagues to the north-west of Mexico, gilded all over with a sort of leaf-gold, which had eluded many Spaniards by its promising colour, for they could never reduce it into a body, either by quicksilver or fusion. This traveller went thither one morning, with an Indian for his guide, and found its situation was pretty high, and in a place very proper for the generation of metals. As he entered into it, the light of the candle soon discovered on all sides, but especially over his head, a glittering canopy of these mineral leaves ; at which he greedily snatching, there fell down a great lump of sand, that not only put out his candle, but almost blinded him ; and calling aloud to his Indian, who stood at the entrance of the cave, as, being afraid of spirits and hobgoblins, *it occasioned such thundering and redoubled echoes,* that the poor fellow, imagining he had been wrestling with some infernal ghosts, soon quitted his station, and thereby left a free passage for some rays of light to enter, and serve him for a better guide." (Univ. Displayed, vol. i., p. 397.)

his cries might not be heard. Thus was he conducted
through caverns slippery with half congealed blood;
damp, gloomy, and full of terror. His ears are saluted
with heavy groans. His heart throbs as they seem to
rise from beneath his feet. His fears are realized; for
here lay the quivering frame of a dying victim, whose
heart had been violently rent from its living sepulchre,[42]
and offered up in sacrifice to the sanguinary gods.[43] The
candidate averts his eyes, and trembles for his own
security. He turns to his guide and is about to break
through the strict injunction of silence which he received
at his entrance into these subterranean chambers of
death. His guide, with an expressive look, lays his finger
on his lips, and the candidate restrains his indignation.
He pauses and looks around him. He finds himself in a
spacious vault, through which an artificial sun or lambent
flame darted its feeble lustre ;[44] and in the roof observes
a small orifice, through which the wretched victim had
been precipitated; for they were now immediately beneath the high altar of Vitzliputzli.[45]

Hurried on from one horror to another, it was only
the rapidity of his movements that prevented him from
sinking under the trial ; it was only the change of scene
and situation which, dissipating reflection, supported him
under the arduous ceremony. At length they arrived at
a narrow chasm or stone fissure at the termination of
this extensive range of caverns, through which the

[42] We have already seen that the priests were clothed in the skins
of victims ; and they had another disgusting practice of a similar nature,
which is thus related. "It was a custom among them on certain
festivals, to dress a man in the bloody skin, just reeking from the body
of one of their victims. A Spanish author assures us that even their
kings and grandees did not think it derogatory to their honour to disguise themselves in this manner, when the captive sacrificed was a
person of distinction. Be that as it will, the disguised person used to
run up and down the streets, and places of public resort of the city, to
beg the charity of all those he met with, and to beat such as refused.
This bloody kind of masquerade continued till such time as the skin
coat began to stink. The money that was collected in this devout
ramble, was employed in pious uses. Not to mention another festival,
when they used to slay a woman, and clothe an Indian with her skin,
who, thus equipped, danced for two days together with the rest of his
fellow-citizens." (Univ. Dis., vol. i., p. 189, 192.)

[43] Acosta. Hist. Ind., p. 382.   [44] Fab. Pag. Idol., vol. iii., p. 189.
[45] Humb. Res., vol. i., p. 222.

aspirant was formally protruded, and was received by a shouting multitude in the open air as a person regenerated or born again.[46]

During the secret celebration of the rites, the females without, divesting themselves of the little clothing which they usually wore, sang and danced[47] in a state of nudity like the frantic Bacchantes.[48] This dance they repeated three times; after which they welcomed the new-born aspirant at his deliverance from the sepulchral process of initiation, and gave themselves up to boundless licentiousness and prostitution.[49] The most outrageous acts of indecency were now committed and tolerated; and the services misnamed sacred, were stained with every species of impurity.[50] And thus were closed the primary initiations of this savage race.

However the general doctrines of this religion might be communicated to the initiated, there were certain degrees of information respecting the most occult rites which were absolutely unattainable, except by the priests; and not even by them until they were qualified to receive the distinguished appellation of Ministers of sacred things by the sacrifice of a human victim;[51] and this dignity once attained, they were eligible to the highest offices of the priesthood. An hour was chosen for the performance

[46] This was undoubtedly the Pastos of the eastern mysteries, and constitutes an additional proof that they were all derived from one common source; for the cavern symbolized the Ark, and the chasm the door through which the great Father proceeded into the renovated world, and was hence said to be a second time born.

[47] The quadrangle in which the temple of Vitzliputzli was situated was so extensive, that "eight or ten thousand persons used to dance therein on solemn days with the greatest ease." (Univ. Dis., vol. i., p. 187.)

[48] Purch. Pilg., b. 8, c. 4.   [49] Rel. Cer. of Var. Nat., p. 289.

[50] Purchas (ut supra) tells us that the young females prostituted themselves without ceremony from 14 or 15 to about 20 years of age, when they were considered eligible to enter into the marriage state!

[51] Prisoners of rank, or approved courage, had a faint chance afforded them of escaping the horrid rite of immolation, by publicly "fighting six Mexican warriors in succession. If the prisoner were fortunate enough to conquer them, his liberty was granted, and he was permitted to return to his own country; if, on the contrary, he sunk under the strokes of one of his adversaries, a priest called Chalchiuhtepehua dragged him, dead or living, to the altar, and tore out his heart." (Humb. Res., vol. i., p. 267.)

of these solemn rites, and it was at midnight only that
the most ineffable degrees of knowledge were communicated; and that under severe obligations, whose penalty
was death without remission.

Their instruction was symbolical, and referred princi
pally to the Deluge, and the wanderings and subsequent
settlement of their ancestors on the lake in which Mexico
was built.   They were ignorant of the means used to
create the world; but asserted that four suns had been
created and destroyed;[52] the first was destroyed by

[52] " The Mexicans believed, according to a very ancient prediction,
that the end of the world would take place at the termination of a
cycle of fifty-two years; that the sun would no more appear in the
horizon; and that mankind would be devoured by evil genii of hideous
appearance, known under the name of Tzitzimimes.   This belief was,
no doubt, connected with the Tolteck tradition of the Four (Suns or)
Ages, according to which the earth had already undergone four great
revolutions, three of which had taken place at the end of a cycle.   The
people passed in the deepest consternation the five complimentary
days, and on the fifth the sacred fire was extinguished in the temples
by order of the high priest; in the convents, the monks devoted
themselves to prayer; at the approach of night, no person dared light
the fire in his house; the vessels of clay were broken, garments torn,
and whatever was most precious was destroyed, because everything
appeared useless at the tremendous moment of the last day.   Amidst
this frantic superstition, pregnant women became the objects of peculiar horror to the men; their faces were hidden with masks! they
were imprisoned in the storehouses of maize, from a persuasion, that
if the cataclysm took place, the women, transformed into tigers, would
make common cause with the evil genii, to avenge themselves of the
injustice of the men.   In the evening of the last day began the festival
of the new fire.   The priests took the dresses of their gods; and,
followed by an immense crowd of people, went in solemn procession
to the mountain of Huixachtecatl, two leagues from Mexico.   This
lugubrious march was termed the march of the gods (teonenemi), a
denomination which reminded the Mexicans that the gods had quitted
the city, and that, perhaps, they would see them no more.   When the
procession had reached the summit of the mountain, it waited the
moment when the Pleiades ascended the middle of the sky, to begin
the horrible sacrifice of a human victim.   The body of the victim
remained stretched on the ground, and the instrument made use of to
kindle the fire by rubbing, was placed on the wound which the priest
of Copulco, armed with a knife of obsidian, had made in the breast of
the prisoner destined to be sacrificed.   When the bits of wood detached
by the rapid motion of the cylinder, had taken fire, an enormous pile,
previously prepared to receive the body of the unfortunate victim,
was kindled.   The flames of the pile were seen from a great part of
the valley of Mexico, on account of the height of the mountain on
which this sanguinary rite was performed; and the people filled the
air with joyful exclamations.   All those who were not able to follow

water; the second by giants; the third by fire, and the
fourth by a tempest of wind, which was succeeded by a
darkness of twenty-five years' duration. The sun which
now enlightens the world they held to be the fifth; and
he was the object of their adoration.[53] They spake of
Tonacateuctli, the great father, and Cihuacohuatl, the
great mother of mankind, and her serpent,[54] which was
ultimately crushed by the mighty spirit Teotl; they
taught that, in the early ages, long before the Incas
began to reign, the sea overflowed its banks, covered
the whole continent with water, and drowned all the
inhabitants except one family who were enclosed in a
box.[55] After a confinement of some length, they sent

the procession, were stationed on the terraces of houses, or the tops
of the teocallis, or the hills that arose in the middle of the lake; their
eyes were fixed on the spot where the flame was to appear, a certain
presage of the benevolence of the gods, and of the preservation of
mankind during the course of a new cycle. Messengers posted at
respective distances, holding branches of the wood of a very resinous
pine, carried the new fire from village to village, to the distance of
fifteen or twenty leagues; it was deposited in every temple, whence it
was distributed to every private dwelling. When the sun began to
appear on the horizon, the acclamations redoubled. The procession
returned to the city, and the people thought that they beheld their
gods return to their sanctuaries. The women were now released from
prison; every one put on new dresses, and everything went on in its
usual course." (Humb. Res., vol. i., p. 380.)

[53] The Floridans worshipped the sun in a deep cavern, under the
form of a cone or phallus. (Ban. Myth., vol. i., p. 144.)

[54] Humb. Res., vol. i., p. 195. Evidently referring to our first parents
in paradise, and the serpent tempter.

[55] The cosmogony of the North American savages is thus given by
Hennepin in his voyage to a country larger than Europe. "The
world was created by a spirit to which the Iroquois have given the
name of Otkon, those of Virginia, Okee, and other savages, who inhabit
the mouth of St. Lawrence's river, Atahauta, and that one Messou
destroyed it after the Flood. They tell us that, as Messou was one
day hunting, his dogs lost themselves in a great lake, which happening
to overflow, soon spread itself over all the earth. They add that, by
the help of some animals, he restored the world. The savages that
inhabit the head of St. Lawrence's river, and the Mississippi, tell us,
that a woman descended from heaven, and hovered some time in the
air, seeking where to rest her foot; that the tortoise offered his back,
which she accepted, and chose that place for her residence; that
afterwards the filth of the sea gathered itself about the tortoise, and
insensibly expanded itself to a great extent of ground. However, as
this woman did not delight in solitude, a spirit descended from above;
who, finding her asleep, drew near to her; that the result of his approach was, her being with child; that she was delivered of two sons.

out birds, by which it was ascertained that the waters
had subsided, for one of them brought back in its mouth
the branch of a tree; when they quitted their asylum
and repeopled the earth. They inculcated the immortality of the soul, and worshipped a triad consisting of
Vitzliputzli—Tlaloc—Tescalipuca. Then followed an
account of their original population, which bears such a
striking analogy with the settling of the Israelites in the
promised land, as to induce some authors to suspect that
it proceeded from a tradition of the deliverance of that
people from their Egyptian captivity, and their subse-

who came out of her side. When the children were grown up, they
exercised themselves in hunting; and as one of them was a much
more skilful hunter than the other, jealousy soon occasioned discord.
They lived together in irreconcilable hatred. The unskilful hunter,
who was of a very savage temper, treated his brother so ill, as forced
him to leave the earth, and withdraw to heaven. After he had thus
withdrawn himself, the spirit returned again to the woman, and from
this second interview a daughter was born, who is the grand parent
of the North Americans." (Rel. Cerem. of Var Nat., p. 298.) In
commenting on the above legends, it will be needless to say that they
bear a decided reference to the Creation and the Deluge. The learned
Grotius tells us (De verit., l. i., s. 16), that " in many parts of America is preserved the memory of the Deluge, and the preservation of
animals, particularly the raven and the dove." Messou and his dogs
are but a transcript of Pwyll in the mysteries of Britain, for dogs
were a legitimate token of the diluvian celebrations; and it is remarkable how generally this belief has prevailed in every region of the
world. The woman who descended from heaven resembles the Grecian Juno (Yuneh), or the dove; and the tortoise reminds us of the
Courma Avater of the East, in which the same animal supports Vishnu
on his back while the Deluge is produced. The contact of the Spirit
with the sleeping woman is an evident specimen of the confusion
which pervades every idolatrous system. The act of Creation is so
intimately blended with the Deluge, as certainly to refer to the
doctrine of an endless succession of worlds; for destruction was ever
considered but as a necessary prelude to reproduction; and creation
but the act of renewing matter which had been previously destroyed.
The two sons thus begotten were the Cain and Abel of Moses; and,
perhaps, the manner in which they were born might have some indistinct reference to the creation or birth of Eve from the side of her
husband. The second meeting of the Spirit and the woman produced
a daughter, who corresponds with the Great Mother of the eastern
world; and the repeopling of the earth by means of these infant
deities was annually commemorated by a solemn sacrifice. The people
assembled on a lake or river in innumerable canoes to witness the
ceremony. A boy and girl of great beauty were produced by the
priests, and, after certain mysterious rites, they were placed in a leaky
boat, and abandoned to the miserable fate of perishing in the waters.
(Purch. Pilgr., b. viii., c. 13. Fab. Pag. Idol., vol. i., p. 271.)

quent wanderings in the wilderness. A warlike tribe of
North Americans, says the legend, under an experienced
chief, and directed by the god Vitzliputzli, who, holding
in his hand a rod formed like a serpent,[56] was seated in a
square Ark,[57] made of reeds,[58] called the throne of the
god,[59] (teoicpalli) the four angels of which were surmounted by serpents' heads.[60] The ark was borne by
four priests;[61] and thus protected, the people set out in
quest of a settlement, assured by the god that they
should conquer every enemy who might be rash enough
to oppose their design.[62] They marched and encamped
by the direction of Vitzliputzli;[63] who, during the continuance of an extended rest, revealed the mode of worship[64] which was most acceptable to him; and dictated
a code of laws to be used when they had taken possession
of the land of promise; and also distinctly marked the
place of their settlement to be upon a lake,[65] abounding
with the lotos,[66] on the borders of which they should find
a fig-tree growing out of a rock, where was perched an
eagle in the act of devouring its prey. In the midst of
their encampments a tabernacle was erected, which contained an altar[67] for the reception of the sacred ark, on
which their god was triumphantly seated. After a long
and tedious expedition they arrived at the precise spot

[56] Could this primitive people have any tradition that the Rod of
Moses was changed into a serpent? (Exod. iv., 3.)

[57] The Israelites were accompanied by an Ark (Josh. iii., 1), which
was esteemed the throne of God. (Exod xxv., 22; xl., 38; Psalm
lxxx., 1; Isai. xxxvi., 16.) And Moses was concealed in an Ark of
bulrushes.

[58] Purch. Pilgr., b. viii., c. 10.   [59] Humb. Res., vol. i., p. 216.

[60] These correspond with *the horns* of the Israelitish altar. (Exod.
xxxviii., 2.)

[61] Vid. Deut. xi., 8.   Josh. vi., 6.

[62] "If thou shalt say in thine heart, These nations are more than I,
how can I dispossess them? Thou shalt not be affrighted at them;
for the Lord thy God is among you, a mighty God, and terrible."
(Deut. vii., 17, 21.)

[63] Robertson, Amer., b. iv., s. 8.   Vid. Exod. xl., 36.

[64] Exod. xxiv., 12.

[65] The Mexican tradition of the Deluge, and the building of a tower
to reach the heavens, may be found in Signs and Symbols, Lect. 5.

[66] It will be altogether unnecessary here to point out the resemblance which the Ark, the serpent-rod, the lotos, and the lake, bear to
the rites of the eastern world. It will be apparent to the most casual
reader of the preceding pages.   [67] Exod. xl., 2, 3.

which had been pointed out, and, finding the prescribed tokens, they built the city of Mexico on an island in the midst of the water;[68] furnished it with a pyramidal temple,[69] and soon became a populous and flourishing nation

Their knowledge was wrapped up in hieroglyphical symbols;[70] and they were acquainted with a most complete system of picture writing,[71] by the use of which they perpetuated their history, as well as their philosophy. Like all other early nations, they bore a particular affection for amulets, which were considered the habita-

[68] Purch. Pilgr., b. viii., c. 10.

[69] Ibid. b. ix., c. 9. Humb. Res., vol. i., p. 81.

[70] The Mexican temples were covered over with hieroglyphics sculptured in relief. Thus to express the rapid progress of time, they introduced a serpent; for suffering innocence, a rabbit was the symbol. Drawings of feet denoted a public road. A living man was represented by a human figure with small tongues painted near his mouth; a dead man had none of those appendages. To live is to speak, say they; and hence a volcano was symbolized by a cone with tongues over its summit, to denote the mountain that speaks, &c. (Vid. Humb. Res., vol. i., p. 140. Warb. Div. Leg., vol. ii., p. 67.)

[71] The first method of recording public events, used by this people, was by knots or quippus (Marm. Incas., vol. i., p. 32); but the imperfection of this system caused it soon to be abandoned, and hieroglyphics were introduced; and at the conquest of Cortes they formed an exclusive profession in which thousands of persons were employed. Their books were rolled in a zigzag form, and the paintings were executed on the folds. They had "real simple hieroglyphics for water, earth, air, wind, day, night, the middle of the night, speech, motion; they had also for numbers, for the days and the months of the solar year. These signs, added to the painting of an event, marked, in a very ingenious manner, whether the action passed during the day or night; the age of the persons they wished to represent; whether they had been conversing, and who among them had spoken most. We even find among them vestiges of that kind of hieroglyphics which is called *phonetic,* and which indicates relations, not with things, but with the language spoken. Among semi-barbarous nations the names of individuals, of cities and mountains, have generally some allusion to objects that strike the senses, such as the form of plants and animals, fire, air, or earth. This circumstance has given the Azteck people the means of being able to write the names of cities and those of their sovereigns. The verbal translation of Axajacatl is, *face of water;* that of Ilhuicamina, *arrow which pierces the sky;* thus to represent the kings Monteuczoma Ilhuicamina and Axajacatl, the painter united the hieroglyphics of water and the sky to the figure of a head and of an arrow. In this manner the union of several simple hieroglyphics indicated compound names, and by signs which spoke at the same time to the eye and to the ear." (Humb. Res., vol. i., p. 159.)

tion of benevolent spirits, whose intervention would preserve them from every species of calamity in this life; and convey them, after death, to a happy and flourishing country; blest with perpetual peace and plenty; abounding with game and fish; free from storms and tempests, blight and mildew, and all the terrible judgments inflicted on the wicked by the agency and wrath of the vindictive Tescalipuca.

"The Incas of Peru boasted of their descent from the two great luminaries of heaven; or, in other words, from Noah and the Ark, worshipped in conjunction with the Sun and Moon."[72] The rites of initiation were essentially the same as those of other nations; varied, indeed, in a succession of ages from the system of the original planters. They were said to have been introduced by Manco Capac and Mama Ocello,[73] who were descended from one of the persons saved at the Deluge.[74] They taught the natives to worship a god called Pacha-Camac—a name so venerable, that those who were intrusted with it were bound by solemn oaths never to expose it to profanation. They termed the Creator Viracocha,[75] which signifies "the froth of the sea;" and the evil power Cupai.[76]

[72] Fab. Mys. Cab., c. 4. "They worshipped every object in Nature from which they derived any advantage; mountains, the sources of rivers, rivers themselves, and the fountains which watered and fertilized the earth; the trees which afforded them fuel; those animals of a gentle and timid nature upon which they fed; the sea abounding with fish, and which they denominated their Nurse. But objects of terror had the most numerous votaries.—Whatever was hideous, or horrible, they converted to a god, as if man delighted to terrify himself. They worshipped the tiger, the lion, the vulture, and large snakes; they adored the elements, tempests, the winds, thunder caverns, and precipices; they prostrated themselves before torrents the noise of which depressed them with fear; before gloomy forests and at the foot of those dreadful volcanos, which cast forth upon them torrents of flame and rocks of fire." (Incas, vol. ii., p. 4, 5.)

[73] Abbé Raynal, Hist. Ind., vol. iii., p. 17. Garcil., b. i., c. 15. These personages were the Osiris and Isis, Bacchus and Rhea, Hu and Ceridwen, &c., of the old world.

[74] They say also that Manco Capac, like Mithras, was born from a Rock or Cave (Purch. Pilgr., b. ix., c. 9); but in all nations there was such an intimate connection between a cave and the Ark, that the one was frequently mistaken for the other.

[75] To this god the father of a family would offer his son as a vicarious sacrifice to avert sickness from his family. (Acosta, p. 380.) He was also identified with the Sun. (Purch., b. ix., c. 10.

[76] Cerem. of Var. Nat., p. 329.

10*

They worshipped a Triad of deity, for Acosta says,[77] they had an idol whom they called Tangatanga, which signifies, *One in Three, and Three in One;*[78] and paid divine honours to the Sun[79] as the fountain of Light,[80] and the parent of the Incas.[81]

On their great annual festival, which was held on the first day of the September moon, their secret mysteries were celebrated, which they believed would convey a

[77] Cerem. of Var. Nat., p. 412.

[78] Faber (Pag. Idol., vol. i., p. 269) says they entertained a belief in two other triads. "The first consisted of Chuquilla—Catuilla—Intylappa, or the father-thunder, the son-thunder, and the brother-thunder; the second of Apomti—Churunti—Intiquaoqui, the father-Sun, the son-Sun, and the brother-Sun."

[79] "At Cusco was that wonderful temple of the sun, the beauty and riches whereof surpassed imagination.—I shall transcribe the description which one of their Incas, called Garcilasso, has given us thereof. His words are as follow: 'The high altar of this pompous edifice stood eastward; and the roof, which was made of timber, was thatched over, they having no tile or brick among them. The four walls of the temple, from the top downwards, were all covered over with plates of gold, and the ceiling was also of gold. On the high altar was the figure of the sun, represented on a gold plate, twice as thick as those which covered the walls. This figure, which was made of one continued piece, represented a round face, surrounded with rays and flames, in the same manner as our painters usually draw the sun. It was of so prodigious a breadth, that it almost covered one side of the wall, on which there was no other representation of any kind.—This was the only one the Peruvians had, either in that or any other temple. On each side of the image of the sun, the several bodies of their deceased incas, or monarchs, were ranged in order, according to the course of their respective reigns, and so embalmed (the manner of which is not known to us) that they seemed to be alive. They were seated on thrones of gold, raised on plates of the same metal, with their faces looking towards the bottom of the temple.—This temple had several gates, which were all covered with plates of gold, the chief of which looked towards the north, as it still does to this day. Moreover, round the walls of this temple, on the outside, was a cornice of gold, in the shape of a crown or garland, more than a yard broad. On one side of the temple was a cloister, built in a quadrangular form; and in its highest enclosure a garland of pure gold, an ell broad, like the above-mentioned. Round this cloister were five square pavilions, or houses, covered over in the shape of a pyramid. The first was built for the habitation of the moon, the sun's wife, and stood the nearest to the great chapel of the temple. The doors and enclosures of it were covered with silver plates; its white colour denoting that it was the apartment allotted to 'the moon, whose figure was represented like that of the sun; but with this difference, that it stood upon a silver plate, and was represented with a woman's face." (Univ. Dis., vol. i., p. 268, 269.)

[80] Raynal. Hist. Ind., vol. iii., p. 20.   [81] Marm. Incas, vol ii., p 40

general lustration, cleanse the soul from all its impurities, and render the body healthy and less susceptible of disease. They prepared for this solemnity by a fast of four and twenty hours' continuance; and then kneaded the purifying element, which was a sort of dough[82] mixed with blood, and called Cancu.[83] After washing their bodies, they anointed them with this dough, and fixed the remainder on the door of their habitation. Thus purified, the people watched the rising of the sun[84] with great emotion; and when his radiance burst upon their view, the eastern doors of their temple were expanded, and his image in burnished gold was illuminated with the blazing splendour of his beams. The whole multitude, in devout prostration, chanted the sacred hymn, led by the High Priest.[85] After this, the mild and equitable laws of Peru were rehearsed; and the Inca, with the chief officers of the realm, swore to administer justice with strict impartiality. A procession of young men and maidens succeeded, habited in white and spotless garments, and bearing garlands of flowers. These paraded round the temple until the Sun had attained his meridian height,[86] when the Inca and High Priest offered up a solemn prayer to that deity. The consecrated virgins then approached, and were presented to the Inca, and heard from the unpolluted lip of the High Priest, the awful denunciations attached to violated vows of perpetual celibacy.

[82] "The night after the fast, they used to knead pieces or balls of a dough which they called cancu. They par-boiled these in earthen kettles, till such time as they were collected into one great lump. Of this they made two sorts, one of which was mixed with blood, which they drew from between the eyebrows and nostrils of young children." (Univ. Dis., vol. i., p. 271.)

[83] How similar is this ceremony to a rite practised by the idolatrous Israelites when the fury of the Lord was ready to be poured upon them. "The children gather wood and the fathers kindle the fire, and *the women knead the dough to make cakes to the queen of heaven*, and to pour out drink offerings unto other gods, that they may provoke me to anger, saith the Lord." (Jer. vii., 18. See also xliv., 15–19.)

[84] The first dynasties of Incas were dignified with the names of the sun and moon. (Horn. de Orig. Gent. Amer., p. 105.

[85] Marm. Incas, vol. i., pp. 25–27.

[86] "Upon twelve mountains that surrounded the city of Cusco, there were twelve stone columns, dedicated to the sun, and answering to the twelve months of the year." (Fab. Pag. Idol., vol. iii., p. 230.)

Four Incas then made a progress through the city, armed in the day with lances richly adorned, and at night furnished with blazing torches.[87] The inhabitants flocked around them, and hailed their arrival with loud and joyful acclamations; for this auspicious ceremony was believed to purge the city from disease and calamity for the ensuing year. The lustration was closed with a grand procession to the temple of the Sun, where the secret rites were concluded by public sacrifices, accompanied with divination, which it was not lawful for the High Priest to reveal but to the Inca alone.[88]

---

[87] Univ. Dis., vol. i., p. 272.

[88] Marmontel has furnished a beautiful specimen of divination from the setting of the sun after a public festival, which foretold the approach of the Spaniards. "The people and the grandees themselves waited in silence without the court. The king alone ascended the steps of the portico, where the High Priest was waiting for his sovereign, to whom alone the secrets of futurity were to be imparted.— The heaven was serene; the air calm and without vapours; and for the instant one might have taken the setting for the rising sun. On a sudden, however, from the bosom of the Pacific Ocean, there arises over the top of Mount Palmar, a cloud resembling a mass of bloody waves; an appearance which, on a solemnity like this, was looked upon as an omen of calamity. The High Priest shuddered at the sight; he comforted himself, however, with the hopes that, before the sun should be quite gone down, these vapours would be dispersed. Instead of that they increase, they pile themselves one upon another, in appearance like the tops of mountains, and, as they ascend, seem to brave the god as he approaches, and defy him to break the vast barrier they oppose to him. He descends with majesty, and, summoning forth to him all his rays, he rushes on the purple flood; he opens through it many a flaming gulf; but then on a sudden the abyss is closed. Twenty times he shakes off, as many times he seems to sink under the burden. Overwhelmed awhile, then putting forth a few scattered rays, he expends the whole remaining force of his enfeebled light, till at length, exhausted with the struggle, he remains deluged, as it were, in a sea of blood.—A phenomenon still more tremendous showed itself in the sky. It was one of those luminaries which were thought to wander without a plan, before the piercing eye of Astronomy had traced them in their course through the immensity of space. A comet, resembling a dragon vomiting forth fire, and whose flaming mane bristles round upon his head, advances from the east, as if he were flying after the sun. To the eyes of the people it appears but as a spark in the blue firmament; but the High Priest, more inquisitive, fancies he can distinguish all the lineaments of that portentous monster. He sees the flames issue out of his nostrils; he sees him flap his fiery wings; he sees his flaming eye-balls pursue the sun in his path from the zenith to the horizon, as if eager to get up with him and devour him. Dissembling, however, the terror which

The Peruvians, according to the testimony of Bartholomew Las Casas, were as innocent as lambs;[89] and Columbus said, in a letter to the King of Spain, "I swear to your majesty, there is not in the world a people more gentle, or more inoffensive." The Inca was distinguished by the title of Whaccacuyas, the friend of the poor.

the prodigy had struck into his soul, 'Prince,' says the Pontiff to the King, 'follow me into the temple,' " &c., &c. (Marm. Incas, vol. i., pp. 53, 54, &c.)

[89] Las Casas was, however, a partial judge, for Acosta tells us, that they "sacrificed young children from foure to six yeares old unto tenne," in prodigious numbers, to avert misfortune and procure blessings. "They did likewise sacrifice virgins; and sometimes a sonne would be sacrificed to the Sunne for the life of the father." (Hist. Ind., p. 380.) Thus, like the idolatrous Israelites of old, they sacrificed their sons and their daughters unto devils. (Psalm cvi., 36.)

COROLLARY.

Such were the famous mysteries of idolatry. I have designedly omitted to draw any formal comparison, for the purpose of shewing what portion of the true Freemasonry they retained amidst all their abominations, because the intelligent Brother will not fail to discover the points of resemblance wherever they occur. It will appear evident that all the mysteries of antiquity originated in some common source, which was familiar to the primitive leader of every tribe that formed the nucleus of great and powerful nations; because the ceremonies, in all cases, bear a striking similarity to each other. They were all funereal. The legend celebrated the death and resurrection of some imaginary being in whom their affections were interested, and to whom their devotions were directed to be paid. The rites were always solemnized in lamentation, terminating in joy. Severe tests and probations accompanied the ceremonial; and the initiations were performed in secret caverns, which were alike the object of horror and dread to the uninitiated, and the vehicles of a mystical regeneration to the epopt which conferred personal and political distinction. Ablutions and purifications formed a distinguishing feature in all these institutions; the efficacy of which was not a little augmented by the supposed virtues of amulets and talismans, that constituted a perpetual shield of protection, under the cover of which, the enlightened candidate expected to surmount all the evils of life.

The doctrines of the mysteries formed another, and more decisive evidence of their common origin and primitive application. They exhibit traces, which cannot be mistaken, of the unity and trinity of the godhead; of the creation and fall of man; the promise of a Mediator, who should expiate sin by a voluntary death; the doctrine of redemption by blood, of a vicarious sacrifice, by the efficacy of which a single life would be accepted as a sacrifice for all. We discover, in these remarkable institutions, fables which bear an undoubted reference to the sin of our first parents, and their exclusion from the garden of bliss, where they were originally placed by their beneficent Creator—a sin produced by the intervention of a serpent tempter; to the first fratricide, and the transactions of the antediluvian world; to the destruction of the human race, for their iniquities, by the waters of a deluge, and the salvation of one just family, in a boat or Ark, for the repeopling of the earth; to the Egyptian bondage, and the deliverance under the conduct of the Jewish lawgiver; to the sacrifice of Isaac, and many other facts in the early history of the world, which are of the utmost importance to the present and future condition of man.

Above all, the reader will be struck with the remarkable fact, that the abstruse doctrines of the resurrection and a future state, which were not perfectly understood, even by God's favourite people, were embodied in the ceremonies of initiation; where the candidate not only is figured to die and be restored to life, but the torments of a place of punishment are broadly contrasted with the happiness of the final reward which good men are sure to enjoy after death.

These coincidences are remarkable, and leave no doubt on the mind but they were learned by the planters of all nations, when the inhabitants of the earth dwelt together as one family; worshipping the same God; participating in the same privileges, and practising the same rites and ceremonies. It is impossible that the above truths could have been invented; they must have been derived; and they could not have been derived from any system but that which had been revealed from heaven to the first race of men, before they were contaminated by error, or polluted by the abominations of an idolatrous worship. In this view, the mysterious institutions of antiquity, explained in these pages, form a striking corroboration of the Mosaic history and records. The evidence is extremely valuable, because it is undesigned. Nor did the heathen nations suspect—when they were burning incense to the spurious deities of their teeming pantheon, and fostering their secret institutions to uphold alike the supremacy of their religious and political creed, and their own assumption of divine honours—that they were furnishing an unsuspected evidence to the cause of religi-

ous truth, which, at the appointed time, should uproot
their system, and triumphantly found the true plan of
human salvation on its ruins.

It will be seen that every system of mystery practised
throughout the world has been applied to religion and
the worship of the deity.[1] How diversified soever in

---

[1] I subjoin, without comment, the following observations of the
learned and intelligent Faber, on the *machinery* of the Apocalypse,
which he thinks was borrowed from that of the mysteries.   In this
Book, "we find the pure Church described as a woman clothed with
the sun, and standing upon the crescent of the moon; while a corrupted Church is exhibited to us, both under the image of a female
floating upon the surface of many waters, and under that of a harlot
using a monstrous beast as her vehicle.   The former of these women,
when about to bring forth her first-born, is attacked by a monstrous
serpent, which spouts out, against her offspring, a deluge of water;
but the earth opens its mouth, and receives the mighty inundation
into the centrical abyss.   The latter of them, under the mystic name
of *the false prophet*, together with her bestial supporter, is said to be,
at length, plunged alive into an infernal lake, burning with fire and
brimstone.   I cannot but think it sufficiently clear, that the whole of
this machinery is palpably diluvian; and I believe it *to have been
derived from that received imagery of the Patriarchal Church, which
by a corrupted channel was admitted into Paganism.*   It is impossible
not to perceive that the woman standing upon the crescent is the very
figure of the Samian Juno, or of the Egyptian Isis, who were represented in a precisely similar manner with reference to the lunar boat;
that the attack upon the woman and her offspring, by the deluging
serpent, which is frustrated by the Earth's absorption of the waters,
is perfectly analogous to the attack of the diluvian serpent Python or
Typhon upon Latona and Horus; which is similarly frustrated by the
destruction of that monster; and that the false Church, bearing the
name of *Mystery*, floating on the mighty waters, or riding on a
terrific beast, and ultimately plunged into the infernal lake, exhibits
the very same aspect as the Great Mother of Paganism sailing over
the ocean, riding on her usual vehicle, the lion, venerated with certain
appropriate Mysteries, and during the celebration of those Mysteries,
plunged into the waters of a sacred lake, deemed the lake of Hades.
I take it, that in the representation of the pure Church, *an ancient
patriarchal scheme of symbolical machinery*, derived most plainly from
the events of the Deluge, and borrowed with the usual perverse mis-
application by the contrivers of Paganism, has been reclaimed to its
proper use; while, in the representation of the false Church, which,
under a new name, revived the old Gentile demonolatry, the very
imagery and language of the Gentile hierophants has, with singular
propriety, been studiously adopted. (Rev. xii., xvii., 1–5, xix., 20.)   I
need scarcely remark that I am speaking solely of the apocalyptic
machinery ; of this, the origin will still be the same, however we may
interpret the prophecies which are built upon it.   *The whole machinery
of the Apocalypse, from beginning to end, seems to me, very plainly, to
have been borrowed from the machinery of the ancient Mysteries :* and

other respects, this is a broad and distinguishing feature
which undisguisedly pervades the whole. If the deities
were false, the system was false also; and if the worship
was directed to its true fountain, the system remained
pure and uncontaminated by error or delusion : Religion,
so called, was the ostensible design of each; for, however the world may have been infested and overrun by
idolatry, it has suffered little from professed atheism.
There is a principle implanted in the heart of man,
which prompts him to the belief and acknowledgment
of a superior and superintending power, under whatever
name he may have been personified; endowed with
attributes of infinite knowledge and infinite wisdom.
Sophism cannot overwhelm it; philosophy cannot succeed in erasing it from the heart; it is engraven there
in characters broad and deep, and spake the same language to the ignorant savage, amidst trackless woods
and barren wastes, and to the proud philosopher of
antiquity, as it did to the learned Jew or the enlightened

this, if we consider the nature of the subject, was done with the
very strictest attention to poetical decorum. St. John, himself, is
made to personate *an aspirant* about to be initiated ; and, accordingly,
the images presented to his mind's eye closely resemble the pageants
of the Mysteries, both in *their nature*, and in *order of succession*. The
prophet first beholds a *door opened* in the magnificent temple of heaven;
and into this he is invited to enter by the voice of one, who plays *the
hierophant*. Here he witnesses the unsealing of *a sacred book;* and,
forthwith, he is appalled by a troup of *ghastly apparitions*, which flit
in horrid succession before his eyes. Among these are pre-eminently
conspicuous, *a vast serpent*, the well-known symbol of the Great
Father ; and two portentous *wild beasts*, which severally come up out
of the sea and out of the earth. Such hideous figures correspond with
the canine phantoms of the Orgies, which seemed to rise out of the
ground, and with the polymorphic images of the principal hero god,
who was universally deemed the offspring of the sea. Passing these
terrific monsters in safety, the prophet, constantly attended by his
angel-hierophant, who acts the part of an interpreter, is conducted
into the presence of a *female*, who is described as closely resembling
the Great Mother of Pagan theology. Like Isis, emerging from the
sea, and exhibiting herself to the eyes of the aspirant. Apuleius, this
female divinity, upborne upon the marine wild beast, appears to float
upon the surface of many waters. She is said to be *an open and sys-
tematical harlot;* just as the Great Mother was the declared female
principle of fecundity ; and as she was always propitiated by literal
fornication reduced to a religious system, and as the initiated were
made to drink a prepared liquor out of a sacred goblet, so this harlot
is represented as intoxicating the kings of the earth with the *golden
cup* of her prostitution. On her forehead, the very name MYSTERY is

Christian. It displays a God of Nature who loves virtue
and abhors vice, and teaches man the doctrine of personal responsibility. And this is the extreme boundary
of Natural Religion. But Revelation, which opens our
eyes to futurity, directs us how to worship this omnipotent Being, so as to attain the reward, and escape the
punishment consequent on our actions, and instructs us
how to walk in that pure and perfect way which leads
to eternal life.

inscribed; and the label teaches us that, in point of character, she is
the *great universal mother* of idolatry. The nature of this Mystery
the *officiating hierophant* undertakes to explain, and an important
prophecy is most curiously and artfully veiled under the very language
and imagery of the Orgies. To the sea-born Great Father was ascribed
a threefold state; he lived, he died, and he revived; and these changes
of condition were duly exhibited in the Mysteries. To the sea-born
wild beast is similarly ascribed a threefold state; he lives, he dies,
and he revives. While dead, he lies floating on the mighty ocean,
just like Horus, or Osiris, Siva, or Vishnu; when he revives again,
like those kindred deities, he emerges from the waves; and, whether
dead or alive, he bears seven heads and ten horns, corresponding in
number with the seven ark-preserved Rishis, and the ten aboriginal
patriarchs. Nor is this all; as the worshippers of the Great Father
bore his special mark or stigma, and were distinguished by his name,
so the worshippers of the maritime beast equally bear his mark, and
are equally designated by his appellation. At length, however, *the
first or doleful part* of these sacred Mysteries draws to a close, and
the last or joyful part is rapidly approaching. After the prophet has
beheld the enemies of God plunged into a dreadful lake, or inundation
of liquid fire, which corresponds with the infernal lake, or deluge of
the Orgies, he is introduced into *a splendidly illuminated region*
expressly adorned with the characteristics of that *Paradise* which
was the ultimate scope of the ancient aspirants; while, *without* the
holy gate of admission, are the whole multitude of the profane, *dogs,
and sorcerers, and whoremongers, and murderers, and idolaters, and
whosoever loveth or maketh a lye.*" (Fab. Pag. Idol, vol. iii., p.
640–643.

LIST OF BOOKS

PUBLISHED AND FOR SALE BY THE

MASONIC PUBLISHING AND MANUFACTURING CO.,

430 Broome street, New York.

☞ *Postage prepaid, on printed books, on receipt of the price.* The *money must, in all cases, accompany the order.*

THE GENERAL AHIMAN REZON AND FREEMASON'S GUIDE, containing Monitorial Instructions in the Degrees of Entered Apprentice, Fellow-Craft and Master Mason, with explanatory notes, emendations and lectures: together with the Ceremonies of Consecration and Dedication of New Lodges, Installation of Grand and Subordinate Officers, Laying Foundation Stones, Dedication of Masonic Halls, Grand Visitations, Burial Services, Regulations for Processions, Masonic Calendar, etc. To which are added a Ritual for a Lodge of Sorrow, and the Ceremonies of Consecrating Masonic Cemeteries: also an Appendix, with the forms of Masonic Documents, Masonic Trials, etc. By DANIEL SICKELS, 33°. Embellished with nearly 300 Engravings.
Bound in fine Cloth—extra—large 12mo.................. $1 50
"   "   Morocco, full gilt, for the W. Master's table, with appropriate insignia of the East...... 3 00

Freemason's Monitor, containing all the Degrees in the Lodge, Chapter, Council, and Commandery. By Daniel Sickels. (*An enlarged edition of Macoy's Masonic Manual.*)
.... Tucks. 1 50
Same work, bound in cloth............................ 1 00

The Historical Landmarks and other Evidences of Freemasonry Explained in a series of Practical Lectures, with
copious Notes. By George Oliver, D. D. 2 vols. Large
Duodecimo—with Portrait of the Author.

BINDING — { Cloth—Uniform Style............ ...... $5 00
{ Half Morocco—Uniform Library Edition. 7 00

Signs and Symbols, Illustrated and Explained in a Course of
Twelve Lectures on Freemasonry. By Geo. Oliver, D. D.
Large Duodecimo.

BINDING — { Cloth—Uniform Style................... 1 50
{ Half Morocco—Uniform Library Edition. 2 50

The History of Initiation, in Twelve Lectures; comprising a
Detailed Account of the Rites and Ceremonies, Doctrines,
and Discipline of the Secret and Mysterious Institutions
of the Ancient World. By George Oliver, D. D. Royal
Duodecimo—300 pages.

BINDING — { Cloth—Uniform Style................... 1 50
{ Half Morocco—Uniform Library Edition. 2 50

The Symbol of Glory, showing the Object and End of Freemasonry. By George Oliver, D. D.

BINDING — { Cloth—Uniform Style................... 1 50
{ Half Morocco—Uniform Library Edition. 2 50

The Lights and Shadows of Freemasonry; consisting of
Masonic Tales, Songs, and Sentiments never before published. By Rob. Morris, K. T.

BINDING — { Cloth—Uniform Style................... 1 50
{ Half Morocco—Uniform Library Edition. 2 50

The Theocratic Philosophy of Freemasonry, in Twelve Lectures on its Speculative, Operative, and Spurious Branches.
By George Oliver, D. D. Large Duodecimo.

BINDING — { Cloth—Uniform Style................... 1 50
{ Half Morocco—Uniform Library Edition. 2 50

The Revelations of a Square, exhibiting a graphic display
of the Sayings and Doings of Eminent Free and Accepted
Masons, from the Revival in 1717, by Dr. Desaguliers, to
the Reunion in 1813. By George Oliver, D. D. Royal
Duodecimo.

BINDING — { Cloth—Uniform Style................... 1 50
{ Half Morocco—Uniform Library Edition. 2 50

The Mystic Tie; or Facts and Opinions, illustrative of the
Character and Tendency of Freemasonry. By Albert G.
Mackey, M. D.

BINDING — { Cloth—Uniform Style.................., $1 50
{ Half Morocco—Uniform Library Edition. 2 50

Traditions of Freemasonry and its Coincidences with the
Ancient Mysteries. By A. T. C. Pierson. Large Duodecimo—fine cloth................................... 2 00

Manual of the Order of the Eastern Star, containing Symbols,
Scriptural Illustrations, Lectures, etc., adapted to the
system of Adoptive Masonry. Beautifully Illustrated.
Gilt Edges and Illuminated Cover...................... 1 00

Signet of King Solomon; or, the Freemason's Daughter.
By Aug. C. L. Arnold, LL.D. Splendidly Illustrated..... 1 25

Ancient Constitutions of Freemasons. By James Anderson.
A verbatim copy of the original edition of 1723......... 1 00

Taaffe's History of the Knights of Malta. 8vo. 4 vols.
bound in 2.. 5 00

Text-Book of Masonic Jurisprudence, by A. G. Mackey..... 2 00
Book of the Chapter, by A. G. Mackey................... 1 50
Manual of the Lodge, by A. G. Mackey................... 1 50
Lexicon of Freemasonry, by A. G. Mackey............... 3 00
Familiar Treatise on the Principles and Practice of Masonic
Jurisprudence, by John W. Simons..................... 1 50
Digest of Masonic Law, by G. W. Chase................. 1 50
Origin and Early History of Masonry, by G. W. Steinbrenner 75
Book of the Commandery, by John W. Simons............ 75
Manual of the Chapter, by Sheville & Gould............. 75
Freemason's Monitor, by Webb......................... 75
Freemason's Hand-Book, by Wm. H. Drew...........Tuck. 1 00
Masonic Manual, by J. Ashe........................... 1 00
Moral Design of Freemasonry, by S. Lawrence........... 1 00
Freemason's Pocket Library and Working Monitor, by G.W.
Chase ....Tuck. 1 50
Rationale and Ethics of Freemasonry, by A. C. L. Arnold... 1 00
Masonic Advocate, containing Mackey's Lexicon and Oliver's
Masonic Dictionary............................. ..... 1 50
Des Freimaurer's Handbuch (German).................. 75

Manual of the Ancient and Accepted Rite, by William M.
  Cunningham...$2 00
Manual de la Masoneria, (*Spanish,*) by A. Cassard.......... 8 00
Craftsman and Freemason's Guide, by C. Moore............ 1 50
Freemason's Manual, by K. J. Stewart..................... 1 50
Masonic Trestle-Board, by C. W. Moore................... 1 50
Masonic Text-Book, by J. L. Cross.....................tuck. 1 50
Masonic Chart, by J. L. Cross............................. 1 50
Templar's Chart, by J. L. Cross........................... 2 00
Star in the East, by George Oliver......................... 1 00
Revelations of a Square, by George Oliver................. 1 50
History of the Ancient and Accepted Rite, by Robt. B. Folger. 5 00
Antiquities of Freemasonry, by George Oliver............. 1 25
Statutes and Regulations of the Ancient and Accepted Rite,
  by A. Pike... 2 00
Beauties of Freemasonry Exemplified, by George Oliver.... 20
Outlines of Speculative Freemasonry, by Salem Town...... 20
Mason in High Places, by an English Rector............... 20
Juryman Mason, by an English Rector..................... 25
Masonic Vocal Manual, by Robt. Macoy............per doz. 3 00
Masonic Harp, by George W. Chase........ .... 1 00
Ancient Constitutions of 1723, by James Anderson......... 75
Keystone of the Masonic Arch, by Charles Scott........... 1 25
Master Workman, by James K. Hall...................tuck. 1 25
  Do.   do.   do. ....cloth. 1 00
Book of Marks for Chapters.............................. 4 00
Ode Cards for the Lodge.......................per doz. 1 50
Ode Cards for the Chapter.................... ... " 1 50
Proposition Book.. 3 00
Receipt Books for Lodge and Chapter................... 3 00
Lodge Register.. 2 00
Draft Books for Lodge and Chapter...................... 3 50
Question Book for Commandery.......................... 4 00
Visitors' Book.. 3 50
Petitions for Membership.......................per 100, 1 25
Black Book... 3 5?
Ledgers and Minute Books. Large and Small BIBLES.

*All Masonic Books now published, and not named in this List
on hand, or furnished to order at the lowest market prices.*